With the compliments of

Social Function in Psychiatry:
The Hidden Axis of Classification Exposed

Social Function in Psychiatry

The Hidden Axis of Classification Exposed

Edited by

PETER TYRER and PATRICIA CASEY

With the compliments of

WRIGHTSON BIOMEDICAL PUBLISHING LTD
Petersfield, UK and Bristol, PA, USA

Editorial Office:

Wrightson Biomedical Publishing Ltd
Ash Barn House, Winchester Road, Stroud,
Petersfield, Hampshire GU32 3PN, UK
Telephone: 01730 265647
Fax: 01730 260368

British Library Cataloguing in Publication Data

A catalogue record for this book is available from the British Library.

Library of Congress Cataloging in Publication Data

Social function in psychiatry: the hidden axis of classification
    exposed / edited by Peter Tyrer and Patricia Casey.
        p. cm.
    Includes bibliographical references and index.
    ISBN 1-871816-23-8 (hbk.)
    1. Social adjustment.   2. Mentally ill—Social networks.
    I. Tyrer, Peter J.   II. Casey, Patricia R.
        [DNLM: 1. Mental Disorders.   2. Social Behaviour.   3. Social
    Adjustment.   4. Social Support.   WM 31 S6763 1993]
    RC455.4.S67S64   1993
        616.89′14—dc20
DNLM/DLC   98-28470
for Library of Congress   CIP

ISBN 1 871816 23 8

Composition by Scribe Design, Gillingham, Kent
Printed in Great Britain by Biddles Ltd, Guildford.

For our mothers,
May Tyrer and Rita Casey

Contents

Contributors

Patricia Casey, *Professor of Psychiatry, University College Dublin, and Consultant Psychiatrist, Mater Hospital, Eccles Street, Dublin 7, Ireland*

Elena Garralda, *Professor of Child and Adolescent Psychiatry, St Mary's Hospital Medical School, Horace Joules Hall, Central Middlesex Hospital, Park Royal, London NW10 7NS, UK*

John Green, *Chief Clinical Psychologist, Department of Clinical Psychology, Paterson Wing, St Mary's Hospital, London W2 1NY, UK*

Fiona Henderson, *Psychologist, Department of Clinical Psychology, Paterson Wing, St Mary's Hospital, London W2 1NY, UK*

Matthew Hodes, *Senior Lecturer, Academic Unit of Child and Adolescent Psychiatry, St Mary's Hospital Medical School, Horace Joules Hall, Central Middlesex Hospital, Park Royal, London NW10 7NS, UK*

Stephen Merson, *Consultant Psychiatrist, St Charles' Hospital, London W10 6DZ, UK*

Mark Rapley, *Principal Clinical Psychologist, Royal Albert Hospital, Ashton Road, Lancaster LA1 5AJ, and Honorary Lecturer, Department of Psychology, University of Lancaster, UK*

Peter Tyrer, *Professor of Community Psychiatry, St Mary's Hospital Medical School, Academic Unit of Psychiatry, St Charles' Hospital, London W10 6DZ, UK*

Preface

Social function is deceptively simple, two words that describe how an individual or a group associate with society at large and in their own personal environment. But like many words in common use in the caring professions, they are very difficult to define. Social function is similar to the word 'health'. Just in the same way as everyone can be an expert on health but have great difficulty in providing a definition for it, we all have an immediate impression of what is meant by social function when these words are mentioned. In methodological parlance, they have face validity; they seem to describe a concept that fits in with our ideas of reality. People can be well or ill but they have to exist with their fellow men and interact with them as well, and social function seems to be bound up with this.

So far, so good. The problem arises when we attempt to set boundaries to this type of function. Does it include our performance in relationship to the rest of society, does it measure how well we are adapted to our roles, does it record the nature of our friendships and other social contacts, or is it just a measure of how much we are satisfied with our place in the scheme of things?

This book explores the subject in full for the first time. We justify this because of evidence demonstrated many times in the pages that follow, that social function is of immense importance in psychiatric practice and yet often remains ignored. We suspect it is overlooked because, like a jelly, it seems to change its shape depending on the constraints imposed, and can be made to encompass almost any aspect of society.

In this book we attempt to tie the concept down, give it added authority and meaning, and emphasise the reasons why it should be studied more and recorded in clinical practice. In the final chapter we introduce a term which we feel is the essence of social function, *sodality*: all those aspects of fellowship with our social environment that are independent of mental state, personality and Shakespeare's 'slings and arrows of outrageous fortune'. We hope to stimulate the reader in opening a debate on this subject and to show that by taking account of social function in all forms of psychiatric disorder we add a rich new dimension to theory and practice.

PETER TYRER AND PATRICIA CASEY

Social Function in Psychiatry: The Hidden Axis of Classification
Edited by Peter Tyrer and Patricia Casey
©1993 Wrightson Biomedical Publishing Ltd

1

What is Social Function?

PETER TYRER

The late Stephen Potter, the originator of the words 'lifemanship' and 'one-upmanship' had a series of stock phrases that he interjected into conversation in order to gain an advantage. One of the more effective ones was used as a response to individuals who dominated conversations by long and often erudite accounts of the peoples of distant countries. By and large discussion at times like this disappears because no one knows anything about the countries or the peoples concerned and either stand back in admiration of the knowledge displayed or wait with irritation for him/her to finish. Potter used to end these soliloquys by looking wise and saying 'yes, but only in the south'. After this nothing more was usually said. The raconteur and his audience immediately felt that Mr Potter must know that little bit more than the speaker so the whole purpose of the conversation, to impress the listeners, was lost.

Equivalent conversations sometimes take place among mental health professionals. The same combination of admiration and irritation is often found when an acknowledged or aspiring expert is giving that account of a mental health problem that displays skills and understanding of the psychodynamic aspects, the descriptive psychopathology or diagnostic virtuosity. At an appropriate point in this dissertation, preferably when the final 'i's have been dotted and 't's crossed, the innocent question, 'what was the level of social function?' has the same effect as Potter's southern focus.

The reason for this is that most professionals in mental health circles do not know too much about social function and once someone starts talking about 'levels' their ignorance is even more exposed. Social function is acceptable when it is some vague sociological concept but when someone discusses its levels they must be regarding it as a science and therefore subject to verification and hypothesis testing. Rather than engage the questioner on such suspect territory the monologue ends and starts again somewhere else to a more receptive audience!

After reading this book, particularly this chapter, the reader should be able to deal with this type of interjection with complete confidence.

We first need to examine the different meanings of social function. These two words have the merit of face validity; they seem to be referring to how the person copes with the human world outside his own psyche and it is reasonable to suppose that such function can be measured in some way. When one looks at a subject more closely, however, social function becomes a much more ambiguous term. Examination of the dictionary reveals that social can be used in many different adjectival forms. It describes the ability to associate and work well with others, friendliness and geniality in the company of other people, a degree of close association because of some common tie, living together in groups and enjoyment of common benefits, the organisation of people into natural groups with common characteristics and, finally, a more legalistic conception of the structure of society.

Although all these descriptions have a common feature, that of describing an individual's relationship to other people, there are differences, both obvious and subtle, between them. It is useful to examine these under six headings which summarise the main features outlined in the description above: co-operation, affability, bonding, community, status and class.

CO-OPERATION

This aspect of human behaviour is best summed up by John Donne's 'no man is an island' and the more mundane quote 'man is a social animal'. The main reason why *Homo sapiens* has achieved such remarkable success in the world has been his capacity to collaborate and communicate with others. In the early history of man such collaboration was necessary for self preservation; the tribe was formed and mutual support ensured its survival. Even in our independent age, where in many countries individuals owe no allegiance to anybody and are not required to, it is usually necessary to have some degree of social support, usually mutual, to induce well being. If in any way the individual is handicapped so that he or she is unable to compete with others, self support becomes essential.

The support is not just necessary in one's personal life. It particularly applies at work, where organisations such as trade unions are set up to represent the common interests of members, in nuclear families, in which there is division of labour to ensure care and concern, and in leisure activities, where co-operation is most obvious in team games.

The number and frequency of social supports necessary to ensure well being varies from individual to individual and in different types of life. When such social supports are entirely lacking the individual will probably suffer, but not necessarily so.

AFFABILITY

In this sense the adjective 'social' becomes closely allied with 'sociable'. The ability of some people to get on with almost everybody else in life, no matter which age group and from which background they come, is sometimes looked on with envy by others. Charles Dickens' Mr Pickwick is a good example of such an individual, and the popularity of Mr Pickwick seems to lie as much in his ability to disregard the many barriers to normal social intercourse that existed in the Victorian age as in any other quality.

At the opposite end of the spectrum is the painfully shy individual who finds it extremely difficult to relate to any person; this in its more severe form becomes an incapacitating social phobia.

This type of social function involves particular skills in detecting cues in conversation and body language so that one can respond to them appropriately and produce social resonance. The subject is recognised in psychiatry by the development of social skills training as a particular, primarily behavioural, technique to improve those who have major difficulty in relating to others (Curran, 1977).

BONDING

Although the ability to get on with other members of the human race and to co-operate in matters of mutual interest are important, they are no substitute for close friendships and intimate relationships. This aspect of social function concerned with close relationships is best described as bonding, even though this word is specifically used to describe the close relationship that develops between a mother and a new born baby. The absence of close social relationships that are personally important was first highlighted many years ago by Emil Durkheim (1897) and is summarised under the name 'anomie'. The development of close social relationships is an important part of child psychiatry and was given major prominence by the work of Bowlby (1973) who was mainly responsible for the science of attachment theory, the study of the processes that go on between child, parents and others during chronological development.

As the development of good and stable attachment figures is considered to be such an important element to positive mental health this could be regarded as one of the prime aspects of social function.

COMMUNITY

The previous aspects of social function are all individually focused; collectively these combine to describe the functioning of large elements of society in geographical areas. People live, work and play together in varying degrees of closeness but are rarely completely isolated. Good social function could therefore describe good citizenship, the ability to conform to the rules of the community without causing offence or distress.

The absence of this community aspect of social function is best shown in the conditions described as personality disorders. These are disorders in which, to varying degrees, the sufferer causes distress to society taken in its broadest sense (e.g. family, friends and the community at large) and then simultaneously or subsequently distress to himself.

STATUS

Man is not only a social animal but a competitive one. He is motivated by ambition and wishes to succeed. Such success is often measured in terms of social status. High status can be measured in several ways including capital wealth, high earning capacity, professional respectability, charitable acts and high media prominence (perhaps best summed up as fame).

Those with excellent social function could therefore be judged to be those with the greatest social status. This can however be misleading as the public image of a person may be quite separate from their private, personal behaviour. Indeed, the exposure of personal social dysfunction by going behind the mask of public social success is one of the most common themes in literature, perhaps most clearly expressed in Hardy's *Tess of the d'Urbervilles*.

CLASS

Social function is formalised in society in various ways and, particularly in the United Kingdom, has been enshrined in the concept of social class. Although this concept is often considered to be redundant (our current Prime Minister exhorts us to be a 'classless society'), it nonetheless exists and is likely to continue to do so. Good social function could therefore be regarded as that which is appropriate for the class concerned. To take perhaps the most extreme example, in Aldous Huxley's *Brave New World* each class of people (graded between alpha and epsilon) is 'programmed' to act in a certain way from birth onwards. Each class regards its functioning as superior to all others so individuals are not encouraged to rise out of or fall below the class into which they were born.

Although such rigidity is never found in Western civilization nowadays the fact remains that expectations vary greatly from one class to another. This serves to emphasise that there is no common measurement of social function;

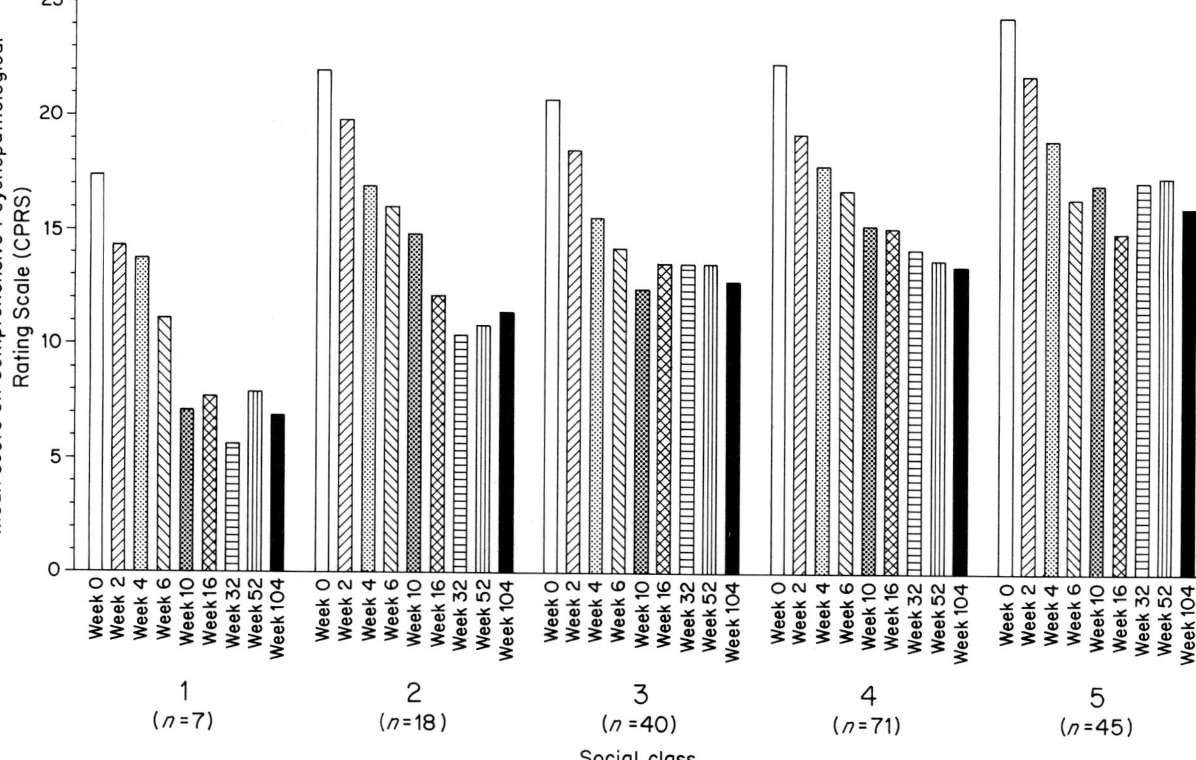

Figure 1.1. Influence of social class on response to treatment in the Nottingham study of neurotic disorder. This illustrates the importance of social class in determining the outcome of treatment (as measured by the Comprehensive Psychopathological Rating Scale (Åsberg *et al.*, 1978) in 181 patients with a defined neurotic disorder (anxiety and depressive diagnoses) and followed up at regular intervals over two years. Patients in social classes 4 and 5 had greater symptomatology at all times of assessment. (After Tyrer *et al.*, 1993.)

there are an innumerable set of norms for each microcosm of society. Nevertheless, most formal studies reveal poorer clinical function in lower social classes; an example is illustrated in Figure 1.1, and when social function is recorded also a similar trend is shown.

Although the exact meaning of social function is open to debate, one interpretation is already demarcated clearly in psychiatry, the classification of mental disorders. For many years the only conditions considered worthy of classification were the disorders of mental state — melancholia, dementia praecox and the schizophrenias, neuroses, childhood disorders, mental handicap and the addictions — and other aspects, particularly the psychosocial ones, were barely mentioned except as features which might help to facilitate the correct diagnosis. Since the widespread adoption of the American classification (DSM) for research purposes following the publication of its third revision (DSM-III) (American Psychiatric Association, 1980), there has been greater interest in the other axes of classification. The subsidiary title of this book, *The Hidden Axis of Classification Exposed*, indicates that social function is one of the axes of this classification, albeit a rudimentary one. In DSM-IIIR (American Psychiatric Association, 1987) and in DSM-IV (American Psychiatric Association, 1993), social function is mainly covered in Axis V (Global Assessment of Functioning) (see Chapter 3 this volume), whereas in the international classification, ICD-10 (World Health Organisation, 1992) it has just been introduced in the form of the WHO Disability Diagnostic Scale (see Chapter 10 this volume) and is undergoing field trials before being introduced as the second axis of psychiatric classification. Social factors and life events that might be responsible for precipitating episodes of illness are identified on separate axes.

This book, in prising open this axis of classification, hopes to justify the presence of social function as an important aspect of mental illness that is related to, but in many ways independent of, mental state. It may also offer the opportunity of expanding the classification from its present, predominantly global description, into a more detailed system.

Where are we at present? It is worth looking at the most frequently used social function measurement, the Global Assessment of Functioning (GAF) Scale, a revision of the Global Assessment Scale (GAS) (Endicott *et al.*, 1976), which is unique in that it alone constitutes a whole axis of classification in DSM-IIIR (and in DSM-IV). This scale, reproduced later in this book (Figure 3.4), was developed from a much earlier instrument, the Global Scale of the Health–Sickness Rating Scale (Luborsky, 1962) and also incorporates the Children's Global Assessment Scale (CGAS) (Shaffer *et al.*, 1983), so that the instrument covers all age groups.

However, close examination of the GAF reveals that it covers much more than social function. It is a measure of 'overall level of functioning' including clinical symptoms, coping abilities, general social function and, in its more impaired scores, measures self preservation skills, the ability to stay alive by avoiding self-harm and maintaining self-care. Unfortunately this overall scale also includes 'overall' in its other sense, an 'outer garment that hides and protects what is underneath'. It covers every aspect of living and therefore correlates with any other measure of mental function. Thus it is impossible to score the maximum on the scale, 100, and have any form of mental distress, as the criteria for this score are 'superior function in a wide range of activities, life's problems never seem to get out of hand, is sought by others because of his [sic] many positive qualities. No symptoms' (American Psychiatric Association, 1987). This paragon of perfection offers no scope for any form of disability, yet, as will be shown in later chapters of this book, it is possible to be functioning extremely well in spite of significant mental illness and, conversely, to disintegrate in social function in the presence of little or no mental illness. Two short vignettes illustrate this.

Vignette 1

An advertising executive aged 48 was seen in a general practice psychiatric clinic because of concern by his wife that he was doing too much and might be ill. He had recently taken on the responsibility for advertising a new branded product and had been working on this for about 14 hours each day. When seen, he was ebullient and over-talkative, insisting the interview must end early as he had to get back to work on promoting his product, a new cigarette.

He insisted that the doctor gave an opinion on the new slogan he had just thought of that morning, repeatedly interrupted questions during the interview, maintained frequently that he was not ill but just in an 'extraproductive' phase of his life, and terminated the interview prematurely. Information obtained from other sources revealed that he had two previous episodes, the second treated successfully with lithium carbonate. A diagnosis of bipolar affective disorder with current hypomania was made. The patient refused treatment subsequently and when his wife was seen three months later she reported that his advertising campaign had been a great success and that he had made over £100 000 in fees from its adoption.

Vignette 2

An unmarried woman of 42 years who had gradually worked her way to a senior position in an industrial company was unexpectedly made redundant when a dramatic fall in orders led to a restructuring of the company. She was informed about her redundancy in a typed letter from the senior personnel officer and given 24 hours to clear her desk. She had no previous history of psychiatric disorder but after her dismissal she refused to leave her flat because she could not face the humiliation of being seen by fellow workers and was referred for a psychiatric opinion after she said she would be better off dead and had contemplated various forms of suicide. At interview she was subdued at first but later became extremely angry about the way she had been treated.

This was developed further at interview by the therapist adopting the role of the managing director of the firm and encouraging her to express these feelings directly. She became incandescent with rage during this psychodrama, which was aggravated by the therapist/managing director justifying his decision to sack her. She left the interview saying that he was no different from her former bosses and that she had wasted her time. Two weeks later the therapist received a letter from the patient apologising for her behaviour and thanking him for his help. She had immediately felt better, lost her suicidal feelings and had already been seen by an 'outreach agency' that had found some attractive positions in other companies, for one of which she had been short-listed.

In the first case a major mental disorder, bipolar affective (formerly named manic–depressive psychosis) was clearly present and yet associated with what can only be described as superior social function, whereas in the second a relatively minor mental condition, an adjustment disorder following the loss of a job, was associated with severe impairment. Despite this obvious discrepancy between symptoms and functioning the scores of both patients were very close on the GAF Scale, the first patient scoring 45 and the second 42. This is because both symptoms and behaviour can affect scoring and if neither is impaired the score is adjusted accordingly. In the words of the advice given in scoring, 'in making a rating, one should select the lowest interval that describes a subject's functioning during the preceding week. For example, if a subject has behaviour considerably influenced by delusions (a range of 21–30) as well as "marked impairment in several areas" (range 31–40), the lower range should be chosen'.

It is therefore clear that this axis of functioning is not just a measure of social function and even if there was full agreement about what constituted social function the GAF scale would still not be an appropriate measure. Although this criticism is not as applicable to the ICD-10 axis it remains a powerful argument against the value of social function as an independent measure in mental illness, or indeed, in medicine generally.

Despite all these difficulties, it is worthwhile trying to answer the question posed by the title of this chapter. Social function can be defined as 'the level at which an individual functions in his or her social context, such function ranging between self preservation and basic living skills to the relationship with others in society'. There are many influences that have an impact on social function, shown in approximate proportions in the pie chart (Figure 1.2) but, despite their intimate associations, they are not synonymous with social function and need to be recognised as independent.

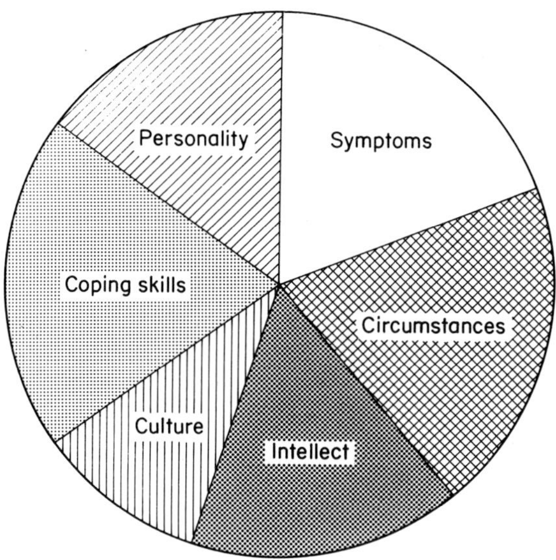

Figure 1.2. The confluence of social function: factors that affect social function and which, to varying degrees, may be confused with it.

One of the most common areas of confusion is in the vexed issue of quality of life, a subject that is discussed later in this book and which creates even more arguments over nomenclature than social function in its various guises. We cannot pretend that 'quality of life' is a satisfactory concept but neither is it a redundant one, as is clear from the keen interest expressed in the subject from a large number of people ranging from politicians to health economists. However, whatever quality of life is, it is not the same as social function. It is probably better to regard quality of life as a global measure of health that includes social function among its elements, as is clear from examination of instruments recording quality of life such as the Nottingham Health Profile (Hunt *et al.*, 1986) but which also includes physical (P), cognitive (C), affective (A), economical (E) and ego function (personality) (E), which make up the PCASEE scale suggested by Bech (1992). In short, quality of life includes social function but social function is only one of the aspects of quality of life.

We hope to convince the reader that social function is not an epiphenomenon of mental illness, a measurement of personality disorder, a consequence of social policy or intellectual endowment, or a chimera of political theory. It is a separate domain from all others. Exactly what makes it separate and distinct and worthy of classification, discussion and measurement should become clear in the following chapters.

REFERENCES

American Psychiatric Association (1980). *Diagnostic and Statistical Manual of Mental Disorders, 3rd edn.* American Psychiatric Association, Washington DC.

American Psychiatric Association (1987). *Diagnostic and Statistical Manual of Mental Disorders, 3rd edn, Revised.* American Psychiatric Association, Washington DC.

American Psychiatric Association (1993). *Diagnostic and Statistical Manual of Mental Disorders, DSM-IV Draft Criteria.* American Psychiatric Association, Washington DC.

Åsberg, M., Montgomery, S.A., Perris, C., Schalling, D. and Sedvall, G. (1978). A comprehensive psychopathological rating scale. *Acta Psychiatrica Scandinavica,* **271** (Suppl.), 5–29.

Bech, P. (1992). Measuring quality of life: the medical perspective. *Nordisk Psykiatrisk Tidskrift,* **46**, 85–89.

Bowlby, J. (1973). *Attachment and Loss. Vol. 2: Separation.* Basic Books, New York.

Curran, J.P. (1977). Skills training as an approach to the treatment of heterosexual social anxiety: a review. *Psychological Bulletin,* **84**, 140–157.

Durkheim, E. (1897). *Suicide (Trans. 1952).* Routledge and Kegan Paul, London, pp. 777–789.

Endicott, J., Spitzer, R.L., Fleiss, J.L. and Cohen, J. (1976). The global assessment scale: a procedure for measuring the overall severity of psychiatric disturbance. *Archives of General Psychiatry,* **33**, 766–771.

Hunt, S.M., McEwen, J. and McKenna, S.P. (1986). *Measuring Health States.* Croom Helm, London.

Luborsky, L. (1962). Clinicians' judgements of mental health: a proposed scale. *Archives of General Psychiatry,* **7**, 407–417.

Shaffer, D., Gould, M.S., Brasic, J., Ambrosini, P., Fisher, P., Bird, H. and Aluwahlia, S. (1983). A Children's Global Assessment Scale (CGAS) for children 4 to 16 years of age). *Archives of General Psychiatry,* **40**, 1228–1231.

Tyrer, P., Seivewright, N., Ferguson, B., Murphy, S. and Johnson, A.L. (1993). The Nottingham study of neurotic disorder: impact of personality status on response to drug treatment, cognitive therapy and self-help over two years. *British Journal of Psychiatry,* **162**, 219–226.

World Health Organisation (1992). *International Classification of Diseases, 10th Revision.* WHO, Geneva.

Social Function in Psychiatry: The Hidden Axis of Classification
Edited by Peter Tyrer and Patricia Casey
©1993 Wrightson Biomedical Publishing Ltd

2

The Importance of Social Function in Psychiatry

PATRICIA CASEY

One of the many criticisms meted out to psychiatrists is that they are nothing more than agents of social control who incarcerate those whose behaviour is deemed by society to be odd, eccentric or unacceptable in some way without understanding the dynamics or the rationale for such behaviour. This argument further states that it is society rather than any inherent deficit which labels the person's functioning as unusual. Thus mental illness is a myth which doctors have failed to understand and as Szasz (1973), the most vociferous opponent of traditional psychiatry, claims, psychiatric practice is composed of 'prescribing drugs, operating on the brain and imprisoning persons labelled as mentally ill'.

As with many overstatements there are elements of truth in this caricature. It is true that behaviour which is believed to be unacceptable is often referred to psychiatry for appraisal. Indeed at times such people are detained in hospital. The falsehood in the above arguments lies in failing to identify the element of personal distress and suffering often accompanying such impairment to functioning and in assuming that only one element of the patient's totality is brought to bear on intervention decisions. This argument also manifestly fails to take into account advances in our understanding of the biological basis for psychiatric disorders. Interestingly this unidimensional view of emotional disturbance held by the antipsychiatry school is the mirror image of the unidimensional approach adopted by traditional psychiatry. This holds that symptoms are sacrosanct and placed in isolation above all other aspects of the patient and his environment. The poverty of both of these approaches lies in their failure to recognise the link between symptoms and functioning, a view proferred by Adolf Meyer and implicitly recognised by the nosologists of ICD-10 and DSM-IIIR.

For many years psychiatrists played shadow-boxing with the notion of social dysfunction and little more than cursory inquiry was made about such areas as employment satisfaction, capacity to form confiding relationships, management of money and the numerous other components of daily life which constitute what was commonly called 'social performance' or, even then, 'social functioning'. Only in those suffering from schizophrenia did social function come to be recognised as a valid area of inquiry and an important measure of outcome. This led to developments in the treatment of this aspect of the illness, encompassing the 'negative symptoms', with the debut of behaviour and other psychological therapies. In the past decade attempts have been made to develop pharmacological agents to improve functioning and reduce the negative symptoms of schizophrenia.

The importance of psychosocial dysfunction in engendering vulnerability to or causation of psychiatric illness has a more venerable history although tending to be anecdotal rather than scientific until the recent past. Unemployment, inadequate social supports and homelessness are just a few of the variables which have been investigated in this regard. A distinction has been drawn between those aspects of social dysfunction which have an aetiological role and those which maintain a disorder. This will be discussed below.

RECENT ADVANCES

The first official recognition of the independence of social function from symptoms and of its potential importance came in DSM-III in 1980 when social function was included as a separate axis in the classification of psychiatric disorders. Although those involved in the classification and nosology of psychiatric disorders in Europe have generally been tardy, there are proposals to include two aspects of the social environment in ICD-10, i.e. social stressors on axis IV and disabilities or social function on axis V as well as axes dealing with syndromes, with developmental conditions (including personality, mental retardation and specific developmental delays) and physical conditions (Mezzich, 1988). The reasoning behind such a move stems from the influence of such researchers as Rutter *et al.* (1975) and Bech *et al.* (1987). The advantage of this approach is that abnormalities such as personality disorder are not regarded as exclusive of illness. The adverse effects of prioritising illness and symptoms over their consequences such as social impairment are avoided leading to a fuller appreciation of the spectrum of difficulties which the patient experiences. This multi-axial approach can thus be viewed as straddling the strictly biological, psychological and social approaches to psychiatric disorder leading to a more enriched view of the patient, his environment and his disorder.

SOCIAL DYSFUNCTION AND THE GENESIS OF PSYCHIATRIC DISORDER

The aetiology of psychiatric disorder is generally not fully understood and the truism that aetiology involves biological, social and psychological factors is easily recognised. It is pertinent to ask what is the exact role of social factors in the genesis and maintenance of psychiatric disorder.

Depressive illness is the area which has been most extensively investigated. The major contribution of Brown and Harris (1978), who suggested that social dysfunction in the form of poor marital relationships and unemployment outside the home render women vulnerable to depressive disorder in the face of adverse events, must be recognised. Other workers are even more insistent that unsatisfactory social relationships have a direct aetiological role independent of adverse events (Henderson *et al.*, 1978; Lin *et al.*, 1979). In particular they cite a lack of close friends and of contacts outside the home and an unsatisfactory relationship with the principal attachment figure so that time spent together is unpleasant. This latter view stems from the work of Bowlby (1969) on attachment in childhood and has been used as a model for the social causes of neurotic disorders. The hypothesis is that their symptoms are analogous to separation anxiety and to the absence or loss of the affectional bonds necessary for emotional well-being.

The role of social dysfunction in the genesis of behaviours such as suicide and parasuicide has also received considerable attention. In particular unemployment has been cited as increasing vulnerability to parasuicide and suicide. This will be discussed further in Chapter 6.

HOMELESSNESS

Homelessness requires special consideration in relation to social dysfunction since it represents the apogee of social dysfunction and may occur without any psychiatric disorder. It is indeed correct that some homeless people have psychiatric disorders (Lin *et al.*, 1990) although many more data are required. Since psychiatric disorder is in itself associated with social disadvantage and incapacity it would be necessary to control for this factor in assessing the relative contribution of mental illness and disadvantage. The implication of the view that homelessness is unequivocally linked to psychiatric disorder is that the homeless should be treated in settings appropriate to their disorder. Lamb (1990) advocates the hospitalization of all such persons on the basis of their right to treatment — a position which is not sustainable on present evidence and on principles of civil liberty. However this area requires further study in order that planning care for the homeless can be guided by coherence and knowledge rather than anecdote.

SOCIAL FUNCTION AND SYMPTOMS

Although there is now a commitment to recording social function in both DSM-IIIR and ICD-10 it is pertinent to ask if this is likely to serve any useful purpose. Many regard abnormalities of social function as being largely an epiphenomenon of psychiatric disorder and therefore conveying little useful information other than that recorded in symptomatic assessment of the individual. If this hypothesis holds true then recovery of symptoms should parallel changes in social function and vice versa. On the other hand, if both symptoms and social function can be demonstrated to be distinct from each other then the case for recording them on separate axes becomes more than theoretical.

The relationship between social function and psychiatric symptoms has been shown to be positive with increasing social incapacity as symptom severity worsens (Casey *et al.*, 1985). This association is hardly surprising since many symptoms also measure or imply changes to social function. Thus anergia and psychomotor retardation are highly likely to be associated with impairment of day to day activities. However the relationship is not a direct association and many patients, although highly symptomatic, may function well in their social roles. For instance the patient with a paranoid psychosis is often not recognised as such for many years since the symptoms do not intrude upon behaviour or functioning unless the focus of them is at hand. Many depressive symptoms such as anhedonia, appetite disturbance or free-floating anxiety do not inevitably lead to impairment. Hurry and Sturt (1981) demonstrated a correlation (*r*) of 0.68 between the social function score as measured by the Social Performance Schedule and the PSE symptom score in a community sample. Weissmann and co-workers (1978) in an earlier study also found a positive correlation (*r*) of 0.44–0.59 between social function and three different measures of symptomatology. An even higher correlation was shown by Casey and Tyrer (1986) who found that the PSE total score achieved a correlation (*r*) of 0.75 with the mean social function score derived from the Social Functioning Schedule in a random community sample and a correlation of 0.69 in a sample of patients in primary care with conspicuous psychiatric morbidity (Casey *et al.*, 1985). Surprisingly, there was little difference in the correlation when those who were in contact with the psychiatric services were compared with those who were not.

Studies of hospital populations show that this association is less powerful than among community samples as illustrated above and Hurry and Sturt (1981) believe this dilution to be due to the diversity of the hospitalised population with patients at various stages of recovery when compared with community samples. Support for the disparity between hospital and community samples is not upheld universally (Casey and Tyrer, 1986) although in the latter study the hospital population were out-patients rather than in-patients and therefore more likely to resemble a community rather than an in-patient sample. A more recent study conducted by the author (Casey and Butler, 1993) investigating social function among those with severe depressive illness who were being treated with ECT found a low correlation between symptoms and social function ($r = 0.31$, NS) at the time of first receiving ECT and this had increased at discharge to $r = 0.69$, $p<0.01$, lending support to the view of Hurry and Sturt above.

During recovery from illness there are several studies which point to the discordance between symptomatic and social recovery. During recovery from depressive illness in particular, which has been studied in greatest depth, the correlation between symptoms and functioning changes with the stage of recovery, being lowest during the acute phase and increasing as symptomatic recovery takes place. The explanation lies in the relatively slower improvement in social dysfunction when compared with symptomatic recovery which proceeds more quickly (Paykel and Weissman, 1973). This has obvious implications for the advice given to patients about return to work and other aspects of social interaction. It should also be borne in mind when considering changes in treatment because of what appears to be a protracted illness with delayed social recovery — this may be no more than the natural course of events. This aspect of social function will be considered in greater depth in Chapter 5.

SOCIAL FUNCTION AND DEMOGRAPHY

Social function has also been shown to change with age when severity of illness is partialled out (Weissman and Paykel, 1974; Casey *et al.*, 1985) and improvements with increasing years have been documented. This is hardly surprising as more mature styles of interacting develop with increasing age and experience although in extreme old age social function may deteriorate. Indirect support for this is provided from studies of the natural history of personality disorders — the group of disorders which *par excellence* have a long-term impact on social relationships. Many of these attenuate with increasing age and this change is likely to be most clearly manifested in changes in social function (Tyrer and Seivewright, 1988).

The effect of sex in determining the level of social function and incapacity has been inferred in some studies and made explicit in others. A consistent finding has been that for equivalent severity of symptoms men are more likely to be referred to the specialist services (Robertson, 1979). A likely reason is the greater impact illness has on the social role, especially that which is work related, of the traditional breadwinner. In addition those with significant social dysfunction are more likely to be referred by general practitioners to the specialist psychiatric services than those with lesser degrees of social impairment for equivalent severity of symptoms (Casey *et al.*, 1985). This suggests that difficulties in social functioning are indeed important contributors to the decision to refer and lends support to the view that symptom assessment alone provides an incomplete understanding of the patient and the disorder.

Finally urban–rural differences have been described, even in community samples (Casey and Tyrer, 1986). Functioning has been shown to be significantly better in rural than in urban populations. The explanation for this is obscure at present but is likely to be due to the effects of variables such as educational level, employment status and integration of social networks as well as the drift of the mentally ill to the anonymity of the inner city (Leighton *et al.*, 1963).

SOCIAL FUNCTION AND OUTCOME

Recovery

The importance of social function in relation to outcome is two-fold — first, the extent of social impairment generated by a disorder itself may have predictive power in relation to both short-term and long-term prognosis. Secondly, social function itself and the extent to which it has been restored following an episode of illness may be a more pragmatic and appropriate measure of outcome than symptom severity.

Mann and his co-workers (1981) have verified the former approach in their study of the one year outcome of patients with neurotic (mainly depressive) illness seen in general practice. They demonstrated that social function at the outset was a significant contributor to the outcome of illness at one year and that a good family life distinguished those who improved early in the course of follow-up from those who did not. The effect of social factors on outcome among in- and day-patients with first episode neurotic disorders was also shown by Sims (1975). The predictive value of social function has also been demonstrated by Huxley *et al.* (1979) in their study of minor psychiatric disorders in an out-patient setting. Social circumstances, including social functioning, and constitutional factors were superior to clinical variables in determining the outcome at one year.

Surprisingly, social assets such as social supports did not have any effect on outcome, a finding at variance with that of Keitner and Miller (1990), who demonstrated that patients from hostile families had a higher relapse rate than those from supportive families. Huxley and colleagues concede that this unexpected finding may have resulted from the inadequacy of the measures they used or that it may have been a valid finding. The role of social function in relation to outcome among hospitalised depressives is less clear (Tanner *et al.*, 1975). In a study conducted by the author, social function at outset did not contribute to the outcome at six months after discharge from hospital among those with severe depressive illness treated with ECT. However when social function was used as an outcome measure, personality rather than severity of symptomatology was the main contributing variable, a finding which has been underlined by Paykel *et al.* (1978) who states that social function measures an element of personality although the two are not synonymous since other factors also contribute to the degree of social impairment or functioning.

Relapse

The theory that abnormal family relationships such as schism, skew and 'double bind' were the cause of schizophrenia has long been relegated to history. However there has been an increasing recognition that family pathology may be responsible for relapses even when protected by medication. The view that high expressed emotion (EE) is associated with relapse even when patients are protected by medication (Vaughn and Leff, 1976) is not without its challengers (MacMillan *et al.*, 1986) although the belief in this is now ascendent and has led to practical methods to resolve the problems posed by this abnormal family environment such as family therapy and reduction in face to face contact between patient and family members.

The beneficial effects of social supports and networks in relation to relapse and the long-term prognosis of depressive illness have a body of knowledge attesting to their importance (Miller *et al.*, 1989; Brugha *et al.*, 1990). Interestingly the nature of the relationship between social support and outcome shows gender differences with the size of the patient's close social network predicting outcome in women. However in men, but not women, the presence of a partner had a positive effect on outcome. More specifically family hostility at the index episode has been shown to predict a poorer long-term prognosis (Swindle *et al.*, 1989) although whether the degree of conflict is indicative of the severity of the illness itself rather than the cause of the poor outcome has not been clarified. Studies of expressed emotion have been applied to depressive illness as well as to schizophrenia by several workers in their investigation of relapse. The findings are similar to those in the schizophrenic population with relapse being higher among those from high EE families compared with the low EE families. Interestingly relapse seemed to occur in depressives at lower levels of criticism than is the case with schizophrenics (Hooley and Teasdale, 1989; Vaughn and Leff, 1976).

SOCIAL FUNCTION AND QUALITY OF LIFE

Quality of life (QOL) measures have developed as a result of the impetus for the rehabilitation of patients with severe and incapacitating psychiatric disorders. Indeed the *raison d'être* for rehabilitation policies has been to improve the quality of life of psychiatric patients, specifically those who have been institutionalised. At present more than 100 QOL measures exist, many of which are aimed at assessing the impact of physical illnesses (in particular heart disease, rheumatoid arthritis and cancers) on day to day life. There is no consensus on whether these should be constructed so as to provide objective or subjective measures of QOL and indeed there is no agreement on the relationship if any between one method of measurement and the other. It will be noted that the same issue presents itself in considering social function and social adjustment (see Chapter 1) with the former being viewed as non-value laden and the latter as laying down *a priori* grounds for what constitutes 'normal' functioning. Moreover the contribution that psychopathology makes to QOL also has to be fully clarified if the latter is not to be regarded as a mere epiphenomenon of symptomatology — again an issue which has been raised and clarified in relation to social function. Finally, the development of measures specific to certain disorders needs to proceed apace since it is likely that the areas of concern will vary with differing psychiatric groups and treatment settings.

The World Health Organisation (1980) issued a policy statement outlining the dimensions to be included in QOL measures. These were physical, cognitive, social, economic and affective. It is obvious that such comprehensive measures include social function as one aspect of QOL although its association with other aspects needs to be clarified. However when one examines some of the commonly used QOL measures it is apparent that these are no different from social function scales except in name.

Finally, QOL measures have been used to aid in cost–benefit analysis of various health programmes. Using this approach the impact of treatments for a variety of conditions is assessed in terms of physical and social well being. In this way comparisons are made between, say, hip replacements and cognitive therapy thereby enabling governments to prioritise the financial aid given to various specialties and to different treatments. Needless to say this approach, dubbed QUALYs (quality adjusted life years), is fraught with ethical difficulties as well as philosophical and methodological ones and has yet to gain acceptance in psychiatric evaluation (Wilkinson *et al.*, 1990). This is discussed in greater detail in Chapter 9.

REFERENCES

Bech, P., Hjorts, S., Lund, K., Vilmar, T. and Kastrup, M. (1987). An integration of DSM-III and ICD-8 by global severity assessments for measuring multidimensional outcomes in general hospital psychiatry. *Acta Psychiatrica Scandinavica*, **75**, 297–306.

Bowlby, J. (1969). *Attachment and Loss. Vol. 1: Attachment.* Hogarth Press, Institute of Psychoanalysis, London.

Brown, G.W. and Harris, T.O. (1978). *The Social Origins of Depression. A Study of Psychiatric Disorder in Women.* Tavistock, London.

Brugha, T.S., Bebbington, P.E., MacCarthy, B., Sturt, E., Wykes, T. and Potter, J. (1990). Gender, social support and recovery from depressive disorders: a prospective clinical study. *Psychological Medicine,* **20,** 147–156.

Casey, P.R. and Butler, E. (1993). Social functioning and recovery from severe depressive illness. *Journal of Affective Disorders,* submitted.

Casey, P.R. and Tyrer, P. (1986). Personality, functioning and symptomatology. *Journal of Psychiatric Research,* **20,** 353–374.

Casey, P.R., Tyrer, P. and Platt, S. (1985). The relationship between social functioning and psychiatric symptomatology in primary care. *Social Psychiatry,* **20,** 5–9.

Henderson, S., Duncan-Jones, P., McAuley, H. and Richie K. (1978). The patient's primary group. *British Journal of Psychiatry,* **132,** 74–86.

Hooley, J.M. and Teasdale, J.D. (1989). Predictors of relapse in unipolar depressives: expressed emotion, marital distress and perceived criticism. *Journal of Abnormal Psychology,* **98,** 229–235.

Hurry, J. and Sturt, E. (1981). Social performance in a population sample: relation to psychiatric symptoms. In: Wing, J.K., Bebbington, P. and Robins, L.N. (Eds), *What is a Case? The Problem of Definition in Psychiatric Community Surveys.* Grant-McIntyre, London.

Huxley, P.J., Goldberg, D.P., Maguire, C.P. and Kincey, V.A. (1979). The prediction of the course of minor psychiatric disorders. *British Journal of Psychiatry,* **135,** 535–543.

Keitner, G.I. and Miller, I.W. (1990). Family functioning and major depression: an overview. *American Journal of Psychiatry,* **147,** 1128–1137.

Lamb, H. (1990). Will we save the homeless mentally ill? *American Journal of Psychiatry,* **147,** 649–651.

Leighton, D.C., Harding, J.S., Macklin, D.B., Hughes, C.C. and Leighton, A.H. (1963). Psychiatric findings of the Stirling County Study. *American Journal of Psychiatry,* **119,** 1021–1026.

Lin, N., Ensel, W.M., Simeone, R.S. and Kuo, W. (1979). Social support, stressful life events and illness: a model and an empirical test. *Journal of Health and Social Behaviour,* **20,** 108–119.

Lin, N., Gelberg, L. and Leake, B. (1990). Substance abuse and mental health status of homeless and domiciled low-income users of a medical clinic. *Hospital and Community Psychiatry,* **41,** 307–310.

MacMillan, J.F., Gold, A., Crow, T.J., Johnson, A.L. and Johnstone, E.C. (1986). Expressed emotion and relapse. *British Journal of Psychiatry,* **148,** 133–143.

Mann, A.H., Jenkins, R. and Belsey, E. (1981). The twelve month outcome of patients with neurotic illness in general practice. *Psychological Medicine,* **11,** 535–550.

Mezzich, J.E. (1988). On developing a psychiatric multiaxial schema for ICD-10. *British Journal of Psychiatry,* **152** (Suppl. 1), 38–43.

Miller, P. Mc., Kreitman, N.B., Ingham, J.G. and Sashidharan, S.P. (1989). Self-esteem, life-stress and psychiatric disorder. *Journal of Affective Disorder,* **17,** 65–75.

Paykel, E.S. and Weissman, M.M. (1973). Social adjustment and depression. A longitudinal study. *Archives of General Psychiatry,* **28,** 659–663.

Paykel, E.S., Weissman, M.M. and Prusoff, B.A. (1978). Social maladjustment and severity of depression. *Comprehensive Psychiatry,* **19,** 121–128.

Robertson, N.C. (1978). Variation in the pattern of psychiatric referrals from general practitioners. *Psychological Medicine,* **9,** 355–364.

Rutter, M., Shaffer, D. and Shepherd, M. (1975). *A Multiaxial Classification of Child Psychiatric Disorders*. World Health Organisation, Geneva.

Sims, A. (1975). Factors predictive of outcome in neurosis. *British Journal of Psychiatry*, **127**, 54–62.

Swindle, R.W. Jr, Cronkite, R.C. and Moos, R.H. (1989). Life stressors, social resources, coping and the 4-year course of unipolar depression. *Journal of Abnormal Psychology*, **98**, 468–477.

Szasz, T. (1973). *Ideology and Insanity*. Calder Boyars, London.

Tanner, J., Weissman, M.M. and Prusoff, B. (1975). Social adjustment and clinical relapse in depressed outpatients. *Comprehensive Psychiatry*, **16**, 547–556.

Tyrer, P. and Seivewright, H. (1988). Studies of outcome. In: Tyrer, P. (Ed.), *Personality Disorders. Diagnosis, Management and Course*. Wright, London.

Vaughn, C.E. and Leff, J.P. (1976). The influence of family and social factors on the course of psychiatric illness. A comparison of schizophrenic and depressed neurotic patients. *British Journal of Psychiatry*, **129**, 125–137.

Weissman, M.M. and Paykel, E.S. (1974). *The Depressed Woman — a Study of Social Relationships*. University of Chicago Press, Chicago.

Weissman, M.M., Myers, J.K. and Harding, P.S. (1978). Psychiatric disorders in a US urban community: 1975–1976. *American Journal of Psychiatry*, **135**, 459–462.

Wilkinson, G., Croft-Jeffreys, C., Krekorian, H., McLees, S. and Falloon, I. (1990). QALYs in psychiatric care? *Psychiatric Bulletin*, **14**, 582–585.

World Health Organisation (1980). *International Classification of Impairments, Disabilities and Handicaps*. WHO, Geneva.

Social Function in Psychiatry: The Hidden Axis of Classification
Edited by Peter Tyrer and Patricia Casey
©1993 Wrightson Biomedical Publishing Ltd

3

Measurement of Social Function

PETER TYRER

The first chapter of this book indicated many of the difficulties involved in measuring social function. Social function covers a variety of different domains and although to some extent these are related they are sometimes contradictory. The researcher who wishes to have a measure of what is conveniently called 'overall social functioning' has many scales to choose from but these are unlikely to produce as good an estimate as when a specific part of social function is being addressed. Such scales of overall social function will be discussed initially but these have different underlying assumptions and investigators need to be aware of these before they begin using them.

In particular, one issue needs to be highlighted straight away. We live in an overcrowded planet and social function involves getting on reasonably well with our neighbours. Together our neighbours constitute society and therefore, in addition to individuals having a view of social function, society as a whole also has a valid view. This introduces the concept of 'normative behaviour', an issue first raised in the measurement of social function by Barrabee and colleagues in 1955. It would be extremely valuable if society could set down norms for social function which could be applied across the board and be easy to validate externally as there would then be a common base.

Unfortunately, life is not quite like that, and there are many different 'norms' of social behaviour in different cultures and between different elements of society. Irresponsibility in one setting becomes entrepreneurial verve in another, and the same behaviour can be described as either conscientiousness or obsessive preoccupation, prudence or paranoid suspicion, caution or anxious avoidance, depending on the societal norms adopted in their interpretation. Social function always involves some sort of interaction between subject and society and although attempts have been made to 'purify' assessments so that only one of these is measured such attempts are bound to fail. It is therefore impossible to produce a norm for 'good' functioning within society without imposing external value judgments that have no factual basis.

The reason why this issue is important is not just a fundamental, philosophical one. Measurement can always be made more reliable by imposing definitions that are unambiguous and inflexible. This is exemplified by the use of operational criteria in the American classifications DSM-III and DSM-IIIR (American Psychiatric Association, 1980, 1987). Although it is possible to argue that we do not yet have sufficient knowledge to impose such operational criteria there is no doubt that their introduction has improved the reliability of psychiatric diagnosis. In the case of social function it would be quite wrong to impose similar criteria because good social function is as much a subjective as objective phenomenon. If subjective and objective judgments disagree there are no satisfactory ways of determining which should take priority.

This does not mean of course that social function cannot be measured adequately; it only serves to emphasise caution in interpreting the findings. In fact social function has been recognized as a separate axis of measurement and classification for several years and has been given an equivalent status to mental state classification in DSM-III and DSM-IIIR. In the most recent classification, ICD-10, there is also a separate axis (Axis II) measuring disability (WHO Disability Diagnostic Scale) (WHO–DDS) which has been developed from earlier measurements (World Health Organisation, 1980) and which measures 'the best estimate of the degree of dysfunction in relation to the maximum level of expected functioning in the sociocultural context of the patient' (World Health Organisation, 1993, see also Chapter 10). In these classifications social function is used almost synonymously with social competence and describes the ability of the person to cope with the demands imposed by the main spheres of living: work, household responsibilities, financial commitments, leisure time, family relationships, and wider social interactions. Social function can equally be regarded as a description of an individual's network and social contacts, or, more particularly, those to whom the individual is particularly attached, social status and social role performance (Weissman *et al.*, 1981).

Rather than examine each of these individually, the research worker wishing to measure social function usually has to make a decision about which of three types of measurement is most desirable: measurement of (a) social competence as judged by the individual in his or her environmental setting, (b) the person's social function in the eyes of society at large (best viewed as social role performance), or (c) the number and extent of supportive and other relationships for the person (social networks). Although these distinctions are not usually made formally in the description of measuring instruments they can be identified, if only by implication.

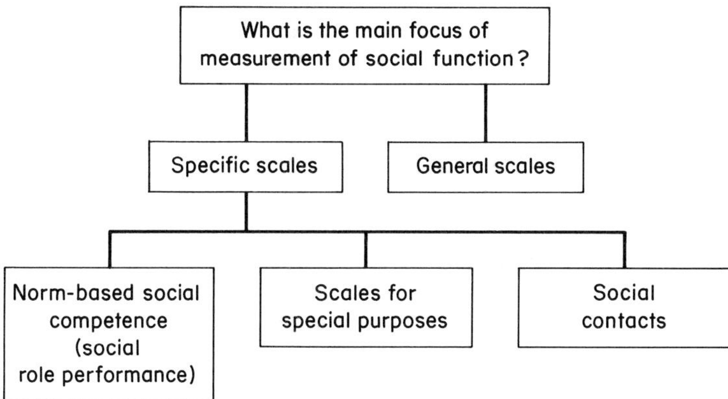

Figure 3.1. Flowchart to measurements of social function described in this chapter.

In recent years it has become clear that social function and psychiatric symptomatology are not always highly correlated and a measurement of social function as well as symptomatology is a useful combination. Even scales such as the Global Assessment Scale (GAS) (Endicott *et al.*, 1976), which attempt to measure total function in a single measurement, not only include the measurement of social function but give it sufficient weight so that it is equivalent to the recording of symptomatology. The choice of measurement is discussed under the headings outlined in the flowchart and in the following sections (Figure 3.1).

GENERAL SCALES

The main general scales used to record social function are listed in Table 3.1. It is difficult to be guided as to which scale to use and a great deal depends on the time available, the specific use of the instrument, and its availability. The most popular scales are the Social Behaviour Schedule (SBS) (Sturt and Wykes, 1986) and the Social Adjustment Scale (SAS) (Paykel *et al.*, 1971) which, although having some of the characteristics of a social role performance scale has some of the characteristics of a general scale also.

Almost all these scales assess, to varying degrees, functioning in work and daily tasks, household responsibilities, financial management, childcare, social and family relationships, and use of spare time. Table 3.2 shows the social function component derived from the Global Assessment Scale (GAS). The shortest of the general scales, the Social Functioning Questionnaire (SFQ), is reproduced in Table 3.3, together with the full GAS

Table 3.1. General scales for measurement of social function for administration to subjects or informants.

Scale[a]	Authors (source of scale)	Main features
Katz Adjustment Scales (S and I)	Katz and Lyerly (1963)[b]	205 items rated by patients (55) and relatives (150) on 4-point scales (30–35 mins)
Social Adjustment Inventory (I)	Berger et al. (1964)	33 items rated by close informant on 6-point scale (10 mins)
Social Dysfunction Rating Scale (SDRS) (S)	Linn et al. (1969), McDowell and Newell (1987)	21 items rated on a 6-point scale (not present–very severe); administered as semistructured interview (15–40 mins, this variation is because some items may require careful assessment if scored positive)
Levels of Function Scale (S)	Strauss and Carpenter (1972)	4-item scale covering both social adjustment and symptoms (20 mins)
KDS-15 (S and I)	Frank and Kupfer (1974)	80-item scale to assess marital function (40 mins)
Psychosocial Adjustment to Illness Scale (PAIS)	Derogatis (1976)	Seven sections involving 45 questions covering attitudes to health care (25 mins)
Social Adjustment Scale — Self-report (SAS–SR) (S)	Weissman and Bothwell (1976), McDowell and Newell (1987)	42-item scale developed from interview version (SAS) (20 mins)
Global Assessment of of Functioning Scale (O)	Endicott et al. (1976)	Global scale assessed by interviewer that is now an integral part of DSM-IIIR. Although it includes both mental state and social function components in one scale these can also be separated
Social Functioning Schedule (SFS)	Remington and Tyrer (1979)[c]	Record of social function in work/tasks, money, personal, social and childcare relationships, and spare time (20 mins)
Standardised Interview to Assess Maladjustment (S)	Clare and Cairns (1978)	Six sections covering 42 items on 4-point scales (45 mins). Planned for studies of neurotic disorders
Social Functioning Questionnaire (SFQ) (S)	Tyrer (1990)[d]	8-item scale each scored on 4 points (5 mins). Correlates well with scores on SFS (Table 3.3) (Tyrer et al., 1990)

[a]S, subject; I, informant; O, observer.
[b]Department of Psychiatry, Albert Einstein College of Medicine, Bronx Municipal Hospital, New York 10461, USA.
[c]St Charles Hospital, London W10 6DZ, UK.
[d]See Table 3.3.

Table 3.2. Global Assessment of Functioning Scale (GAF): social function and performance (from Endicott *et al.*, 1976).

90 – 81	Able to function well in occupational, social and spare time activities with no difficulties.
80 – 71	Some minor stress or difficulties limiting full function but having little effect on general performance.
70 – 61	Mild but definite problems in social, school or occupational functioning.
60 – 51	Moderate impairment of function at work, school or spare time with definite handicaps.
50 – 41	Serious impairment of occupational and social functioning, with persistent handicaps and difficulties in at least some relationships.
40 – 31	Major impairment in several areas of social function with inability to maintain or develop satisfactory relationships except with a few people.
30 – 21	Impairment in social function so serious that normal activities impossible except in sheltered situations (e.g. hospital, clinic).
20 – 11	Gross social dysfunction leading to personal neglect or conflict in behaviour towards others that is threatening or dangerous.
10 – 1	Social dysfunction so serious that intervention necessary to prevent death to self or others through injury or neglect.

A score of between 90 and 100 can be obtained but would indicate no dysfunction at all.

(Table 3.4). Many of the other scales concentrate on special areas of social function or on special populations. Almost all have a potential problem with scoring. If, for example, the scale referring to work performance is not scored because the person is unemployed then the item is missed out when adding up the scores, and those which are scored are averaged to produce a score of mean social function. If, subsequently, the person gets a job but does not perform particularly well at first and is under more stress, the item referring to work performance is scored poorly and the mean social function score may be reduced somewhat. In reality, however, the person's function has probably improved. This potential for error is reduced if the scales are scored

Table 3.3. The Social Functioning Questionnaire (SFQ).

Please look at the statements below and tick the reply that comes closest to how you have been over the past two weeks.

		Score
I complete my tasks at work and at home satisfactorily.	Most of the time	0
	Quite often	1
	Sometimes	2
	Not at all	3
I find my tasks at work and at home very stressful.	Most of the time	3
	Quite often	2
	Sometimes	1
	Not at all	0
I have no money problems.	No problems at all	0
	Slight worries only	1
	Definite problems	2
	Very severe problems	3
I have difficulties in getting and keeping close relationships.	Severe difficulties	3
	Some problems	2
	Occasional problems	1
	No problems at all	0
I have problems in my sex life.	Severe problems	3
	Moderate problems	2
	Occasional problems	1
	No problems at all	0
I get on well with my family and other relatives.	Yes, definitely	0
	Yes, usually	1
	No, some problems	2
	No, severe problems	3
I feel lonely and isolated from other people.	Almost all the time	3
	Much of the time	2
	Not usually	1
	Not at all	0
I enjoy my spare time	Very much	0
	Sometimes	1
	Not often	2
	Not at all	3

in sections or if work and tasks are regarded as equivalent — even those without work have tasks they expect to, or are expected to, perform.

The Social Adjustment Scale — Self-report (SAS–SR) (Weissman and Bothwell, 1976) is one of the best tested of scales and is particularly

Table 3.4. The full Global Assessment of Functioning Scale (GAF Scale)
(Endicott *et al.*, 1976).

Note: Use intermediate codes when appropriate, e.g., 45, 68, 72.

90 Absent or minimal symptoms (e.g. mild anxiety before an exam), good functioning in all
| areas, interested and involved in a wide range of activities, socially effective, generally
| satisfied with life, no more than everyday problems or concerns (e.g. an occasional
81 argument with family members).

80 If symptoms are present, they are transient and expectable reactions to psychosocial
| stressors (e.g. difficulty concentrating after family argument); no more than slight
| impairment in social, occupational, or school functioning (e.g. temporarily falling behind
71 in school work).

70 Some mild symptoms (e.g., depressed mood and mild insomnia) OR some difficulty in
| social, occupational, or school functioning (e.g. occasional truancy, or theft within the
| household), but generally functioning pretty well, has some meaningful interpersonal
61 relationships.

60 Moderate symptoms (e.g. flat affect and circumstantial speech, occasional panic attacks)
| OR moderate difficulty in social, occupational, or school functioning (e.g. few friends,
51 conflicts with co-workers).

50 Serious symptoms (e.g. suicidal ideation, severe obsessional rituals, frequent shoplifting)
| OR any serious impairment in social, occupational, or school functioning (e.g. no friends,
41 unable to keep a job).

40 Some impairment in reality testing or communication (e.g. speech is at time illogical,
| obscure, or irrelevant) OR major impairment in several areas, such as work or school,
| family relations, judgement, thinking, or mood (e.g. depressed man avoids friends,
| neglects family, and is unable to work; child frequently beats up younger children, is
31 defiant at home, and is failing at school).

30 Behaviour is considerably influenced by delusions or hallucinations OR serious
| impairment in communication or judgment (e.g. sometimes incoherent, acts grossly
| inappropriately, suicidal preoccupation) OR inability to function in almost all areas (e.g.
21 stays in bed all day; no job, home, or friends).

20 Some danger of hurting self or others (e.g. suicide attempts without clear expectation of
| death, frequently violent, manic excitement) OR occasionally fails to maintain minimal
| personal hygiene (e.g. smears faeces) OR gross impairment in communication (e.g.
11 largely incoherent or mute).

10 Persistent danger of severely hurting self or others (e.g. recurrent violence) OR
| persistent inability to maintain minimal personal hygiene OR serious suicidal act with
1 clear expectation of death.

commended by McDowell and Newell (1987). The scale has mainly been
used with depressed patients although an enlarged version (SAS–II), a semi-
structured interview containing 56 items, has been used in the assessment of
schizophrenic patients.

The Social Maladjustment Schedule (Clare and Cairns, 1978) has a certain inherent face validity, with the separation of material conditions (e.g. family income, housing status), social management (e.g. financial affairs) and satisfaction in each of the main areas of function. However, there is limited evidence of its reliability and validity. Factor analysis of the data shows that the main areas of measurement overlap greatly. The same criticisms apply to the Social Dysfunction Rating Scale (SDRS) (Linn *et al.*, 1969) which has scores divided into three systems (self, interpersonal and performance), a division that is not supported by factor analysis of the data (Linn *et al.*, 1969). Despite this, the scale has enjoyed considerable use and has been of value in assessing schizophrenic and psychogeriatric patients in particular (Goodman *et al.*, 1969; Linn *et al.*, 1979).

The Social and Behaviour Schedule (SBS) (Sturt and Wykes, 1986) is an excellent scale for assessing behaviour rapidly with an informant, particularly in psychotic patients. It takes about 10 minutes to complete but requires an informant (usually a carer) who has had a reasonable degree of recent contact with the person concerned. The Social Functioning Schedule (SFS) is simple to use and involves scoring on an analogue scale for each area of social function on both behavioural and stress items. It is applicable across the range of psychiatric disorders and has also been used in psychiatric studies of discharged in-patients (Goering *et al.*, 1983, 1984; Casey *et al.*, 1985) and in other community studies (Burns *et al.*, 1993).

The Katz Scales are not now recommended as they have not been adequately tested for reliability and validity (McDowell and Newell, 1987) but are of considerable interest as they antedate most of the other scales.

SOCIAL ROLE PERFORMANCE

Because the bias of interviewers can enter into allegedly objective assessments of social competence the importance of norm-based and subject-based assessments becomes more important. The norm-based scales (Table 3.5) mostly owe their origin to the Normative Social Adjustment Scale (NSAS) (Barrabee *et al.*, 1955) in which normal function was in effect defined in advance by the investigators and assessments were made to determine 'the degree to which a person fulfils the normative social expectations of behaviour that constitute his roles' (Barrabee *et al.*, 1955). Such scales became very popular in the United States in the 1970s and, to coin a cliché, became the norm. These scales imply that certain numbers of social contacts, types of relationships, satisfactory employment, and 'good' use of leisure time are ideals to be aimed for by all members of the population, and, if for some reason the ideal of a heterosexual relationship, preferably marital, with sexual intercourse two to three times weekly, high job aspirations with an

Table 3.5. Scales of social function that primarily measure social performance.

Scale[a]	Authors (source of scale)	Main features
Normative Social Adjustment Scale (NSAS) (O)	Barrabee *et al.* (1955)	27 key items, each rated on a 5-point scale (up to 60 mins)
Social Role Adjustment Instrument (SRAI) (O)	Cohler *et al.* (1968)	Semi-structured interview of 200 items specifically to assess women in their adjustment to their roles in society
Structured and Scaled Interview to Assess Maladjustment (SSIAM) (S and O)	Gurland *et al.* (1972)	60-item scale, each 11-point, covering work, social relations, family, marriage and sex, but also including 15 items rated by the interviewer, including personality strengths (30 minutes)
Social Adjustment Scale (SAS) (O)	Paykel *et al.* (1971)	54-item scale which contains alternative questions for some items so only 42 are recorded together with 6 global judgements (45–60 mins)
Social Functioning Scale (SFS) (S and I)	Birchwood (1983)[b]	Records assessment of function and needs in seven areas, primarily used in schizophrenic patients and is most appropriate for this population and others in which basic living skills may be impaired

[a]S, subject; I, informant; O, observer.
[b]Psychology Department, All Saints Hospital, Birmingham B18 5SD; also published as
   appendix in Barrowclough and Tarrier (1992).

increasing income and manageable debts, and a broad ranging social network of friends with good, but not too close, relationships with blood relatives, was not considered to be worth striving for, this was a criticism of the person's social attitudes, not a criticism of the method of assessment.

The main advantage of the norm based scales is that they tend to be associated with better reliability and the assessor is spared the embarrassment of seeing an individual who, for example, is homeless and unemployed but contented with their lot and without any social distress; the happy tramp. This is illustrated by the following example, taken from clinical practice, in which several scales were used to make an assessment of social function. The individual concerned is not homeless, but would have been without the intervention of his concerned family and the local psychiatric services. He does not work, but regards this as a normal state of affairs where he lives, as unemployment rates are 20% and much higher in his ethnic group, the Afro-Caribbean one. He smokes cannabis at times and sometimes drinks to excess (but not recently for financial reasons). He has been assessed on many occasions by the psychiatric services and on one occasion was admitted compulsorily because of self-neglect, but after full assessment was felt either to have simple schizophrenia or a schizoid personality disorder, rather than an active psychotic disorder. He did not respond to antipsychotic drug treatment and was found to lack motivation for any form of retraining for work or improving his social contacts. He visits his family, who live nearby, and occasionally drinks with friends.

Despite these apparent problems he is always cheerful and accommodating when seen and complains of no problems. He can do what he wants when he likes and does not ask for anything more from his life. He has no special ambitions and although his flat is bare, dirty and uninviting, he likes it and has no wish to move. He is well-fed and whenever he visits home his mother gives him a large hot meal which helps to balance the somewhat restricted diet he has at other times. He tends to avoid contact with other people and has a restricted social network.

This man scores very low on scales for social role performance and much higher on general scales. Thus, for example, in the SSIAM he score poorly on all areas, having no interest in work, with relative social isolation, friction with his family who want him to do more, no heterosexual relationships, and few personal strengths. Similarly, on the Social Functioning Scale (Birchwood, 1983) he scores poorly on social engagement (spends most of his time alone), interpersonal communication (no friends apart from drinking partners), independence (scores somewhat higher but still needs help from family), recreation (no hobbies apart from watching television), prosocial behaviour (unmotivated for active involvement in social and leisure activities) and employment (unemployed and avoiding prospects of work). On general scales, however, particularly those completed with the subject, he scores much higher. For example, the question from the Social Adjustment Scale (SAS) 'Have you felt bored with your spare time during the last two weeks?' he answers 'I never felt bored', and on the Social Functioning Questionnaire he scores a total of 3 (out of a maximum score of 24 (with higher scores indicating worse functioning).

The reasons for the discrepancy in scoring is quite clear when one looks at an individual case such as this. Society does not look kindly on what it sees as a parasitic couch potato, who does nothing to earn his keep and, what is worse, shows no desire to change. The subject sees himself, and many in his immediate generational ethnic group share his view, as alienated from the mainstream of society and has no particular desire to become integrated. This is partly cultural and partly clinical as he probably has a psychiatric illness, but he has made what could be regarded as a reasonable adjustment to a difficult situation and has achieved a stability of sorts. He is therefore within normal limits when examined from his immediate social microcosm but highly abnormal when examined from society in general and from the standpoint of thrusting middle-class mental health professionals in particular. Whenever an external or allegedly 'objective' view of his social function is taken he will score badly.

When social role performance is assessed from a common origin, the putative measure of good social adjustment in society, which is productive, sharing and involved, it is much easier to get good agreement in ratings than when the assessment is made from the normative values of the subject or his intimate societal framework.

When does this matter? Is it just an academic issue or has it real importance in recording social function? It is important, because we are attempting in this axis of classification to identify something which is not the same as general affluence, life satisfaction or a measure of integration in society, although it is correlated with all three of these. The important distinction is between social satisfaction and social role; sometimes they are congruent but at others are widely disparate. As with all measures the choice is not which is the 'best scale' but which is most fitted for the purposes of the investigator (Kendell, 1975). If, for example, the measurement is being used as part of an investigation to improve the mental status (and also the social competence) of a defined population (e.g. with schizophrenia) then the best measurement is probably one which incorporates social role to some extent (e.g. Social Functioning Scale (Birchwood, 1983)) as this would detect quite small changes in degree of independence and daily living skills. If the measurement is concerned with, for example, the general social function of populations in different geographical areas, then a general scale concerning social satisfaction is preferable, as it would not be biased by sociodemographic influences to nearly the same extent as a social role performance scale.

Of the scales recording social performance, the SSIAM (Gurland *et al.*, 1972) and the SAS (Paykel *et al.*, 1971) are the most widely used but the other scales have their uses in particular populations. The Social Functioning Scale (Birchwood, 1983) which can easily be confused with the Social Functioning Schedule (Remington and Tyrer, 1979) is well tested for reliability and structure but has been used primarily in the assessment of schizophrenic patients and is particularly suited to this group (Birchwood *et al.*, 1990).

SCALES FOR SPECIAL PURPOSES

The difficulties of defining social function have been alluded to on many occasions throughout this book. It is therefore to be expected that some interpretations of social function lend themselves to special instruments. However, in this section there are several disparate scales that have no natural inter-relationships; they are listed together for those investigators

Table 3.6.   Rating scales for special purposes.

Scale[a]	Authors (source of scale)	Main features
Personal Resources Inventory (PRI) (S)	Clayton and Hirschfeld (1977)[b]	41-item interview assessing best social function in a defined period (usually over past year) (20 mins)
Social Disability Questionnaire (SDQ) (S)	Branch and Jette (1981)	A self-report scale useful in surveys of elderly population
General Health Questionnaire (GHQ) (S)	Goldberg (1972)	A 60-item questionnaire (also available in 12, 20, 28 and 30 items) with questions that include social function
Social Behaviour Assessment Schedule (SBAS) (S and I)	Platt *et al.* (1980)	A comprehensive 239-item interview schedule that is best used to assess function/behaviour over the past month; includes assessment of impact of behaviour on others

[a]S, subject; I, informant; O, observer.
[b]Department of Psychiatry, Washington University School of Medicine, St Louis, Missouri 63110, USA.

who have a clear idea of what they wish to measure and understand the issues well.

The scales for special purposes (Table 3.6) cover screening to the closest of evaluations of social dysfunction. The Personal Resources Inventory (Clayton and Hirschfeld, 1977) assesses the best level of social function achieved over a set time period, and reflects the interest of this subject in the DSM-III classification, where best social function in the past year was one of the axes of classification. The scale is a measure of both potential and positive functioning and has merits in determining what people can achieve rather than merely recording how they are at a single time point.

Both the Social Disability Questionnaire (SDQ) (Branch and Jette, 1981) and the General Health Questionnaire (GHQ) (Goldberg, 1972) are useful in screening social function. The SDQ also includes a measure of risk and can therefore be used to anticipate further problems. Although the GHQ is primarily used to screen for mental illness, particularly common ones in defined populations, it contains many questions that measure primarily social function and which have been identified as such in factor analytic studies (e.g. Worsley and Gribben, 1977). A simple way of screening for social dysfunction is to score the items referring to social dysfunction separately. However, the appropriate cut-off points for poor and good function have not been identified. The questions specifically referring to social function in the GHQ are listed in Table 3.7.

Table 3.7. Twelve items from the GHQ-60 that primarily measure social function.

Number of question in GHQ 60-item scale	Subject
21	Managing to keep busy and occupied
22	Taking longer over the things you do
23	Losing interest in your personal appearance
25	Taking less interest in your clothes
28	Felt on the whole you were doing things well
29	Been late getting to work, or getting started on your housework
30	Been satisfied with the way you've carried out your task
32	Been finding it easy to get on with other people
33	Spent much time chatting to people
35	Felt you were playing a useful part in things
36	Felt capable of making decisions about things
42	Been able to enjoy your normal day-to-day activities

The Social Behaviour Assessment Schedule (SBAS) is perhaps the most objective measure of social function available. It concentrates on a dispassionate record of social behaviour both with the subject and close informants. By examining every part of an individual's behavioural repertoire with only the barest minimum of subjective impression an assessment is made which is in the spirit of true ethology; a record of actual behaviour and its impact. Unfortunately the scale can take up to two hours to complete and is not used as widely as it deserves because of this handicap. For investigators who have the need and the time to look at all social behaviour it remains a most valuable instrument. It is also completely lacking in the social role distortions induced by other scales. Many of the components and principles of this instrument have been adopted in the assessment of social function in care management, e.g. Care Management Carer's Questionnaire (CMCQ) (Research and Development for Psychiatry, 134–138 Borough High Street, London SE1 1LB).

SOCIAL CONTACTS AND NETWORKS

There is increasing interest in the nature and quality of social relationships in psychiatry. This has been highlighted in particular by studies of expressed emotion in various psychiatric illnesses, particularly in schizophrenia, but it is also important in developing rehabilitation programmes and in predicting the vulnerability to conditions such as depression. However, although the subject is important, it is not easy to measure. This is not because it is intrinsically difficult, but that at times it can be extremely boring. If one considers the number of social interactions that the average person has during the

Table 3.8. Interview measures for social attachment and support.

Scale[a]	Authors (source)	Main Features
Social Interaction Schedule (SIS) (S)	Henderson *et al.* (1978)[b]	Assesses all social interactions over the previous seven days (may take over an hour)
The Interview Schedule for Social Interaction (ISSI) (S)	Henderson *et al.* (1980)[b]	Similar to SIS but no fixed time interval. Uses a complex system of scoring availability and adequacy of social attachment and integration
Social Relationships Scale (SRS) (S with O)	McFarlane *et al.* (1981)[c]	Measure of quality of relationships in 6 areas of functioning
Family Relations Inventory (FRI) Work Relations Inventory (WRI)	Holohan and Moos (1983)	Measurement of frequency and quality of relationships within family and at work
Social Support Questionnaire (S)	Sarason *et al.* (1983)[d]	Measures the number (SSQ–N) and perceived satisfaction (SSQ–S) of social relationships
Self-evaluation and Social Support Schedule (SESS)	O'Connor and Brown (1984)	Detailed assessment of close relationships (may take up to 2 hours)
Interview Measure of Social Relationships (IMSR) (S)	Brugha *et al.* (1987)[e]	Modified version of the SIS (above) which is shortened to include important social contacts only (can still take 30–60 min)
Social Network Scale (SNS)	Dunn *et al.* (1990)[f]	Short interview scale to establish the social networks of psychiatric patients, with simple measures of both quality and quantity

[a]S, subject; I, informant; O, observer.
[b]See Henderson *et al.* (1981).
[c]Department of Psychiatry, McMaster University, Hamilton, Ontario, Canada L86 3Z5.
[d]Department of Psychology, University of Washington, Seattle, Washington 98195, USA.
[e]Department of Psychiatry, University of Leicester, PO Box 65, Leicester LE2 7LX, UK.
[f]Team for the Assessment of Psychiatric Services, Friern Hospital, London N11 3BP, UK.

course of the day it can be extremely difficult to record all of these accurately and reliably.

Considerable time can be saved by the use of questionnaires to record the type and frequency of contact and its direction (either negative or positive). These are shown in Table 3.8. Each of these instruments has satisfactory reliability; the social Support Questionnaire (SSQ) is perhaps the best known.

The SSQ is self-administered and consists of 27 questions, each of two parts. The first lists the people who the person can count on for support in specified circumstances (availability) and the second asks how satisfied the people are with the type and level of support usually offered (satisfaction). A maximum of nine people can be listed in the support network. The questions include a good range of everyday issues; some examples of which are given below, with the item number indicated in parentheses:

(6)   Whom can you talk with frankly, without having to watch what you say?

(18) Whom do you feel would help if a family member very close to you died?

(26) Whom can you really count on to support you in major decisions you make?

The scale has received some validation from a positive correlation between the number of positive (favourable) life events and high scores on the questionnaire (Sarason *et al.*, 1983). It is relatively economical in terms of time and its only disadvantage is that it has not been fully tested in severe mental illness. The questions also require a certain level of psychological understanding which is not universal.

The Interview Schedule for Social Interaction (ISSI) (Henderson *et al.*, 1980) is probably the most comprehensive instrument available. Although it is described as taking only 45 minutes to complete, it usually takes longer. It records both the quality and quantity of social support over a fairly long period, usually a year, and the results are analysed by availability of attachment and social integration and its adequacy. It is a useful instrument in detailed surveys but is perhaps too cumbersome to use in studies using repeated measures. It has been tested mainly in neurotic patients and in normal populations and may make too many demands on those with severe mental illness.

The Social Interaction Schedule (SIS) (Henderson *et al.*, 1978) preceded the ISSI and in many respects is a prototype of it. The Interview Measure of Social Relationships (IMSR) (Brugha *et al.*, 1987) also assesses the number and quality of social interactions and is somewhat shorter. Nevertheless, as is clear from the study described in the next section, it yields a great deal of information, even in its shortened form, and this can be a problem when used repeatedly. The Social Network Scale (SNS) (Dunn *et al.*, 1990) was created specially to assess the social support of long-stay patients discharged from psychiatric hospital and contains questions that are really only suited to this population, (e.g. 'would you visit X if either of you moved from here? Do you just say hello to X, do you do things for each other, or do you have conversations?').

The other scales listed in Table 3.8 are used more in family and psychotherapeutic studies and have not been as widely used as the others. However, almost all seek to record the presence or absence of good support in the form of attachment in the sense used by Bowlby (1973), a close and pleasurable relationship that is mutually satisfying, reinforcing and protecting. I suspect, but this is a hypothesis that remains to be tested, that such relationships are not specifically protecting in themselves and that they are secondary features associated with positive personality attributes. According to their view, if any of these supports are removed from such people by death or transition in another form mental health is sustained because of these underlying personality strengths.

It is of some interest that a psychological variable, information processing, measured by the speed of response in a complex test in which there is a cognitive component as well as simple reaction time, is at least as effective a predictor, and possibly better, than social support at functioning, in predicting outcome in schizophrenia (Wykes *et al.*, 1990). The notion of good social support preventing illness and promoting recovery is seductive but generally lacking in evidence as a prime mover in the generation of and restitution from psychiatric disorder.

MEASUREMENT OF SOCIAL FUNCTION IN A CONTROLLED STUDY OF PSYCHIATRIC SERVICES

To illustrate the value of the measurement of social function in psychiatric services the remainder of this chapter will be concerned with describing the results of a project in which two psychiatric services were compared using the mechanism of the randomized controlled trial. The study concerned compared two psychiatric services, a community-based multidisciplinary team (Early Intervention Service) and a more traditional hospital-based (Standard) psychiatric service. Although both services are based in the same catchment area they do not have a common referral base. The Early Intervention Service operates an open referral system but takes referrals from any source and sees them within a few days whereas the hospital service has a generally slower response to referrals except for severe emergencies, which normally present by the accident and emergency department via the adjacent St Mary's Hospital.

The patients studied were those who presented as emergencies, either to the accident and emergency department, directly to the psychiatrists in the hospital, or to the social work department (also based in the psychiatric unit). Patients were included in the study if they were aged between 16 and 65, were considered after assessment to be suffering from a psychiatric disorder other than primary alcohol or drug dependence, were resident within the catchment area, were not in contact with the psychiatric services and did not require mandatory in-patient care (e.g. compulsory admission under the Mental Health Act). Patients were also required to give informed consent.

Those satisfying the criteria were allocated to the Early Intervention Service (EIS) or hospital (Standard) group via the duty psychiatrist or approved social worker opening a sealed envelope which gave the random allocation. Patients were also stratified for the presence or absence of previous psychiatric contact as this is known to be important in determining outcome.

As the study involved comparison of services there were no restrictions on treatment. Patients referred to the EIS or Standard service received the normal service provisions in that setting and no restrictions were imposed. Most referrals to the EIS were seen at home, at least initially, and referrals to the Standard service were seen at out-patient clinics, social work offices or a day hospital (also based within the psychiatric unit).

The patients were assessed over a period of 12 weeks, at initial randomization, and after two, four and 12 weeks. All assessments were made by psychiatrists who were unaware of the service to which patients had been allocated and at initial assessment the patient too was unaware of the service allocation. Clinical symptoms were scored using the Comprehensive Psychopathological Rating Scale (CPRS) (Åsberg *et al.*, 1978) and its subscales for both depression (Montgomery and Asberg Depression Rating Scale (MADRS) (Montgomery and Åsberg, 1979)) and anxiety (Brief Scale for Anxiety (BAS) (Tyrer *et al.*, 1984)). Social function was measured using the Social Functioning Questionnaire (SFQ) (Tyrer, 1990) (Table 3.3). This is a short self-rated eight item questionnaire which was felt to be most appropriate for the study because many of the patients were expected to be intolerant of research procedures. In such situations research assessments need to be short. In addition the Interview Measure of Social Relationships (IMSR) (Brugha *et al.*, 1987) was administered to record the extent, nature and duration of social contacts and networks.

The IMSR collects data from the number of people in the social network of those being interviewed together with the number of contacts with them. It examines what is called the Primary Social Network (PSN) which consists of household members, close relatives, friends and attachment figures. Attachment figures are those whom the interviewee feels particularly attached to or needs a great deal. In addition, attachment figures are people who the interviewee would find it difficult to manage without. In addition to rating the number of contacts the IMSR also establishes whether the interviewee feels that each contact had an adequate social interaction or whether it was either insufficient or too much. In our study, in which all contacts of the previous two weeks were being assessed on four occasions with each patient, it was felt that more detailed questioning about the quality of the contacts and relationships was not possible and their number and duration were recorded only.

In addition to these measurements of social function personality was assessed at the beginning of the study only. The Personality Assessment

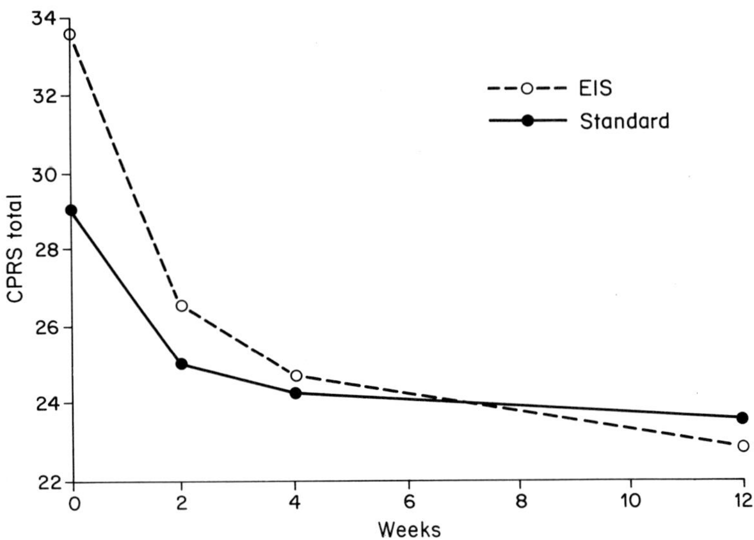

Figure 3.2. Mean changes in clinical symptomatology as measured by the Comprehensive Psychopathological Rating Scale (CPRS) in 100 patients referred to the Early Intervention Service (EIS), a community based service ($n = 48$), and the Standard hospital based service ($n = 52$). Ninety-five patients completed assessments at week 12 and analysis of covariance on ratings adjusted for scores at week 0 and 9; other baseline factors showed significant differences in improvement between the EIS and Standard service (mean improvement = 5.9; 95% confidence limits 0.4, 11.3), $p = 0.037$. (Data derived from Merson *et al.* (1992) and reproduced with permission.)

Schedule (PAS) (Tyrer and Alexander, 1979; Tyrer *et al.*, 1988) was used both with a patient and a close informant wherever possible and from these interviews a final combined personality assessment was made. A separate assessment of both mental state diagnosis and personality status was made using ICD-10 criteria by a panel of three psychiatrists as soon as possible after recruitment of patients to the study.

Main findings

The main findings regarding clinical symptoms and service outcome have been published elsewhere (Merson *et al.*, 1992). Patients referred to the EIS showed greater symptomatic improvement than those allocated to the Standard service, and this was achieved despite those in the Standard service spending eight times longer in psychiatric beds during the study. In addition, the patients seen by the EIS were significantly more satisfied with the service they received than those allocated to the Standard service. Altogether 100

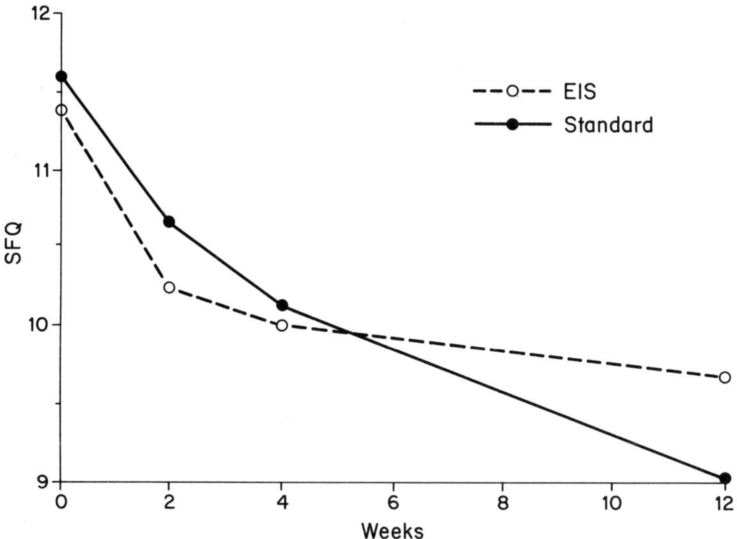

Figure 3.3. Mean changes in social function as measured by the Social Functioning Questionnaire (SFQ) in 98 patients referred to the Early Intervention Service (EIS), a community based service ($n = 47$), and the Standard hospital based service ($n = 51$). Ninety-five patients completed assessments at week 12 and analysis of covariance on ratings adjusted for scores at week 0 and 9; other baseline factors showed no differences in improvement between the EIS and Standard service (mean improvement = –0.5; 95% confidence limits –2.4, 1.4, n.s.). (Data derived from Merson *et al.* (1992) and reproduced with permission.)

patients were seen in the study, 38 of whom had a disorder within the schizophrenic group, with 32 having mood disorders and 25 having a neurotic or stress-related disorder. Four of the patients were subsequently found to have primary alcohol or substance misuse (despite the initial assessment that excluded them as primary disorders) and one patient had a personality disorder only.

Changes in social function

Although symptoms improved to a greater extent in patients referred to the Early Intervention Service (Figure 3.2) this was not shown with social function (Figure 3.3). There was no difference in outcome between the two services and, if anything, the trend was in the opposite direction, with greater improvement in patients allocated to the Standard service.

This is of importance in itself, because it confirms that social function is affected by many other factors apart from mental state abnormality. To state

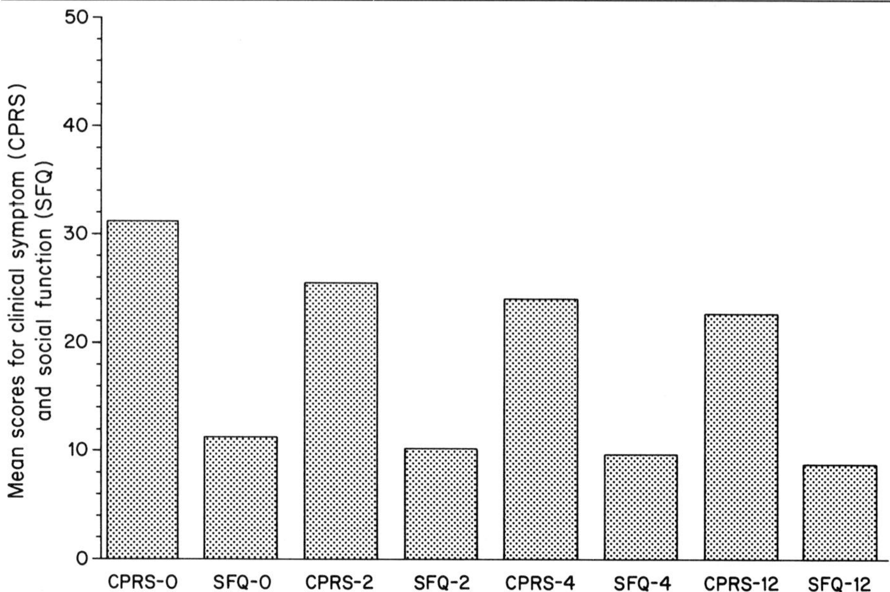

Figure 3.4. Mean changes in social function scores (SFQ) and clinical symptoms (CPRS) in 87 patients assessed on four occasions over 12 weeks in a controlled trial of services. The weighted mean correlation (r) between the two sets of scores on all occasions of testing was 0.55.

one obvious example, if a patient is admitted to hospital because of a severe depressive illness, it is reasonable to expect that social function and feelings of satisfaction will improve much more quickly than if the patient had remained, and received treatment, in the community, and this is supported by other data (Creed *et al.*, 1991); admission to hospital takes away the burdens and responsibilities of daily living and leads to immediate benefit.

It is also clear from the items recorded in the SFQ (Table 3.3) that many aspects of social function will not improve as rapidly as mental state symptoms. This is illustrated in Figure 3.4, in which the mean symptom scores (CPRS) over the course of the 12 week period of the study are shown with the mean SFQ scores. It will be noted that the symptoms change to a much greater extent than those for social function even though there is still a significant correlation between the two. However, it should not be assumed that there is necessarily little change in an individual's social functioning over a short period. Clearly if the poor social function is a direct consequence of a state that can be remedied (e.g. acute mental illness, homelessness) quite dramatic change can take place over a short period.

Despite the small mean changes shown in Figure 3.4 the level of agreement between social function at the beginning of the study and that after 12 weeks was not of a particularly high order (Figure 3.5). In addition to some

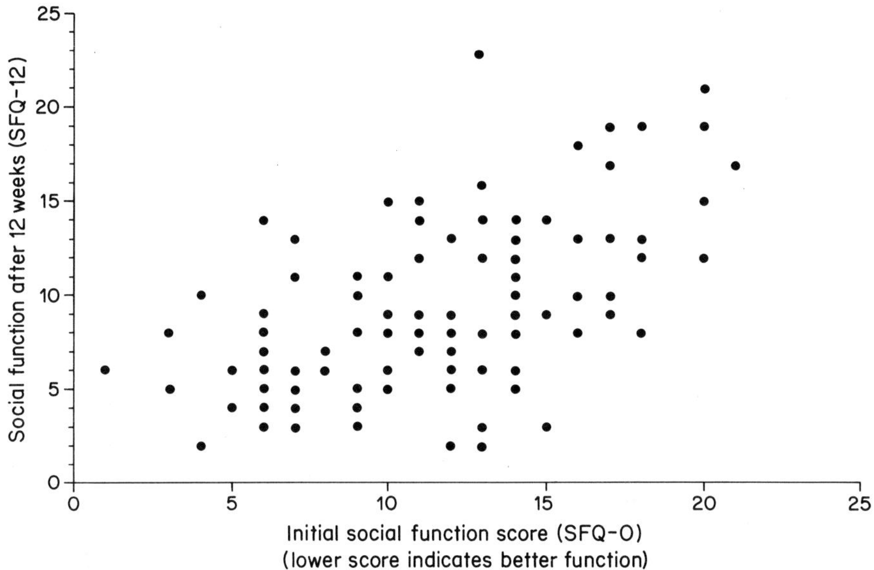

Figure 3.5.   Scattergram of scores of social function (SFQ) in 87 patients at beginning of study and after 12 weeks, illustrating extent of variation in social function during a relatively short period of service contact. The correlation (*r*) between the two sets of scores is 0.53.

dramatic improvements in social function over the 12 week period there were some equally dramatic deteriorations in functioning in several patients. However, the level of agreement was greater than for clinical symptoms (e.g. the product–moment correlation (*r*) between initial and final CPRS scores was 0.34).

Social function, clinical and personality status

As all patients presented as emergencies one might have expected that social function, recorded over the previous two weeks, would be universally poor. This was not the case as can be seen from the scattergram (Figure 3.5). As all types of mental illness were considered for the study (apart from the attempted exclusion of those with drug and alcohol abuse) it also might have been expected that there would be differences in social function between the major groups. This was found to be so, but not perhaps in the direction suspected. Patients with what is commonly regarded as the most severe mental illness, the schizophrenic group of disorders, had the best social function at initial assessment (Figure 3.6). Although there is a general

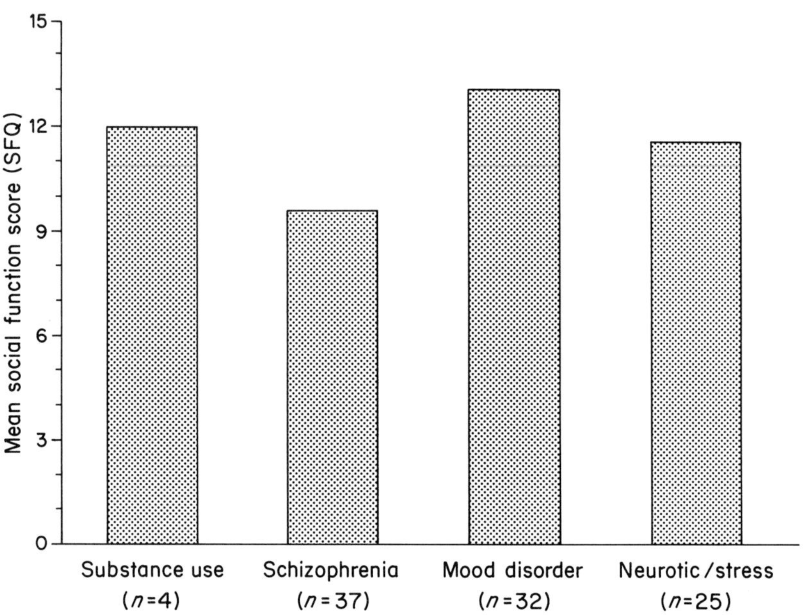

Figure 3.6.   Mean initial scores on the Social Functioning Questionnaire (SFQ) in 98 patients separated by ICD-10 diagnosis (main categories). Two patients not included; one with personality disorder only and one not assessed with SFQ. Analysis of variance of difference between means ($F = 4.2$; d.f. $= 4, 93$; $p<0.01$).

tendency towards major mental illness causing more serious social dysfunction (see Chapter 5), the circumstances in which patients were involved in this study were different from epidemiological surveys. A person with a major reaction to overwhelming environmental stress such as homelessness and unexpected loss of a partner, not only has major symptoms (most of which are understandable) but also is unable to function adequately in other respects. Conversely, many patients with schizophrenic disturbance have been unwell for a much longer period and, however imperfectly, show some adjustment to their handicap. Of course, patients are also seen in acute schizophrenic breakdown and in such instances social function is poor.

The relationship between social function and personality disorder was much more pronounced. The subject is discussed in more detail in Chapter 6 but, as discussed earlier, the intimate association between social dysfunction and disordered personality leads one to expect a closer relationship than between social function and mental state disorder. Indeed, one can almost define personality disorder as a state of perpetual social dysfunction. In the Personality Assessment Schedule (PAS) personality abnormality is scored on

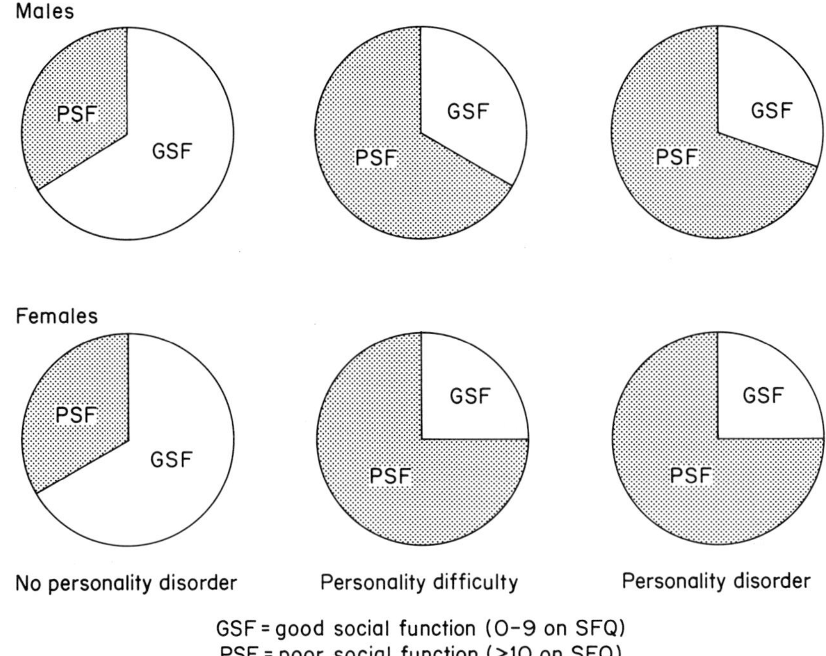

Figure 3.7. Relationship between initial scores on the Social Functioning Questionnaire (SFQ) and personality status measured using the Personality Assessment Schedule (PAS) and separated into three categories. In both sexes there is clear impairment of social function in both personality difficulty and disorder.

a dimensional scale, with four types of severity of personality disorder (simple, combined, severe and gross), personality difficulty, and no personality disorder constituting the groups.

In Figure 3.7 the relationship between initial social function scores and personality status are shown in both sexes. This demonstrates good social function in those without personality disorder and an almost converse association with poor social function in the patients with both personality difficulty and personality disorder. Bearing in mind that all those assessed were presenting as psychiatric emergencies, these findings show the paramountcy of personality disturbance as an associate of social dysfunction.

Social function and admission to hospital

In the psychiatric service the process of being admitted to hospital is like crossing the Rubicon; once the community–hospital boundary has been

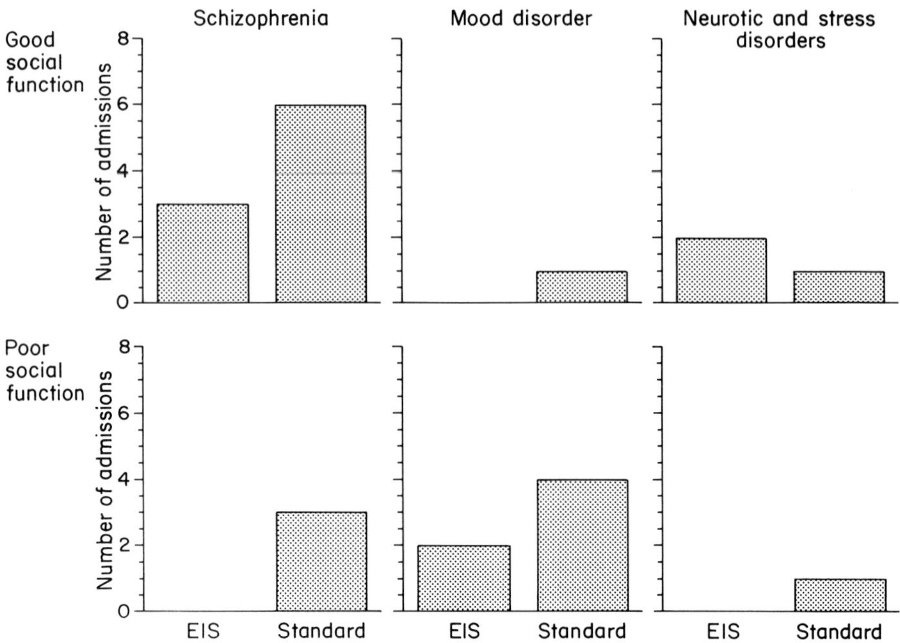

Figure 3.8.   Distribution of the 23 admissions in the study separated by service (Early Intervention Service (EIS) and Standard hospital service), ICD-10 diagnosis (main categories) and social function measured by the Social Functioning Questionnaire (SFQ) (good social function = 0–9; poor social function = 10 or greater). No patients with substance abuse were admitted during the study. One patient with personality disorder only was admitted after a stressful episode; this is included under the neurotic and stress disorders. Social function had no influence on the overall number of admissions but patients with mood disorders (depression and mania) had more admissions with poor social function than other diagnoses ($X^2 = 7.3$, d.f. = 2, $p<0.03$).

crossed it affects the life of the patient forever. Classifications of patients based on whether or not they have ever been in-patients are common and decisions such as the emigration status of people who wish to live in other countries are often based on whether or not they have been admitted to a psychiatric hospital; this is regarded as synonymous with 'real' mental illness in official minds.

This implies that there is something inexorable about admission to hospital that makes it difficult to avoid. This is far from the truth and it is useful to examine the various factors, which include social function, to determine their contribution to the decision to admit a patient at a given time.

Twenty-three of the 100 patients were admitted during the course of the 12 weeks of the study (seven (15%) of the 48 patients allocated to the Early

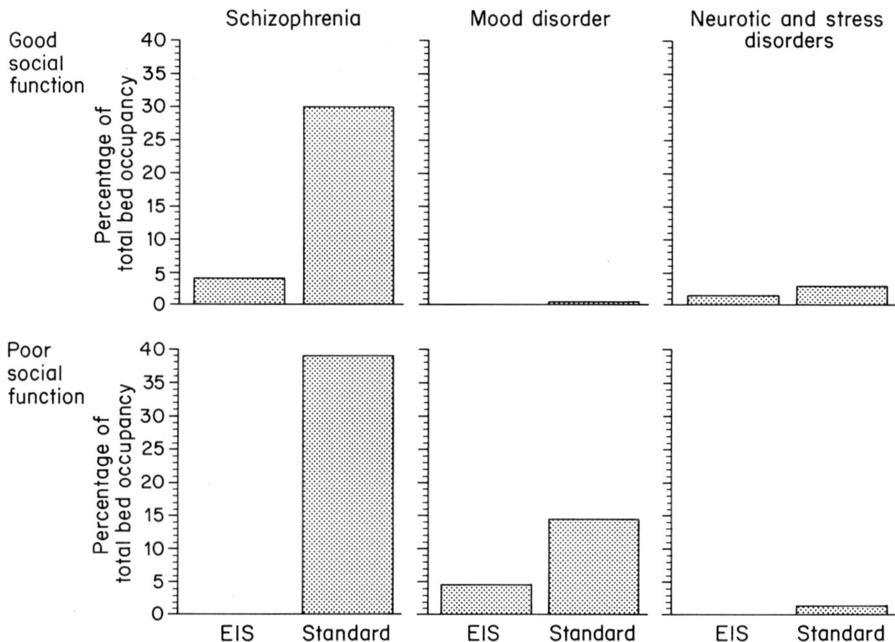

Figure 3.9. Proportion (%) of total bed occupancy (540 days) (mean = 5.4 per patient) during the study separated by service (Early Intervention Service (EIS) and Standard hospital service), ICD-10 diagnosis (main categories) and social function measured by the Social Functioning Questionnaire (SFQ) (good social function = 0–9; poor social function = 10 or greater). Social function had no significant influence on bed occupancy but patients in the Standard service with schizophrenia had greater bed occupancy than other diagnoses and EIS patients ($F = 5.1$; d.f. = 5, 90; $p<0.001$).

Intervention Service and 16 of the 52 patients (31%) allocated to the Standard hospital service). Of these admissions only two of the EIS patients were admitted for more than 10 days compared with 11 (21%) in the Standard group (Merson *et al.*, 1992).

The distribution of admissions and their relationship to initial social function scores and diagnosis are shown in Figure 3.8 and their similar relationships with the duration of admission are shown in Figure 3.9. From these results it can be seen that, overall, social function has very little apparent influence on the decision to admit or on how long the patient stays in hospital subsequently. It is also noticeable that allocation to the Early Intervention Service has a much greater impact on the admission statistics, particularly the duration of admission.

Closer examination shows that in mood disorders social function appears to be more important, and depressed or manic patients with poor social function are more likely to be admitted than those with other disorders (Figure 3.8). This refers to small numbers that may turn out to have little significance. However, it is surely relevant that the severity of depressive illnesses in the newer classifications, particularly ICD-10, are influenced heavily by the degree of social dysfunction that each causes. Thus in mild depression the subject is distressed and 'has some difficulty in carrying on with ordinary work and social activities but will not cease to function completely', but in severe depression 'it is unlikely that the subject will be able to continue with ordinary work, family and social activities, whatever the cultural setting' (World Health Organisation, 1992).

Social network and social support

In this study there were repeated measures of social network throughout the study. At initial assessment and on three further occasions during the 12 weeks the social network and nature of contacts were recorded, each time taking the two weeks before the date of assessment. It was therefore possible to measure changes in both the number and frequency of social contacts during the 12 weeks of the study, although as the additional questions in the IMSR concerning the quality of each social interaction and the perception of need were not measured, the more subtle elements of the contacts could not be assessed.

However, despite this one might have expected that during the course of an episode of psychiatric disturbance there would have been some consistent changes in either the number of social contacts or their duration during the course of the 12 week period. There were changes but they were not consistent. Taking the data both separately and together, there were no significant changes in either the number or duration of social contacts during the 12 weeks of the study and there were no differences between the two services.

However, there were clear differences identified between different groups in the study. In Figure 3.10 the mean number of household members, close relatives, friends and attachment figures (see page 36 for definition) are shown for the four main ethnic groups in the study. There were clear differences on all occasions of testing, with all types of contact being more frequent in Afro-Caribbeans than Caucasians and with friends predominating in the social contacts of those originating from Middle Eastern countries.

When the total duration of social contacts was analysed similar findings emerged, suggesting that in Afro-Caribbeans the greater number of contacts were each associated with a substantial period of interaction. Over the four occasions of testing a mean of nearly 125 hours was spent over the previous two weeks in social interaction in Afro-Caribbeans but only half this number in Indo-Asians, and Caucasians only averaging about 70 hours (Figure 3.11).

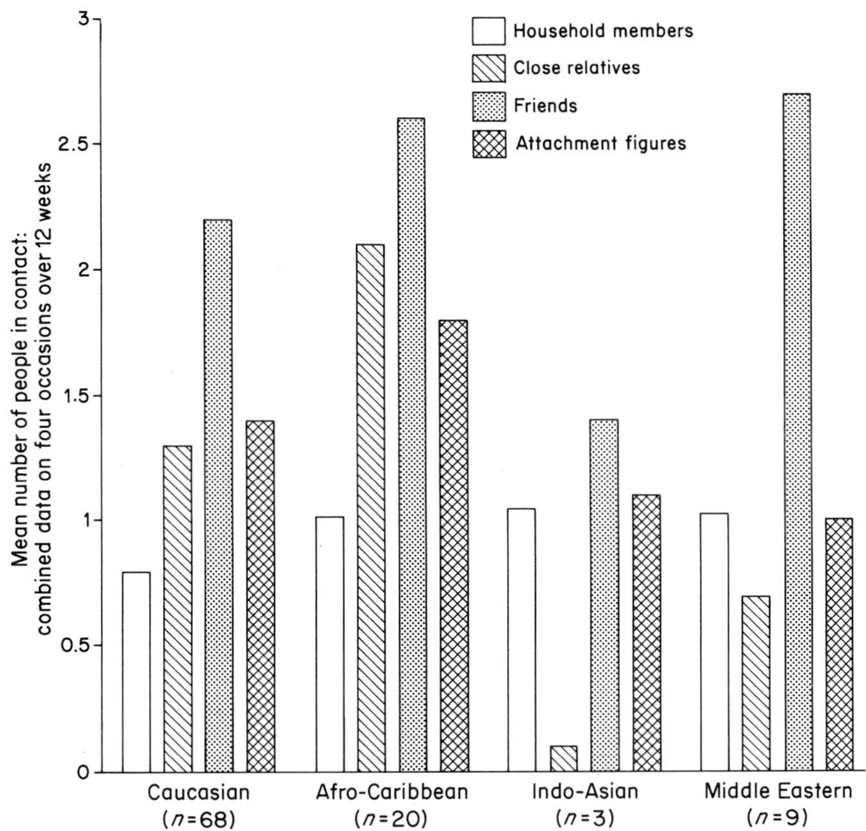

Figure 3.10. Mean number of household members, close relatives, friends and attachment figures seen over the previous two weeks (mean of four occasions) in four ethnic groups in study. All four types of social contact showed significant differences between the ethnic groups using repeated measures analysis of variance ($p<0.001$ for all four analyses). There were no significant differences in the numbers over time.

Implications of the findings

Are there any messages to be learnt about the importance and value of measurement of social function from this review and the detailed analysis of the study of psychiatric emergencies? It is of course quite possible to reach the somewhat cynical conclusion that any additional data recorded about patients will turn up some interesting findings by chance on one occasion in 20!

The findings are too consistent to make this view tenable. First, social dysfunction is a major determinant of use of the more intensive parts of the

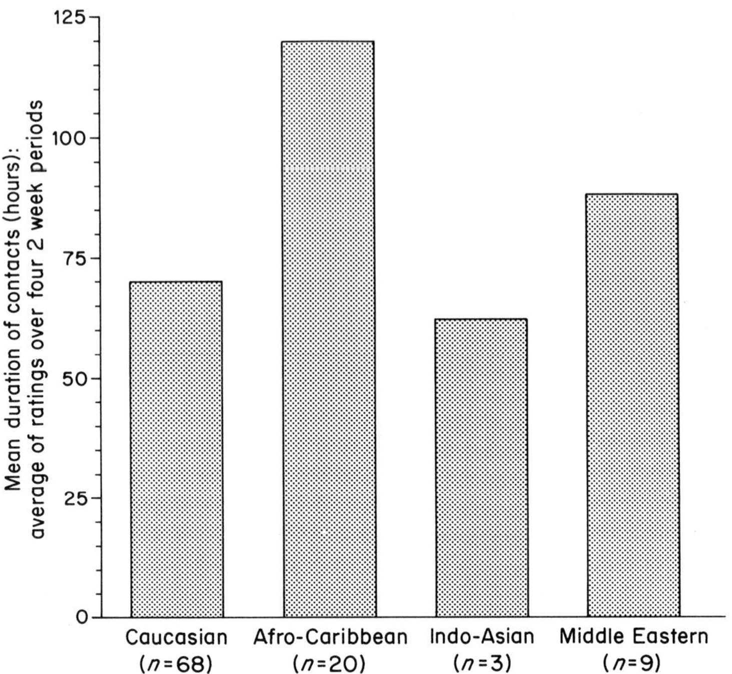

Figure 3.11.   Mean duration of social contacts of all types assessed over the previous two weeks (mean of four occasions) in four ethnic groups in study. Significantly greater duration was found in Afro-Caribbean patients compared with Caucasians ($p<0.001$). There were no significant changes in the duration of contacts over time.

psychiatric services and the uncanny levels of agreement between socio-economic deprivation and admission rates in all developed countries tells its own story. The prevalence of mental illness may show little major geographical change but its treatment does, and services that ignore social function, if not exactly blind, are badly focused.

Secondly, the provision of services must take account of the social structure of the communities which they serve. If they do not, they will alienate and treat many psychiatric problems inappropriately, whatever their level of clinical expertise, as they will fail to reach those who could be helped, antagonise many who do come into contact with the service, and consequently fail to monitor the many who deliberately avoid further contact with a system that is perceived as injuring rather than promoting their health. The success of services in overcoming these difficulties if they promote open access and good liaison in a community orientated model (Stein and Test, 1980; Hoult and Reynolds, 1984; Muijen *et al.*, 1992; Merson *et al.*, 1992) shows that present epidemiological findings need not necessarily be a blueprint for the future.

Finally, there is a question mark placed against the significance of social networks in the outcome of mental illness. The general notion that good social support is like the 'crumple zone' of a well-designed car, protecting the driver from injury even when assailed by major life events (McFarlane *et al.*, 1984; Henderson *et al.*, 1978, 1982), may be correct, but the findings of our study suggest that good social supports are not obtained easily and that little changes over a 12 week period of major crisis in the form of a psychiatric emergency. The alternative suggestion that good social support follows from a stable personality structure needs further testing.

REFERENCES

American Psychiatric Association (1980). *Diagnostic and Statistical Manual of Mental Disorders, 3rd edn.* American Psychiatric Association, Washington DC.

American Psychiatric Association (1987). *Diagnostic and Statistical Manual of Mental Disorders, 3rd edn, Revised.* American Psychiatric Association, Washington DC.

Åsberg, M., Montgomery, S.A., Perris, C., Schalling, D. and Sedvall, G. (1978). A comprehensive psychopathological rating scale. *Acta Psychiatrica Scandinavica*, **271** (Suppl.), 5–29.

Barrabee, R., Barrabee, E.L. and Finesinger, J.E.F. (1955). A normative social adjustment scale. *American Journal of Psychiatry*, **112**, 252–259.

Barrowclough, C. and Tarrier, N. (1992). *Families of Schizophrenic Patients: Cognitive Behavioural Interventions.* Chapman and Hall, London.

Berger, D.G., Rice, C.E., Sewall, L.G. *et al.* (1964). The post-hospital evaluation of psychiatric patients: the social adjustment inventory method. *Psychiatric Study Projects*, **2**, 1–30.

Birchwood, M. (1983). *Family Coping Behaviour and the Course of Schizophrenia.* PhD Thesis, University of Birmingham.

Birchwood, M., Smith, J., Cochrane, R., Wetton, S. and Copestake, S. (1990). The Social Functioning Scale: the development and validation of a new scale of social adjustment for use in family intervention programmes with schizophrenic patients. *British Journal of Psychiatry*, **157**, 853–859.

Bowlby, J. (1973). *Attachment and Loss. Vol. 2: Separation.* Basic Books, New York.

Branch, L.G. and Jette, A.M. (1981). The Framingham Disability Study: 1. Social disability among the aging. *American Journal of Public Health*, **71**, 1202–1210.

Brugha, T.S., Sturt, E., McCarthy, B., Potter, J., Wykes, T. and Bebbington, P.E. (1987). The Interview Measure of Social Relationships: the description and evaluation of a survey instrument for assessing personal social resources. *Social Psychiatry*, **22**, 123–128.

Burns, T., Beadsmoore, A., Bhat, A. V., Oliver, A. and Mathers, C. (1993). A controlled trial of home-based acute psychiatric services. I: clinical and social outcome. *British Journal of Psychiatry*, **163**, 49–54.

Casey, P.R., Tyrer, P.J. and Platt, S. (1985). The relationship between social functioning and psychiatric symptomatology in primary care. *Social Psychiatry*, **20**, 5–10.

Clare, A.W. and Cairns, V.E. (1978). Design, development and use of a standardized interview to assess social maladjustment and dysfunction in community studies. *Psychological Medicine*, **8**, 589–604.

Clayton, P. and Hirschfeld, R. (1977). *Personal Resources Inventory (PRI)*. Washington University School of Medicine, St Louis.

Cohler, B., Woolsey, S., Weiss, J. and Grunbaum, H. (1968). Child rearing attitudes among mothers volunteering and revolunteering for a psychological study. *Psychological Reports*, **23**, 603–612.

Creed, F., Black, D., Anthony, P., Osborn, M., Thomas, P. and Tormenson, B. (1991). Randomised control trial of day-patients vs in-patients' psychiatric treatment. *British Medical Journal*, **300**, 1033–1037.

Derogatis, L.R. (1976). *Scoring and Procedures: Manual for PAIS*. Clinical Psychometrics Research, Baltimore.

Dunn, M., O'Driscoll, C., Dayson, D., Wills, W. and Leff, J. (1990). The TAPS Project. 4: An observational study of the social life of long-stay patients. *British Journal of Psychiatry*, **157**, 842–848.

Endicott, J., Spitzer, R.L., Fleiss, J.L. and Cohen, J. (1976). The global assessment scale: a procedure for measuring the overall severity of psychiatric disturbance. *Archives of General Psychiatry*, **33**, 766–771.

Frank, E. and Kupfer, D.J. (1974). *The KDS-15: A Marital Questionnaire*. Western Psychiatric Institute and Clinic, University of Pittsburgh, Pittsburgh.

Goering, P., Wasylenki, D., Lancee, W. and Freeman, S.J. (1983). Social support and post-hospital outcome for depressed women. *Canadian Journal of Psychiatry*, **28**, 612–623.

Goering, P., Wasylenki, D., Lancee, W. and Freeman, S.J. (1984). From hospital to community: six-month and two-year outcomes for 505 patients. *Journal of Nervous and Mental Disease*, **172**, 667–673.

Goldberg, D. (1972). *The Detection of Psychiatric Illness by Questionnaire*. Maudsley Monograph No. 21. London, Oxford University Press.

Goodman, S.P., Schulthorpe, W.P., Evje, M., Slkater, P. and Linn, M.W. (1969). Social dysfunction among psychiatric and nonpsychiatric outpatients. *Journal of the American Geriatric Society*, **17**, 694–700.

Gurland, B.J., Yorkston, N.J., Stone, A.R., Frank, J.D. and Fleiss, J.L. (1972). The Structured and Scaled Interview to Assess Maladjustment (SSIAM): description, rationale and development. *Archives of General Psychiatry*, **27**, 259–264.

Henderson, S., Byrne, D.G., Duncan-Jones, P., Adcock, S., Scott, R. and Steele, G.D. (1978). Social bonds in the epidemiology of neurosis: a preliminary communication. *British Journal of Psychiatry*, **132**, 463–466.

Henderson, S., Duncan-Jones, P., Byrne, D.G. and Scott, R. (1980). Measuring social relationships: The Interview Schedule for Social Interaction. *Psychological Medicine*, **10**, 1–12.

Henderson, S., Byrne, D.G. and Duncan-Jones, P. (1981). *Neurosis and the Social Environment*. Academic Press, Sydney, Australia.

Hirsch, S.R. (1987). Planning for bed needs and resource requirements in acute psychiatry. *Bulletin of the Royal College of Psychiatrists*, **11**, 398–407.

Holohan, C.J. and Moos, R.H. (1983). The quality of social support: measures of family and work relationships. *British Journal of Clinical Psychology*, **22**, 157–162.

Hoult, J. and Reynolds, I. (1984). Schizophrenia: a comparative trial of community-oriented and hospital-oriented psychiatric care. *Acta Psychiatrica Scandinavica*, **69**, 359–372.

Jarman, B. (1983). Identification of underprivileged areas. *British Medical Journal*, **286**, 1705–1709.

Katz, M.M. and Lyerly, S.B. (1963). Methods for measuring adjustment and social behaviour in the community. I. Rationale, description, discriminative validity and scale development. *Psychological Reports*, **13**, 503–535.

Kendell, R.E. (1975). *The Role of Diagnosis in Psychiatry*. Blackwell, Oxford.

Linn, M.W., Sculthorpe, W.B., Evje, M., Slater, P.H. and Goodman, S.P. (1969). A Social Dysfunction Rating Scale. *Journal of Psychiatric Research*, **6**, 299–306.

Linn, M.W., Caffey, E.M., Klett, C.J., Hogarty, G.E. and Lamb, H.R. (1979). Day treatment and psychotropic drugs in the aftercare of schizophrenic patients. *Archives of General Psychiatry*, **36**, 1055–1066.

McDowell, I. and Newell, C. (1987). *Measuring Health: A Guide to Rating Scales and Questionnaires*. Oxford University Press, New York.

McFarlane, A.H., Neale, K.A., Norman, G.R., Roy, R.G. and Streiner, D.L. (1981). Methodological issues in developing a scale to measure social support. *Schizophrenia Bulletin*, **7**, 90–100.

McFarlane, A.H., Norman, G.R., Streiner, D.L. and Roy, R.G. (1984). Characteristics and correlates of effective and ineffective social supports. *Journal of Psychosomatic Research*, **28**, 501–510.

Merson, S., Tyrer, P., Onyett, S., Lynch, S., Lack, S. and Johnson, A.L. (1992). Early intervention in psychiatric emergencies: a controlled clinical trial. *Lancet*, **339**, 1311–1314.

Montgomery, S.A. and Åsberg, M. (1979). A new depression scale designed to be sensitive to change. *British Journal of Psychiatry*, **134**, 382–389.

Muijen, M., Marks, I., Connolly, J. and Audini, B. (1992). Home based and standard hospital care for patients with severe mental illness: a randomised controlled trial. *British Medical Journal*, **304**, 749–754.

O'Connor, P. and Brown, G.W. (1984). Supportive relationships: fact or fancy? *Journal of Personal and Social Relations*, **1**, 159–175.

Paykel, E.S., Weissman, M.M., Prusoff, B.A. and Tonks, C.M. (1971). Dimensions of social adjustment in depressed women. *Journal of Nervous and Mental Disease*, **152**, 158–172.

Platt, S., Weyman, A., Hirsch, S., Hewett, S. (1980). The Social Behaviour Assessment Schedule (SBAS): rationale contents, scoring and reliability of a new interview schedule. *Social Psychiatry*, **15**, 43–55.

Remington, M. and Tyrer, P. (1979). The Social Functioning Schedule — a brief semi-structured interview. *Social Psychiatry*, **14**, 151–157.

Sarason, I.G., Levine, H.M., Basham, R.B. and Sarason, B.R. (1983). Assessing social support: the social support questionnaire. *Journal of Personal and Social Psychology*, **44**, 127-139.

Stein, L.J. and Test, M.A. (1980). Alternative to mental hospital treatment. 1, Conceptual model, treatment program and clinical evaluation. *Archives of General Psychiatry*, **37**, 392–397.

Strauss, J.S. and Carpenter, W.T., Jr (1972). The prediction of outcome in schizophrenia: I. Characteristics of outcome. *Archives of General Psychiatry*, **27**, 739–746.

Sturt, E. and Wykes, T. (1986). The Social Behaviour Schedule: a validity and reliability study. *British Journal of Psychiatry*, **148**, 1–11.

Tyrer, P. (1990). Personality disorder and social functioning. In: Peck, D.F. and Shapiro, C.M. (Eds), *Measuring Human Problems: a Practical Guide*. Wiley, Chichester, pp. 119–142.

Tyrer, P. and Alexander, J. (1979). Classification of personality disorder. *British Journal of Psychiatry*, **135**, 163–167.

Tyrer, P., Owen, R.T. and Cicchetti, D. (1984). The Brief Scale for Anxiety: a subdivision of the Comprehensive Psychopathological Rating Scale. *Journal of Neurology, Neurosurgery and Psychiatry*, **47**, 970–975.

Tyrer, P., Alexander, J. and Ferguson, B. (1988). Personality assessment schedule. In: Tyrer, P. (Ed.), *Personality Disorders: Diagnosis, Management and Course.* Wright, London, pp. 140–167.

Tyrer, P., Merson, S., Harrison-Read, P., Lynch, S., Birkett, P. and Onyett, S. (1990). A pilot study of the effects of early intervention on clinical symptoms and social functioning in psychiatric emergencies. *Irish Journal of Psychological Medicine*, **7**, 132–134.

Weissman, M.M. and Bothwell, S. (1976). The assessment of social adjustment by patient self-report. *Archives of General Psychiatry*, **33**, 1111–1115.

Weissman, M.M., Sholomskas, D. and John, K. (1981). The assessment of social adjustment: an update. *Archives of General Psychiatry*, **38**, 1250–1258.

World Health Organisation (1980). *International Classification of Impairments, Disabilities and Handicaps.* WHO, Geneva.

World Health Organisation (1992). *International Classification of Diseases, 10th revision.* WHO, Geneva.

World Health Organisation (1993). *WHO Disability Diagnostic Scale (WHO–DDS) — Field Trials Version.* WHO, Geneva.

Worsley, A. and Gribbin, C.C. (1977). A factor analytic study of the twelve item General Health Questionnaire. *Australian and New Zealand Journal of Psychiatry*, **11**, 269–272.

Wykes, T., Sturt, E. and Katz, R. (1990). The prediction of rehabilitative success after three years: the use of social, symptom and cognitive variables. *British Journal of Psychiatry*, **157**, 865–870.

Social Function in Psychiatry: The Hidden Axis of Classification
Edited by Peter Tyrer and Patricia Casey
©1993 Wrightson Biomedical Publishing Ltd

4

Social Function and Psychiatric Services

PETER TYRER and STEPHEN MERSON

A psychiatric service is much more than a collection of treatments for disorders. In addition to *provision* it also comprises the important components of access, assessment, integration, outcome and audit. These all have different implications and are worth discussing separately with regard to social function. One of the reasons why social function has become more important as a measure in mental health is the recognition through service evaluation that it is a potent source of difference between psychiatric services which in other respects may appear to be similar.

ACCESS

An excellent programme of care is useless if no one takes it up. This obvious fact has become more prominent since psychiatric services have been cajoled, and sometimes bullied, into accepting the principles of the market economy. Although in the National Health Service there is no special need to spend large sums on marketing the service for consumers (except by Governments at the time of elections) the issue assumes greater importance in mental health because of the stigma attached to mental illness. There is almost an inverse relationship between the severity of mental illness and perceived personal desire to receive treatment. Although this is to a great extent dependent on the fact that the major mental disorders such as schizophrenia and affective psychosis are associated with loss of insight, so that sufferers do not recognise they are ill and avoid rather than search out treatment, social function is also important.

Epidemiological studies demonstrated close links between socio-economic deprivation, which with its high rates of unemployment, financial hardship, and poor use of leisure time, all increase social dysfunction, and levels of psychiatric disturbance. Professor Brian Jarman at St Mary's Hospital in

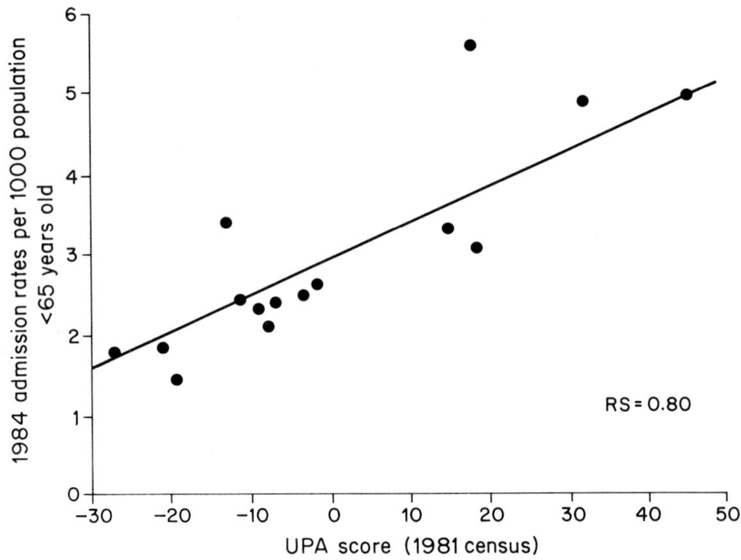

Figure 4.1.   Jarman Underprivileged Area (UPA) scores for districts of the North
West Thames region. Reproduced with permission, from Hirsch (1988).

London has been a pioneer in establishing a hierarchy of socio-economic
deprivation based on census and related figures which enables every district
in the country both to determine its level of deprivation and to have a
weighted score allowing it to be quantitatively compared with other areas
(Jarman, 1983, 1984).

In planning the requirements for the mental health services of a population there is a very high correlation between psychiatric bed use and Jarman
score. This is illustrated in Figure 4.1 in which the admission rates for different boroughs within the North West Thames region near London are highly
correlative with Jarman scores ($r = 0.8$), (Hirsch *et al.*, 1988).

Of course, many factors influence this correlation and more information
is needed to determine the importance of social function and the different
elements concerned in these crude figures, although the Jarman indices have
been shown to be remarkably robust in predicting admission rates when
compared with other models (Thornicroft, 1991).

Several issues are relevant. First of all, patients in socially deprived areas
are more likely to present to psychiatric services through 'unconventional'
channels such as emergency admissions through the police (Section 136) or
compulsory admissions under the Mental Health Act. Many of these patients
have not had any other contact with the psychiatric services before presenting as emergencies. The same finding is shown with what is often the most

Table 4.1. Filter reinforcement to reduce demand on hospital beds.

	The community	Primary medical care		Specialist psychiatric services	
	Level 1	Level 2	Level 3	Level 4	Level 5
	Morbidity in random community samples	Total psychiatric morbidity, primary care	Conspicuous psychiatric morbidity	Total psychiatric patients	Psychiatric inpatients only
Median estimates for 1-year period prevalence	250—315 →	230 →	101.5 →	20.8 →	3.3 (per 1000 at risk per year)
Filter reinforcement		*First filter*	*Second filter* Better psychiatric skills in general	*Third filter* Liaison psychiatry in general practice	*Fourth filter* Greater use of day hospitals to avoid admission

Reproduced, with permission, from Tyrer and Malone (1991). Data quoted are from Goldberg and Huxley (1992) and are reproduced with permission.

socially and economically deprived groups, the ethnic minorities. Such groups are much more likely to be admitted to hospital under emergency powers than the native born population (e.g. Harrison *et al.*, 1988) and, while social dysfunction is only one of the many factors likely to be involved in this differential admission rate, it tends to be underplayed compared with other more emotive factors, such as race.

In Table 4.1 the well known filters on the pathway to psychiatric care described by Goldberg and Huxley (1980) are illustrated together with the additional elements of a comprehensive psychiatric service that can normally prevent individuals from passing beyond each filter (i.e. promoting community care). Patients with poor social function have a tendency to jump these barriers. A typical example is the isolated person who moves from place to place, does not register with the general practitioner, has no links with family or friends and whose social network is extremely limited, and who is unemployed. Such an individual has nowhere to turn to when any form of mental illness strikes. If the conventional forms of medical and psychiatric care are not available it is depressingly predictable that such individuals will either have no contact with the psychiatric services at all if their illness is not a major one, or will present as emergencies at a late stage in their illness, and almost always this is followed by admission, often under a compulsory order.

When social function and attachments are good, contact with services (usually the general practitioner) is achieved early and intervention from specialised services, if necessary, is also earlier, so psychiatric admission does not take place and sometimes is seldom even contemplated.

There is much other evidence that shows poor social function to be associated with late access to psychiatric services (Harrison *et al.*, 1984; Johnstone *et al.*, 1986). It would be wrong to dismiss this as an academic issue that may be of interest to sociologists and epidemiologists but which has little relevance to service planning. Rather than just set aside more in-patient resources for socially deprived areas, new initiatives can help to facilitate access for patients with poorer social function in deprived areas.

One way of doing this is to advertise psychiatric services more widely and allow open referrals. Conventionally psychiatric services accept referrals from other statutory agencies, mainly medical ones. For isolated individuals without contact with statutory services this form of referral process is impractical and the option of any of a range of other agencies, such as housing, voluntary and social work, as well as patients themselves and their relatives making the referral has great attractions. In Figure 4.2 the proportions of referrals to a community psychiatric service (Early Intervention Service) offering open referral is illustrated. Although general practitioners constitute the largest single group of referrers they still only referred a minority of patients. Further analysis showed that housing agencies, the group which had almost the least psychiatric expertise, referred patients who were most

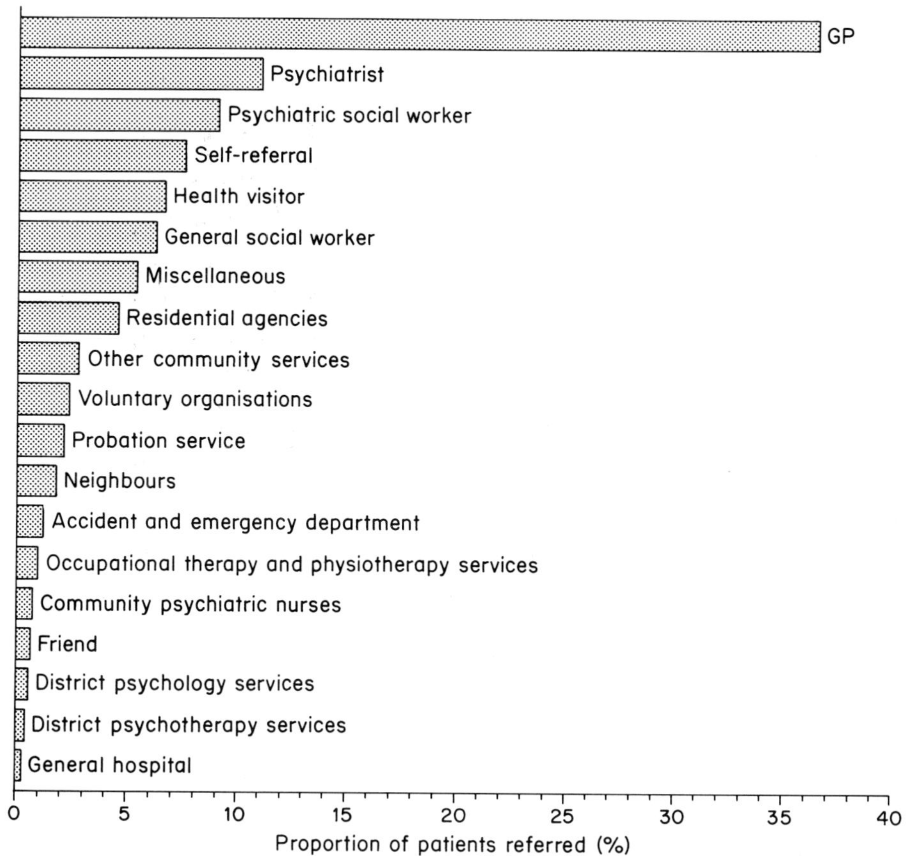

Figure 4.2. Percentage distribution of 695 patients with severe mental illness to a community psychiatric service (Early Intervention Service) offering open referral.

severely ill (Marriott *et al.*, 1993). It is clear that by opening up the referral system those who are socially disadvantaged and less able to seek out help have a better chance of receiving contact.

ASSESSMENT

Increasingly, professionals in the mental health services are taking social function into account when making formal assessments. We have now moved on from the time in which a patient with 'endogenous' depression is deemed to require admission on the basis of their symptoms whereas for example a similar patient with 'reactive depression' is treated outside hospital. Now both the major classification symptoms (ICD-10 and DSM-IIIR) use a multi-axial classification in which social function is one of the axes.

Of course, most clinicians only use the first access of classification, that of mental state disorders. However, even in this group the influence of social function has become more pronounced as the classifications have developed. What has happened is a fundamental change. Instead of identifying clearly demarcated abnormal states of mind as in the past (e.g. involutional melancholia, simple schizophrenia, Alzheimer's disease) and giving clear and unambiguous descriptions of their clinical features, the later classifications have *incorporated* many of the aspects of social function into the classification process.

Close examination of the criteria for diagnosis indicates the importance of social function in attaching the final diagnostic label to a clinical condition. All the following examples come from the diagnostic criteria for research for ICD-10 (DCR-10) (World Health Organisation, 1992).

Organic disorders

The main category in this group is dementia which occurs in many forms. Although there are many different forms of dementia (e.g. Alzheimer's disease, Pick's disease, sub-cortical vascular dementia) the main clinical separation is between mild, moderate and severe impairment. This impairment is almost entirely determined by social function. Thus, for example, in mild impairment the degree of dysfunction is 'not so severe as to be incompatible with independent living', whereas in severe impairment 'the individual is not able to function in the community without close supervision: there is gross decline in personal care'.

Disorders due to psychoactive substance use

These disorders are a consequence of harmful use or abuse of alcohol and other addictive drugs, including stimulants and tobacco. The main category within this group is the dependence syndrome in which continued consumption of the drug is maintained by craving, the production of euphoriant symptoms or the avoidance of withdrawal symptoms, or combinations of these. One of the important components of the dependent syndrome is the 'progressive neglect of alternative pleasures, behaviours, or interests in favour of substance use', together with 'loss of interest in, or reduced participation in activities that previously were important to the individual'.

Schizophrenia

This group includes a range of schizophrenic syndromes, including acute ones, together with persistent delusional disorders. This group might have been expected to have the most pure clinical symptomatology for diagnosis but throughout the descriptions there are criteria that are primarily concerned with social function. For example, in simple schizophrenia it is necessary to have a 'marked decline in social, scholastic, or occupational performance' to achieve the diagnosis and in all these syndromes satisfying the collective diagnosis of schizophrenia the presence of negative symptoms is important and 'these usually result in social withdrawal and lowering of social performance'.

Mood (affective) disorders

The diagnosis of what is now called depressive episode is affected greatly by the assessment of social function. Instead of separation into depressive neurosis and depressive psychosis (as was the case in ICD-9), or older labels such as 'reactive' and 'endogenous' depression, depressive episodes are now separated into mild, moderate and severe forms (together with admixtures of somatic or psychotic symptoms). The separation into these categories of severity is based on the numbers of 13 key symptoms, which include 'marked loss of interest or pleasure in activities which are normally pleasurable', 'decreased energy or increased fatigueability' and 'diminished ability to think or concentrate, such as indecisiveness or vacillation'. These are not in themselves direct measurements of social function but in the clinical description of the three types of depression social dysfunction is one of the major influences that determines the degree of severity (World Health Organisation, 1992). Similarly, among the criteria for the persistent mood disturbance of cyclothymia is social withdrawal, and in the mild chronic depressive disorder known as dysthymia 'a perceived inability to cope with the routine responsibilities of everyday life' is a diagnostic guideline.

Neurotic, stress-related and somatoform disorders

In obsessive–compulsive disorder one of the criteria for the diagnosis is that the symptoms 'cause distress or interfere with the subject's social or individual functioning, usually by wasting time'.

Adjustment disorders

Although social adjustment is not as impaired in adjustment disorders as in more major psychiatric illness social factors are more important in its genesis. In both DSM-IIIR and ICD-10 definitions of adjustment disorder contain words to the effect that the disorder follows immediately after a psychosocial stressor and, in the absence of that stressor, the disorder almost certainly would not have occurred. Following on from this, the persistence of the disorder is to some extent dependent on the persistence of the stressor. Thus, a patient presenting with mixed anxiety and depressive symptoms together with irritability and problems in relationships can be judged to have a primary adjustment disorder. This is considered to be caused entirely by placement in cramped bed and breakfast accommodation with gross overcrowding, though it is clear that only rehousing is going to produce a satisfactory solution to the problem.

Similarly among the subcategories of adjustment disorders are those associated with predominant disturbance of conduct, including aggressive or antisocial behaviour. This category is recorded as a clinical diagnosis but is expressed entirely in terms of social dysfunction without any significant symptomatology.

Behavioural syndromes associated with physiological and physical disturbances

This group includes the eating, sleep and sexual disorders. A diagnosis of the (non-organic) sleep disorders includes the degree of sleep disturbance 'causes marked distress or interferes with social and occupational functioning' and the same applies to hyper-somnia.

Personality disorder

This group of disorders constitutes a separate axis of diagnosis in the American classification (DSM) and, of necessity has to incorporate social dysfunction into the diagnostic criteria for the disorder (Tyrer *et al.*, 1991). All personality disorders lead to behaviour that is 'inflexible, maladaptive, or otherwise dysfunctional across a broad range of personal and social situations' (World Health Organisation, 1992). The importance of social function of these disorders is emphasised in Chapter 6 and is not discussed further here.

Mental handicap and child psychiatry

These are discussed in Chapters 7 and 8. Their separate description in this book indicates the special aspects of social function that are relevant to both these disciplines.

INTEGRATION

Good psychiatric services are well integrated. They have to be because so much of mental illness spans a spectrum from intensive medical and nursing care through to housing needs and relationships with the general public.

The old idea that once you improved a patient's symptoms everything else would improve simultaneously is clearly false. Nonetheless there is a clear correlation between social dysfunction and degree of psychiatric symptomatology as several studies have demonstrated (Hurry and Sturt, 1981; Casey *et al.*, 1985). There are many other factors that can lead to discordance between mental state and social function or in which social dysfunction becomes the prime cause of psychopathology and will need attention if the service is to succeed in helping the patient. These can be discussed under several headings.

A good integrated psychiatric service should be able to detect psychiatric morbidity in its population early, to provide services of the appropriate level of competence in the setting that is most fitting for the needs of the patient, and to return the patient to normal function as quickly as possible with the least degree of adverse affects. One of us (Tyrer, 1985) has suggested that this is best achieved in the hive model of psychiatric care, where each service has a defined catchment area, a core hospital service and community care workers who spend a large part of their time assessing and treating patients at various settings in the community before returning to the central base where they feed back and deploy resources to meet the needs. This involves co-ordination between its hospital, community, local authority and voluntary sectors of mental health care. There is evidence that if such a model is used there is reduced use of hospital beds, achieved both by reducing the number of admissions and the duration of each in-patient episode (Tyrer *et al.*, 1989) and better liaison with primary care services (Ferguson *et al.*, 1992).

Social function has a great deal to do with the success of an integrated service. It is all very well setting up systems of liaison which allow good working between agencies but, as suggested earlier in this chapter, this will not be of value to those in the population that do not enter the system at any level or whose needs are not appreciated when they do make contact. One important element of integration is to make sure that all the agencies concerned are linked together in some formal way. Kingdon (1989) examined 192 health districts in the UK and found that most had no formal planning arrangements or inter-agency collaboration to determine the mental health needs of their population and that very few had the complex structure necessary to support the hive approach.

This may explain the somewhat contradictory data from close examination of the use of psychiatric beds and resources available in psychiatric services (Hirsch, 1988). This working party found that well-endowed hospital services had similar well-endowed community mental health services and the level of community service had little impact on the usage of psychiatric beds. As mentioned earlier, the sociodemographic status of the area was found to be much more important than the resources available to the psychiatric services in predicting numbers of admissions.

The procedure of creating and deploying the essential elements of a good psychiatric service (described as the components model by Strathdee and Thornicroft (1992)) is not the only approach to planning services. The National Institute of Mental Health (1987) has proposed a model based on the needs of each individual with mental illness. These include not only the need for mental health treatment in hospital and community settings, but also housing, money, physical health, family and peer support, and advocacy. Once it is possible to clarify these needs the relevant services can be provided to meet them.

Social dysfunction illustrates the difficulties in defining these. Those who are at the fringes of society, unemployed, homeless or alienated in other ways, often become set in an attitude of hopeless resignation (Jahoda, 1979) and do not seek help even when it might be available. Conversely, those with good social function, especially with good social networks in the professional classes, can also succeed in attracting services that are not necessarily needed. Every doctor, for example, can understand the system that allows them, or members of their families to bypass the normal filters of referral so that specialist care is delivered much earlier in the course of medical problems than would be the case with the general population.

The ideal situation in the service is when needs, demands and provision of services all coincide; unfortunately as Stevens and Gabbay (1991) have illustrated, this only applies to a minority.

The importance of social function and integrated mental health services has been underestimated and largely unresearched. In particular, the phenomenon of *illness behaviour* (Mechanic, 1978), the perception that certain symptoms and feelings constitute illness and therefore need help from a professional, needs to be investigated in different social settings and networks as well as in those with poor and good social function. There is a range of inappropriate illness behaviour that may depend largely on social function. For example, in our personal work we frequently encounter patients who admit freely that their main reason for seeking help is to receive medical reports that will improve their social function. These include letters to housing departments, noting patients as vulnerable in psychiatric terms and therefore deserving priority, similar reports to prisons and local authorities asking for families to be reunited for reasons linked to mental health, and attempts to get into various forms of sheltered employment which are reserved primarily for the mentally ill. This contrasts with the opposite pole of individuals with major psychiatric illness who choose to live on the streets of London with no wish to have contact with any medical services except for the intermittent relief of conditions that cause pain.

On many occasions in other parts of this book the importance of social support in maintaining mental health has been mentioned. Those who have good social support networks are likely to have much better access and involvement with integrated mental health services. However, despite these hypotheses, which have led to the development of many of the instruments described in Chapter 3, there is no good evidence that improving social support has a positive effect on mental health (Brugha, 1991). Understanding this relationship would also help to define the best way of delivering an integrated mental health service. After all, the system of social support available to an individual, and the system of mental health care services available to a community have so many common features they can almost be considered together.

Integration of services is not easy and has been handicapped to some extent by the growth of specialisation in psychiatry. In the past, with fewer organisations and more autocratic systems of management, integration could be achieved much more successfully. Many of us feel we know what needs to be done but feel impotent in implementing change. We are a far cry from the mechanisms invoked to change health systems that were used half a century ago, an example of which is quoted below:

'I put forward the concept that community care and preventive measures were essential in any scheme for mental health services, and that the time has come for the mental hospital to develop these services. The Mental Health Committee, as it was now called, accepted the need for more medical hospital staff to do this, and agreed that we should develop our services in this way by providing community and earlier treatment facilities. The duties of my appointment included the superintendency of the mental hospital, general supervision of the mental division of the institutions, supervision of the out-patient clinics in the hospitals of the city, supervision of the community care of mental defectives, social psychiatry "with all its measures of the prophylaxis of mental illness", the education of the public in such matters, and "the mental health of the city generally". In 1948 the National Health Service Act disrupted the whole scheme by splitting community care from the hospital services; fortunately the local community were very disturbed at this administrative splitting of the mental health service which we had built up, and which had come to full fruition only two years previously. I discussed matters with the Medical Officer of Health, and he agreed that it should be regarded as of the highest importance that existing arrangements should be disturbed as little as possible. A scheme was jointly drawn up, the object of which was to overcome the administrative division, and enable us to carry on essentially as before. This was submitted to the Ministry of Health, and approved in April 1948.'

(MacMillan, 1961).

How would these decisions be reached nowadays? Joint planning teams with representation from local authorities, social work departments, voluntary bodies, housing departments, community health council, and other groups representing patients' interests and health service managers would all have to be involved. If this exercise of the democratic process works well then excellent integration could be achieved, but if it works badly it is less satisfactory than the old autocratic approach.

OUTCOME

In the first chapter of this book the influence of social class in determining the outcome of patients with defined neurotic disorders was illustrated (Figure 1.1). This illustrates a universal and consistent finding in studies of the outcome of a range of psychiatric disorders. This finding can be expressed as a law:

'The outcome of all psychiatric disorder, apart from that of organic origin, can be predicted more successfully through examination of social rather than clinical factors'.

The evidence is unmistakable and comes from studies of neurotic disorder (Huxley *et al.*, 1979; Goldberg *et al.*, 1990), schizophrenia (Wing and Brown, 1961; Curson *et al.*, 1992), depression (Cooper and Paykel, 1992), and old age psychiatry (Pitt, 1992) amongst others.

This is a major blow to those who hope by accurate delineation of psychiatric disorder it is possible to plan treatment and predict outcome independently of influences that can be grouped together as non-clinical ones. It means, for example, that comparisons of diagnoses across cultures and countries are of really no help unless social factors are taken into account.

Social factors cover a wide range of influences, although all have some influence on social function. Social class, although controversial in its divisions, is one of the easiest to measure, and although some measures of social function are independent of class (e.g. SAS; Paykel *et al.*, 1971) most show that the unskilled and the poor have the worst social function (Figure 4.3). Similarly, this group has high levels of family disruption, social isolation, poor housing conditions and other features that together make up the levels of social deprivation that have been found to be so valuable in predicting use of all medical services, not just psychiatric ones (Jarman, 1983). Is social dysfunction therefore like a large dead hand lying over all psychiatric disorder and is it impossible to overcome its malevolent effects? The answer seems to be 'not quite'. In formal studies of community and hospital psychiatric services there is evidence from some studies that social function is improved to a significantly greater extent by community-orientated and home-based treatment than hospital-based services (Stein and Test, 1980; Burns, 1990; Ferguson *et al.*, 1992; Muijen *et al.*, 1993) although the differences are only shown after many months. However, in the study described in more detail at the end of Chapter 3 in which the Early Intervention

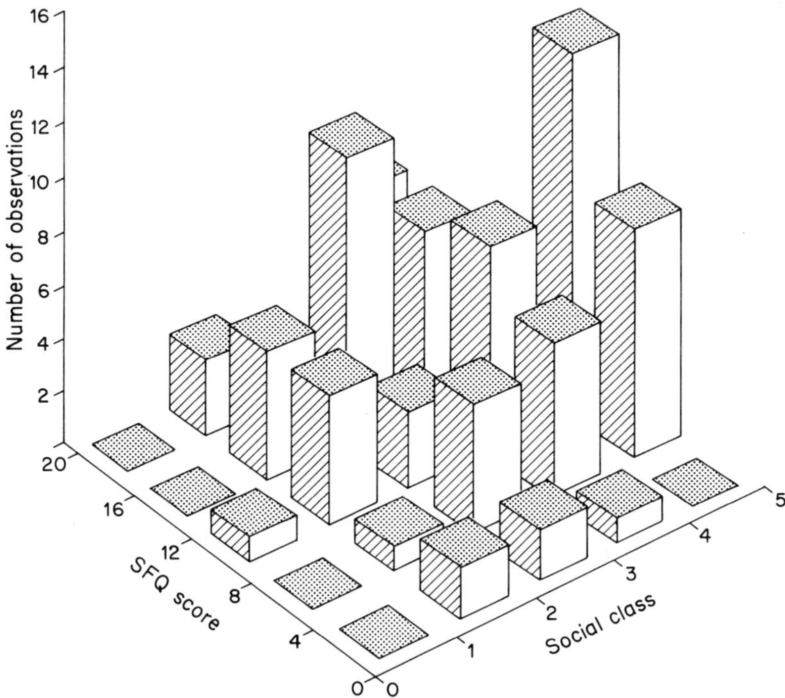

Figure 4.3. Initial scores on the Social Functioning Questionnaire (SFQ) in 100 patients seen in a study of community and hospital psychiatric services (Merson *et al.*, 1992), showing distribution by social class.

Service (EIS) was evaluated after 12 weeks, although there was no difference overall in the social function of patients referred to community or hospital care there was a marked difference in outcome when the patients were separated by personality status (Figure 4.4).

Improvement was greater in those referred to the community service if they had no personality disorder, whereas the opposite was true for those with personality disorder of all degrees of severity. In two other studies in which no difference was shown in the social function of patients referred to community or hospital care (Creed *et al.*, 1991; Burns *et al.*, 1993), reporting of personality status has not yet been made.

In all the studies in which social function has been shown to improve more with treatment from community psychiatric services (apart from the one illustrated in Figure 4.4) there has been a long period of comparison with assessments made over a year or longer. These are important findings, because they suggest that care orientated towards the needs of individuals in

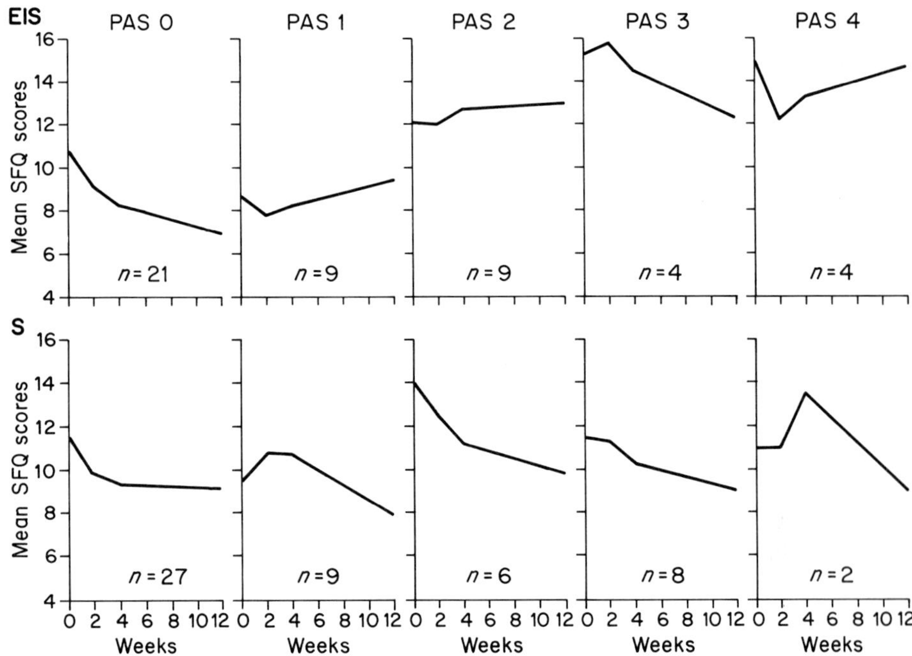

Figure 4.4. Outcome of social function by personality disorder severity measured by the Social Functioning Questionnaire (SFQ) in 99 patients randomly allocated to a community psychiatric service (Early Intervention Service) (EIS)) and a hospital (Standard) (S) service. Personality status recorded using the Personality Assessment Schedule (PAS) with PAS 0 = no personality disorder, PAS 1 = personality difficulty, PAS 2 = personality disorder, PAS 3 = combined personality disorder, PAS 4 = severe personality disorder, (classification after Tyrer *et al.*, 1988). Note the differential response between the services in the personality disordered groups.

the community can be changed in the longer term and that the delayed improvement in social function in comparison with patients treated in hospital settings cannot be explained just by improvement in clinical symptomatology. However, this conclusion remains a tentative one. If, however, it was possible to maintain long lasting improvements in social function in such models of care they would be strong points in favour of introducing these services.

AUDIT

The principles of auditing psychiatric services have become prominent in the last few years with reforms in the National Health Service. Good clinicians have however been practising audit for many years without even knowing it. By taking an interest in any important clinical variable, be it out-patient waiting times, duration of treatment in hospital, incidence of relapse, clinicians become aware of ways in which they can improve their care, both in terms of clinical procedure and administration.

However, despite considerable attention and resources being given to audit in the mental health services, social function is not normally given a high priority. However, there is plenty of evidence in studies of psychiatric patients undergoing rehabilitation, including that after discharge from psychiatric hospitals after long periods of stay, it is greatly affected by social factors that could be important items in auditing (Double and Wong, 1991). In the United Kingdom there is an organisation called Social Audit (PO Box 111, London NW1 8XG) which has been involved primarily in the safety of medicines. As the purpose of the organisation is to 'ask timely questions about the organisations whose decisions and actions shape our lives, and what, in social terms, do these organisations give to and take from the community, and how do they explain and justify what they do?', it is likely at some point that they will examine the issues written about in this book from the viewpoint of the patients being treated and society at large. This type of audit is needed and the caring professions need to anticipate the difficult questions that will be posed to them when such audit begins.

IMPLICATIONS OF SOCIAL FUNCTION IN PLANNING OF PSYCHIATRIC SERVICES

Psychiatry has long been a subject dominated by individuals involved in intense therapy with small numbers of patients. Psychoanalysis as a discipline has had a major impact on literature, drama and journalism, as well as psychiatry, and this is remarkable considering that it has never been a mainline treatment for the mentally ill. The methods of psychoanalysis, even if outstandingly effective, could in no way be applied to large communities. However, even though attitudes have changed to some extent we still tend to think of groups of patients in specialised settings and their response to psychiatric treatments and manipulations without considering the mental health of communities.

There has been a change, not quite a sea change but certainly a considerable swell, in the past 10 years so that now, for the first time, whole psychiatric services with defined geographical catchment areas are being studied and evaluated. Such evaluation needs to be broad-based and to give adequate weight to social factors and social function in all its forms. This also includes quality of life, a concept that is even more difficult to define than social function, and which is discussed in the last chapter of this book.

Despite its theoretical limitations, quality of life is probably the best measure of 'user approval' of a psychiatric service (Huxley *et al.*, 1990) and deserves to be included.

It is clear from the evidence available so far that social function, in all its forms, is a pre-eminent factor in almost all aspects of psychiatric services, and it is not unreasonable to argue that it is the most important of all the factors that should be taken into account when planning and delivering services. The abundant evidence that the amount of psychiatric service needed by a population is best predicted by measures of social deprivation rather than by any clinical or other demographic variable bears witness to the importance of this. This has taken time to penetrate clinical consciousness but as its importance as a predictor of service use has come to the fore social function is unlikely to be neglected again by those who plan, provide and purchase psychiatric services.

REFERENCES

Brugha, T.S. (1991). Human ethology. *Current Opinion in Psychiatry*, **4**, 313–319.

Burns, T. (1990). The evaluation of a home-based treatment approach in acute psychiatry. In: Goldberg, D. and Tantam, D. (Eds), *The Public Health Impact of Mental Disorder*. Hogrefe and Huber, Toronto, pp. 197–205.

Burns, T., Beadsmoore, A., Bhat, A. V., Oliver, A. and Mathers, C. (1993). A controlled trial of home-based acute psychiatric services. I: clinical and social outcome. *British Journal of Psychiatry*, **163**, 49–54.

Casey, P.R., Tyrer, P.J. and Platt, S. (1985). The relationship between social functioning and psychiatric symptomatology in primary care. *Social Psychiatry*, **20**, 5–10.

Cooper, Z. and Paykel, E.S. (1992). Social factors in the onset and maintenance of depression. In: Leff, J. and Bhugra, D. (Eds), *Principles of Social Psychiatry*. Blackwell, Oxford, pp. 99–121.

Creed, F., Black, D., Anthony, P., Osborn, M., Thomas, P. and Tormenson, B. (1991). Randomised control trial of day-patients' vs in-patients' psychiatric treatment. *British Medical Journal*, **300**, 1033–1037.

Curson, D.A., Pantelis, C., Ward, J. and Barnes, T.R.E. (1992). Institutionalism and schizophrenia 30 years on: clinical poverty and the social environment in three British mental hospitals in 1960 compared with a fourth in 1990. *British Journal of Psychiatry*, **160**, 230–241.

Double, D.B. and Wong, T.I. (1991). What has happened to patients from long-stay psychiatric wards? *Psychiatric Bulletin*, **15**, 735–736.

Ferguson, B., Cooper, S., Brothwell, J., Markantonakis, H. and Tyrer, P. (1992). Clinical evaluation of a new community psychiatric service based on general practice psychiatric clinics. *British Journal of Psychiatry*, **160**, 493–497.

Goldberg, D. and Huxley, P. (1980). *Mental Illness in the Community: The Pathway to Psychiatric Care*. Tavistock, London.

Goldberg, D. and Huxley, P. (1992). *Common Mental Disorders: A Biosocial Model*. Tavistock, London.

Goldberg, D., Bridges, K., Cook, D., Evans, B. and Grayson, D. (1990). The influence of social factors on common mental disorders: destabilisation and restitution. *British Journal of Psychiatry*, **156**, 704–713.

Harrison, G., Ineichen, B., Smith, J. and Morgan, H. (1984). Psychiatric hospital admissions in Bristol — II. Social and clinical aspects of compulsory admission. *British Journal of Psychiatry*, **145**, 605–611.

Harrison, G., Owens, D. and Holton, A. (1988). A prospective study of severe mental disorder in Afro-Caribbean patients. *Psychological Medicine*, **18**, 643–657.

Hirsch, S.R. (Chairman) (1988). *Psychiatric Beds and Resources: Factors in Influencing Bed Use in Service Planning*. Gaskell Books, London.

Hurry, J. and Sturt, E. (1981). Social performance in a population sample: relation to psychiatric symptoms. In: Wing, J.K., Bebbington, P. and Robins, L.N. (Eds), *What is a Case? The Problem of Definition in Psychiatric Community Surveys*. Grant-McIntyre, London, pp. 202–213.

Huxley, P.J., Goldberg, D., Maguire, P. and Kincey, V. (1979). The prediction of the course of minor psychiatric disorders. *British Journal of Psychiatry*, **135**, 535–543.

Huxley, P.J., Hagan, T., Hennelly, R. and Hunt, J. (1990). *Effective Community Mental Health Services*. Avebury Press, Aldershot.

Jahoda, M. (1979). The impact of unemployment in the 1930s and the 1970s. *Bulletin of the British Psychological Society*, **32**, 309–314.

Jarman, B. (1983). Identification of underprivileged areas. *British Medical Journal*, **286**, 1705–1709.

Jarman, B. (1984). Validation and distribution of scores. *British Medical Journal*, **289**, 1587–1592.

Johnstone, E.C., Crow, T.G., Johnstone, A.L. and McMillan, J.F. (1986). The Northwick Park study of first episodes of schizophrenia. *British Journal of Psychiatry*, **148**, 115–120.

Kingdon, D. (1989). Mental health services: results of a survey of English district plans. *Psychiatric Bulletin*, **13**, 77–78.

MacMillan, D. (1961). Community mental health services and the mental hospital. *World Mental Health*, **13**, 1–8. Reproduced in: Freeman, H. and Farndale, J. (Eds) (1963). *Trends in the Mental Health Services*. Pergamon Press, London, pp. 303–317.

Marriott, S., Malone, S., Onyett, S. and Tyrer, P. (1993). The consequences of an open referral system to a community mental health service. *Acta Psychiatrica Scandinavica*, in press.

Mechanic, D. (1978). *Medical sociology, 2nd edn*. Free Press, Glencoe.

Merson, S., Tyrer, P., Onyett, S., Lynch, S., Lack, S. and Johnson, A.L. (1992). Early intervention in psychiatric emergencies: a controlled clinical trial. *Lancet*, **339**, 1311–1314.

Muijen, M. (1991). *A Controlled Study of Community Care*. PhD Thesis, University of London.

National Institute of Mental Health (1987). *Towards a Model for a Comprehensive Community-based Mental Health System*. NIMH, Washington.

Paykel, E.S., Weissman, M.M., Prusoff, B.A. and Tonks, C.M. (1971). Dimensions of social adjustment in depressed women. *Journal of Nervous and Mental Disease*, **152**, 158–172.

Pitt, B. (1992). Social factors and old age. In: Leff, J. and Bhugra, D. (Eds), *Principles of Social Psychiatry*. Blackwell, Oxford, pp. 315–330.

Stein, L.J. and Test, M.A. (1980). Alternative to mental hospital treatment. 1, Conceptual model, treatment program and clinical evaluation. *Archives of General Psychiatry*, **37**, 392–397.

Stevens, A.J. and Gabbay, J. (1991). Needs assessment needs assessment. *Health Trends*, **23**, 20–23.

Strathdee, G. and Thornicroft, G. (1992). The principles of setting up mental health services in the community. In: Leff, J. and Bhugra, D. (Eds), *Principles of Social Psychiatry*. Blackwell, Oxford, pp. 473–489.

Thornicroft, G. (1991). Social deprivation and rates of treated mental disorder: developing statistical models to predict psychiatric service utilisation. *British Journal of Psychiatry*, **158**, 475–484.

Tyrer, P. (1985). The hive system. A model for a psychiatric service. *British Journal of Psychiatry*, **146**, 571–575.

Tyrer, P. and Malone, S. (1991). Psychiatry without hospital beds: a review of treatment strategies. In: Granville-Grossman, K. (Ed.), *Recent Advances in Clinical Psychiatry, Vol. 7*. Churchill-Livingstone, Edinburgh, pp. 105–118.

Tyrer, P., Alexander, J. and Ferguson, B. (1988). Personality Assessment Schedule. In: Tyrer, P. (Ed.), *Personality Disorders: Diagnosis, Management and Course*. Wright, London, pp. 140–167.

Tyrer, P., Turner, R., Johnson, A.L. (1989). Integrated hospital and community psychiatric services and use of inpatient beds. *British Medical Journal*, **299**, 298–300.

Tyrer, P., Casey, P. and Ferguson, B. (1991). Personality disorder in perspective. *British Journal of Psychiatry*, **159**, 463–471.

Wing, J.K. and Brown, G.W. (1961). Social treatment of chronic schizophrenia: a comparative survey of three mental hospitals. *Journal of Mental Science*, **107**, 847–861.

World Health Organisation (1992). *Mental and Behavioural Disorders: Diagnostic Criteria for Research. Draft Version*. WHO, Geneva.

5

Social Function in Adult Psychiatric Disorders

PATRICIA CASEY

Most psychiatric disorders lead to impairment of social function to varying degrees. This is a crude generalisation since there are a few disorders which impact very little upon the patient's functioning and are manifest only on direct questioning of the patient. There has been a long-standing debate in psychiatry about the definition of disease and some have suggested that it is best defined in terms of social dysfunction. This is countered by the observation that impairment of social function is not necessarily present in all disorders and at any rate may not become evident until late in the illness. One of the few disorders which does not, initially at any rate, impinge adversely upon social function is paranoid psychosis where the delusions are often harboured secretly for many years whilst the sufferer continues to work, make social contacts and behave in an unremarkable manner. In the early stages of depressive illness and with many phobias there is also unlikely to be any noticeable deterioration in social function. This may explain the delay in seeking treatment which is apparent in clinical practice and there is now firm evidence that it is social incapacity which leads to referral to the psychiatric services rather than symptoms *per se* (Casey *et al.*, 1985) (see also Chapter 4).

The belief that the social impairment evident during an episode of illness is related directly to or is an epiphenomenon of the symptoms is widely held in practice. The implication of this is, first, that as severity of illness increases so social functioning deteriorates and, secondly, that as symptoms improve with treatment so too should social incapacity *pari passu*. However the inclusion of social function as a separate axis in DSM-IIIR and more recently in ICD-10 suggests that the two areas are distinct at least in some respects. The changes in correlation between symptom severity and functioning in relation to various clinical populations have been described in Chapter 2. There is now firm empirical evidence, particularly from studies of recovery, to support the view that symptoms and functioning are indeed separate dimensions and warrant independent assessment as prescribed by DSM-IIIR and ICD-10.

The changes in social function during in-patient treatment for an acute psychiatric disorder have not been studied in detail but point to an initial improvement during the first two weeks of treatment with little change in social function thereafter (Platt *et al.*, 1981). This has been disputed by others who have demonstrated a continuing improvement in social function with the passage of time even after discharge from hospital (Paykel and Weissman, 1973).

SOCIAL FUNCTION AND CASENESS

Despite the intuitive belief that social function deteriorates with increasing severity of illness, there has been little investigation into this using standardised measures of social function and of symptomatology. One such study by Casey *et al.* (1985) examined the relationship between social function and the PSE index of definition. The former was measured using the Social Functioning Schedule (SFS) (Remington and Tyrer, 1979) — a semi-structured interview using a visual analogue scale to measure 12 areas of social function. The index of definition (I/D) is a measure of the degree of certainty with which a diagnosis can be made and by convention an I/D of 4 or less indicates non-caseness, of 5 borderline caseness, and of 6 of more definite caseness. The mean social function scores at various I/D levels are shown in Table 5.1.

In general the degree of social dysfunction (as indicated by higher scores on the SFS) increased as the index of definition increased. Moreover the difference between non-cases, borderline and definite cases is highly significant. Since social function is determined by many factors it is pertinent to ask what is the magnitude of the contribution of some of these likely variables such as age, sex, personality, severity of illness, alcohol abuse, etc. Interestingly, in this study conducted in a general practice setting, only severity of illness as measured by the I/D made a significant contribution.

In other treatment settings these differences are not shown. In general it is to be expected that more serious mental illness will be associated with greater social dysfunction when measured in epidemiological studies, and as a rule 'more psychopathology leads to more social disruption'. However, the evidence already mentioned that it is social dysfunction rather than symptoms that determine referral for specialist treatment and admission to hospital may contradict this. All psychiatric disorder, and this includes acute stress conditions that some would not regard as 'real' disorder, creates problems in social function when it is sufficiently severe. This is illustrated in Chapter 3 in the description of the social function of patients presenting

Table 5.1. Mean social function score and index of definition. ($n = 169$).

Index	Mean score	SD	F	p
1	3.60	6.17		
2	7.71	6.27		
3	18.3	7.86		
4	13.37	10.85	59.37	0.001
5	25.78	14.50		
6	35.5	12.38		
7	46.04	15.80		
8	45.20	26.63		

as psychiatric emergencies. By definition, all patients were in acute distress at the time of initial assessment, and had relatively high scores on the Social Functioning Questionnaire (SFQ). The SFQ was developed from the Social Functioning Schedule (SFS) (Remington and Tyrer, 1979) and correlates well with it.

This is illustrated in Figure 5.1 in which the SFS and SFS scores in patients presenting as emergencies are shown (Tyrer *et al.*, 1990), and in which the

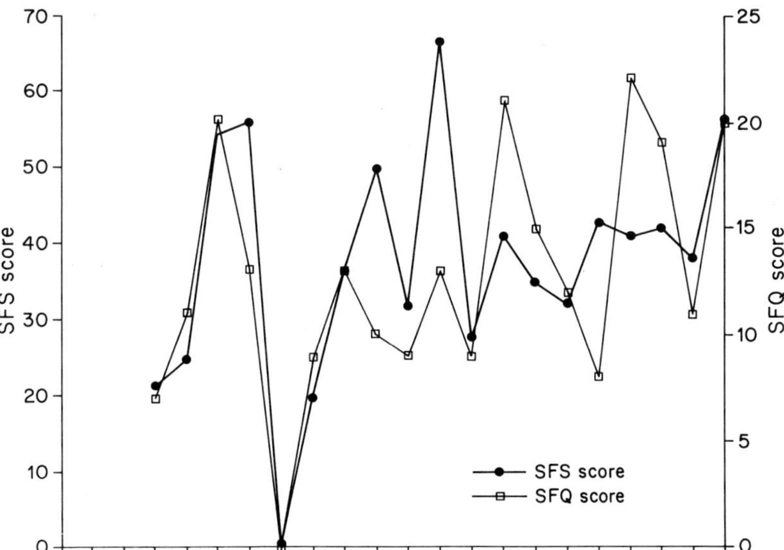

Figure 5.1. Comparison of social function scores using the Social Functioning Schedule (SFS) (Remington and Tyrer, 1979) and the Social Functioning Questionnaire (SFQ) (Tyrer, 1990) in 19 psychiatric patients presenting as emergencies. Reproduced with permission from Tyrer *et al.* (1990).

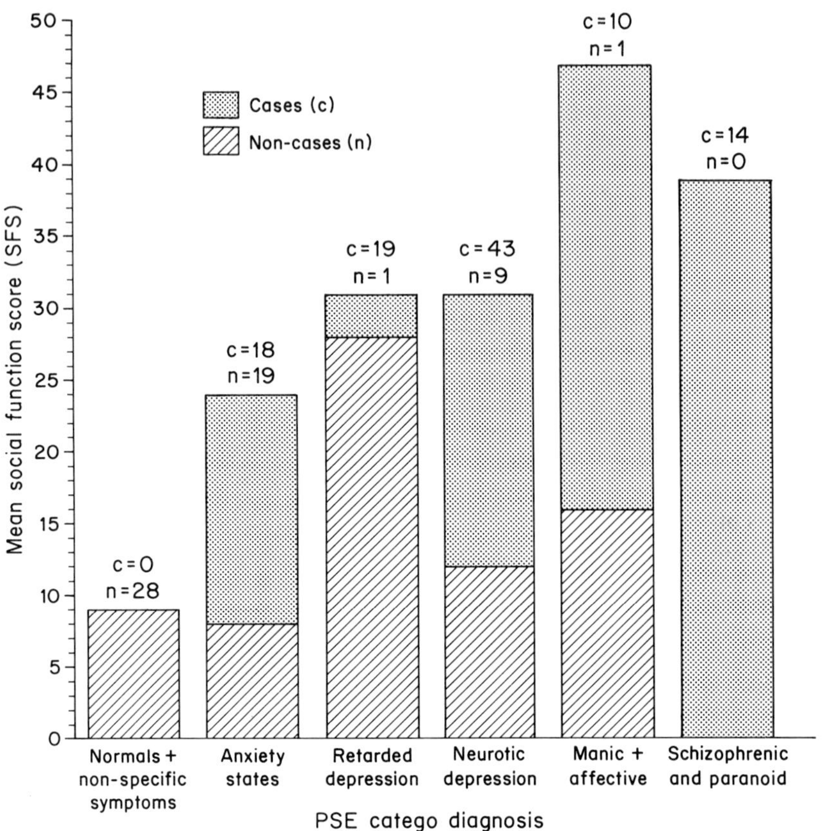

Figure 5.2. Social function of 162 patients with conspicuous psychiatric morbidity seen in primary care, assessed using the Social Functioning Schedule (SFS) and the Present State Examination (PSE), 9th revision, and separated into diagnostic groups, cases (c) and non-cases (n) using the Index of Definition (ID) (score 5 or above indicates caseness). Reproduced with permission from Casey *et al.* (1985).

SFQ scores on the right vertical axis are roughly equivalent to the SFS ones on the left.

In the diagnostic breakdown of psychiatric emergencies patients with schizophrenia had a mean score of 9.3 on the SFQ, lower than that of other diagnostic groups (Figure 3.6). This is equivalent to an SFS score of about 26, which is lower than that in Figure 5.2. Patients with manic depression and other affective psychoses had the highest levels in both studies, but those with neurotic disorders had much higher levels of dysfunction when presenting as emergencies. This illustrates the added information provided by measures of social function. The mental state diagnosis only gives part of the diagnostic picture; social function status adds more.

Some support for the independence of the relationship between functioning and psychopathology comes from community studies where personality status as well as severity of illness makes a contribution (Casey and Tyrer, 1986). Investigation of the relationship between specific areas of social function and psychopathology suggests that in community populations functioning in areas such as marriage and parenting is related to psychopathology whilst in the area of work functioning may be determined by class, gender and ethnic group (Dohrenwend *et al.*, 1981).

SOCIAL FUNCTION AND DEPRESSIVE ILLNESS

The impact of depressive illness on functioning is well recognised in clinical practice. In its crudest terms social incapacity increases during acute episodes of illness, lessens during recovery and deteriorates again at relapse. There however the parallel ends and closer scrutiny of the impact of one upon the other illustrates the simplicity of this viewpoint. The impairment in concentration, the psychomotor retardation and the agitation of depressive illness can all have an impact on how the sufferer relates to family, carries out his or her work or copes with social encounters. Although these symptoms do not directly measure social behaviour, others which are part of the depressive constellation do. These include anergia, irritability, withdrawal, etc. Against this setting of the heterogeneity of depressive symptoms, some measuring social behaviour, others emotions only, it is hardly surprising that the association between both is not as high as might at first seem likely. Several studies have now demonstrated this low correlation between symptoms and functioning during the acute phase of depressive illness. Paykel *et al.* (1978) found a product moment correlation of 0.19 between the social adjustment total score and the three area depression scale score. Casey and Butler (1993) obtained a higher correlation coefficient of 0.35 ($p<0.02$) between the Hamilton rating scale total score and the mean score on the Social Functioning Schedule. In general follow-up studies demonstrate that the correlation between both is higher than during the acute phase of illness and in the intervening period as recovery progresses improvement is not in parallel since symptoms change more rapidly than functioning. Paykel and Weissman (1973) found that improvement in social function is most marked in the first two months of treatment and is particularly noticeable in the area of work. Even after eight months of treatment there are still some residual deficits and these affect the areas of communication and interpersonal friction. Those who relapse exhibit the same deterioration in functioning as was observed at the outset and again work seems to be the area most vulnerable. Interestingly during the acute phase of illness and immediately prior to relapse there was nothing to distinguish this group from the non-relapsers in terms of their functioning. The sudden change in functioning that accompanies relapse has been demonstrated also by Tanner *et al.* (1975).

The discrepancy between symptoms and functioning during improvement has been clearly demonstrated in a family study by Keitner and Miller (1990). They found that family functioning is impaired even after symptomatic recovery and in particular relapse is higher in stressful, hostile and unsupportive home environments. What is unclear is whether family dysfunction is the result of depressive illness or whether it also has an aetiological role. Strikingly many studies have shown that although the dysfunction improves as symptoms remit the families still exhibit more pathology than non-clinical families (Rounsaville *et al.*, 1980; Keitner *et al.*, 1987).

During the acute phase of depressive illness it is surprising that the social incapacity generated by those patients diagnosed as having the so-called neurotic or psychotic forms of the illness is no different (Casey *et al.*, 1985). This further supports the stance adopted by ICD-10 that the distinction should be abandoned, and social function used as one of the means of separating mild, moderate and severe depressive episodes (World Health Organisation, 1992).

In relation to depressive illness these findings have important implications for clinical practice. First, the tendency to underestimate the severity of depressive illness when there is an apparent discrepancy between reported symptoms and function should now be viewed critically since a close relationship between both is not inevitable. Secondly, the finding that social function is slower to improve than symptoms should be borne in mind when advising or reassuring patients about such practical matters as return to work or coping with family and friends. The residual impairment after improvement of symptoms emphasises the need for hesitancy in acceding to requests for changes in medication to bring about more rapid and complete change in functioning. Unfortunately there are no empirical data to guide the psychiatrist in relation to the actual time it takes for full recovery in functioning to occur after symptomatic recovery. Finally, where functioning continues to be impaired it should alert the doctor to the possibility of an underlying axis II disorder with all that this implies. Indeed some would say that the residual impairment in functioning requires a different treatment approach from that recommended during the acute phase of depressive illness. Frank (1961) has emphasised that group psychotherapy primarily enhances social function and others have confirmed the distinction between the impact of pharmacotherapy and psychotherapy in depressed out-patients (Paykel *et al.*, 1975).

The effect of social function, measured at the time of admission to hospital or at the instigation of treatment, upon outcome has been investigated and mentioned in Chapter 2. In general among those seen in general practice with conspicuous psychiatric morbidity the degree of social incapacity at outset has been shown to make a significant contribution to outcome. However among those treated as in-patients in hospital with severe depressive illness, social function at outset had little impact on outcome either at discharge or at six month follow-up (Casey and Butler, 1993). A possible explanation for this disparity lies in the fact that the milder forms of depressive illness, managed in a general practice setting, have multiple aetiologies including social, biological and psychological whereas the severe illnesses requiring in-patient treatment are more likely to have a larger biological component with outcome being determined more by biological than by social factors.

SOCIAL FUNCTION AND PARASUICIDE

Social dysfunction in the parasuicide population has been widely cited. Two aspects require consideration. The first is the role of social factors in predisposing to parasuicide. This has been illustrated by the higher prevalence from those belonging to social classes 4 and 5, among the divorced (Platt *et al.*, 1988), and unemployed (Platt and Kreitman, 1985). In addition poor social circumstances such as overcrowding, single parenthood, financial difficulties and isolation are common (Bille-Brahe *et al.*, 1985; Morgan *et al.*, 1975). However the role of social stress and upheaval in precipitating an episode of parasuicide behaviour has also been described, in particular interpersonal conflict (Morgan *et al.*, 1975).

Although little work has been done on the extent of general social dysfunction in those who parasuicide, focusing instead on specific areas of impairment and immediate stress as outlined above, it is likely that the extent of persistent and general social dysfunction is higher than in the general adult population. Indeed, it is also likely that this may be as high or even higher than in the psychiatric in-patient population in view of the contributory effect of personality disorder found in up to 60% of the parasuicide population (Casey, 1989) combined with the role of immediate stressors, and axis I disorders in a smaller proportion of patients (Ennis *et al.*, 1989). A recent study by Mange-Ingvar *et al.* (1992) found that only 13% of those investigated after a parasuicide had a well-functioning relationship and 66% had occupational difficulties. The persistence of social dysfunction in relation to parasuicide could thus be synthesised as a three-way interaction between vulnerability in terms of poor social supports, especially the absence of a confiding relationship, inability to respond appropriately to the stresses which do arise and the presence of a life event prior to the episode. As a corollary, treatments aimed at secondary prevention, i.e. the prevention of repetition, have focused on improving social function and on changing cognitive restructuring. Disappointingly there has been little success despite vigorous input although there has been a recent suggestion that the teaching of problem solving techniques may have an impact in reducing parasuicide repetition (McLeavy *et al.*, 1987; Salkovskis *et al.*, 1990).

The role of social dysfunction in completed suicide has also received attention most notably from the sociologist Durkheim (1951) although this concept has also been incorporated into the understanding of parasuicide behaviour by modern researchers (Bille-Brahe and Wang, 1985). In relation to suicide the central contribution of such social factors as isolation (called egoism by Durkheim) and anomie (the absence of social cohesion or values) has been clearly documented. The association with increasing age and unemployment as well as with serious psychiatric illness, most notably depression, infer social dysfunction.

ALCOHOL ABUSE

It is a truism to state that alcohol dependency and abuse are associated with a dramatic impairment in social function. This forms at least part of the constellation of features used in making the diagnosis. Unfortunately when serious deterioration in social function occurs the disorder is usually advanced and for this reason Edwards and Gross (1976) do not include this parameter in their classic description of the 'alcohol dependence syndrome' since its inclusion precludes early diagnosis. However the commonly used screening instrument for alcohol, the Michigan Alcoholism Screening Test (MAST), does incorporate social incapacity in its criteria.

The degree of social dysfunction is likely to vary with the population under study and the degree of social impairment may be one factor in leading to help-seeking behaviour as is the case with other psychiatric disorders. There is some evidence in support of this hypothesis from the study by Brennan and Moos (1991) which found that problem drinkers with poor social function, few social supports and who reported life stresses were more likely to seek specialist help than their more functional and supported counterparts. Social function has also been shown to be influenced by the age of onset of the abuse and the later the age of onset the less incapacitated socially is the patient (Brennan and Moos, 1991).

In relation to other disorders it is pertinent to ask if the degree of impairment is similar among those diagnosed as being alcohol abusers. Casey *et al.* (1985), using the MAST, found that alcoholics seen in a general practice setting were significantly more socially impaired than those who were not alcoholic but were less so than those diagnosed as manic depressive. Interestingly there was little difference between alcoholics and schizophrenics (as diagnosed by the PSE). The particular areas of social functioning that relate to family relationships are believed to be important in relation to the high suicide risk associated with the alcoholic population. The triggering effect of a sudden break-up of a once close relationship has been clearly identified as preceding completed suicide (Murphy *et al.*, 1979).

SCHIZOPHRENIA

This is the disorder which represents the apogee of social dysfunction in psychiatry. Not only is functioning impaired during the acute episode but also, and with more serious consequences, in the group who develop the chronic form of the illness. In this group especially, by contrast with the other psychiatric disorders, the relationship between symptoms and dysfunction has been shown to be close (Dohrenwend *et al.*, 1983), probably because factors unrelated to the disorder, such as age, social class, etc., which ordinarily have an impact on functioning, become less important as symptom severity overwhelms the sufferer and creates major disruption in social roles. Thus for this group of patients social function seems to be indeed an epiphenomenon of symptoms. It is likely that those patients who are seen in different treatment settings will display varying degrees of social incapacity although most patients with schizophrenia are in contact with the psychiatric services. Interestingly a group of patients with schizophrenia seen in a general practice setting were no less impaired than those with a Catego 'diagnosis' of manic depression or of depressive neurosis but not surprisingly were significantly more incapacitated than those with anxiety states or with non-specific symptoms (see Figure 5.2) (Casey *et al.*, 1985).

The likely reason for the absence of a difference in incapacity when compared with the affective disorders is that those schizophrenic patients in contact with their general practitioners and referred to a study of conspicuous morbidity in general practice such as this are less severely ill than their counterparts attending the psychiatric services.

Among out-patients with this diagnosis the impact of relapse on one aspect of social function, i.e. employment, was investigated (Scottish Schizophrenia Research Group, 1992). Overall only 19% of patients at five year follow-up were in open employment. Moreover total employment (whether sheltered or in the open market) was strongly associated with relapse of illness. Among relapsers the proportion unemployed rose from 33% to 69% over the five years of the study whilst the converse occurred in the non-relapsers with the number unemployed changing from 38% to 25%.

The importance of social function and of related factors such as personality in determining the symptomatic outcome of schizophrenia has been addressed by Wittenborn *et al.* (1977). Seventy-five newly admitted schizophrenic patients, who were not at the time chronically ill were assessed using the Rutgers Home Inquiry. This interview is conducted in the patient's home by a social worker and is completed over a series of interviews with relatives. It measures aspects of personality, of social function and of the childhood home environment. The relationship between symptoms and measures on the Home Inquiry was low up to 12 months post-admission but thereafter increased and suggests symptoms which persist after the first year can to some extent be predicted on the basis of the Home Inquiry schedule. In particular low self-esteem, lack of self-sufficiency and uncomfortable relationships in the childhood home were shown to be most predictive. Nevertheless the magnitude of the variance accounted for was less than 15%. A similarly modest relationship between social relations and outcome has been described by Strauss and Carpenter (1974).

A study by Johnstone *et al.* (1979) was more conclusive in its findings. A group of acutely ill patients, diagnosed as schizophrenic on the basis of the PSE, were assessed one year after the index admission. Social outcome was significantly related to the degree of social isolation at admission but not to the number of previous admissions or to the presence of positive symptoms. What was interesting however was that among those with negative symptoms a few continued to function well socially. This study did not attempt to address the issue of whether lack of social support predisposed to a poor outcome or whether the patient's withdrawal from society before the index admission augured greater severity of illness but leaned towards the latter view. By contrast Bland and Orn (1979) failed to find any diagnostic or symptomatic criteria predictive of social outcome 14 years after initial hospitalization. An interesting study by Cheadle *et al.* (1978) demonstrated that 'social impairment', measured unsatisfactorily in the form of being unmarried/divorced or unemployed, was greater in men than women. Moreover social isolation was shown to be perceived rather than observed since it was not confined to those living alone. In particular the socially incapacitated group were shown to have more neurotic symptoms than their less incapacitated counterparts and the group was characterised by the absence of psychotic symptoms.

The predictive power of pre-morbid social dysfunction has been demonstrated in many studies which have consistently shown that poor pre-illness functioning was associated with the development of negative symptoms. This has been related to abnormalities in neuropsychological testing of frontal lobe function. However the relationship to ventricular size and to brain cell loss is inconclusive with some demonstrating a clear association with negative symptoms (Williams *et al.*, 1985) whilst others have failed to find an association (Breier *et al.*, 1991).

The aetiology of the chronic impairment seen in schizophrenics is now becoming better understood. Venables (1957) classified the schizophrenic population into two groups — the active and the withdrawn. This seems to mirror the work of Johnstone above. Early studies suggested that the withdrawn group has a greater probability of brain damage than the active group (Depue, 1976).

The impact of rehabilitation on quality of life has received considerable attention in recent years. However the difficulty of making comparisons between patients in different treatment settings is enormous since the severity of psychopathology has a major impact on rehabilitation and placement. A study by Lehman and colleagues (1982) identified the central importance of having a confiding and close friendship in relation to the patient's overall quality of life. Gibbons and Butler (1987) demonstrated that a group of 'new long-stay' patients assessed in hospital and subsequently in a hostel showed the greatest normalisation in the latter although in both settings they felt isolated and lonely.

The impact of schizophrenia on relatives has received increasing attention in recent years with the increased emphasis on brief hospitalisation, day care and out-patient follow-up. The Scottish Schizophrenia Research Group (1992) demonstrated that social function was impaired in the patient's main care-giver and that there was little change in this over the subsequent years despite an improvement in distress particularly in the relatives of those who did not relapse. No attempt was made to address the reason for the absence of change in social function although it is possible that this reflected the unspoken strain of living with a patient who has a potentially serious illness. Further evidence for the uncertain relationship between dysfunction and distress comes from the work of Oldridge and Hughes (1992) who found correlations of around 0.6 between them. They also found that social dysfunction in the carers was particularly related to negative symptoms, a finding consistent with clinical intuition. However a substantial proportion coped very well despite difficulties in the patient.

SOCIAL FUNCTION AND NEUROTIC DISORDERS

One of the essential differences between the neurotic and other psychiatric disorders is that the former apparently disrupt function less than the latter. It is pertinent to ask if this is in fact correct since there are many patients with disorders that belong to this broad group whose functioning is grossly impaired. In particular those with agoraphobia or social phobia are often housebound and isolated to an extreme degree. Moreover, suicide risk is equally high among both the neurotic and psychotic depressives. Both of these observations suggest that the distinction between these broad categories may be an over-simplification. Some support for the view that the neuroses are less incapacitating than other disorders comes from the work of Casey *et al.* (1985) who found that in a general practice setting those with anxiety states were less socially dysfunctional than those with schizophrenia or depressive psychosis. Those with anxiety states, whilst being more socially dysfunctional than those with non-specific symptoms not amounting to disorder on PSE assessment, were not statistically different from the latter. Surprisingly patients assigned to the PSE catego class of neurotic depression did not have a significantly different mean social function score from those with a diagnosis of retarded depression or of depressive psychosis on the PSE. This lends construct validity to the unitary view of depressive disorders, a view shared by Ni Bhrolchain *et al.* (1979) also on the basis of impairment measures as well as symptomatic assessment.

Whilst adjustment disorders in themselves have received little attention in the psychiatric literature and are regarded by some as a 'rag-bag' diagnosis, they are commonly seen in general practice settings and clinically can resemble depressive disorders. Although Casey *et al.* (1985) did not specifically examine the degree of social impairment in those clinically diagnosed as having adjustment disorders, the PSE interview did identify a number of patients belonging to the catego class of 'non-specific symptoms', the class to whom this diagnosis is most likely to apply. Social function was significantly less impaired in this group than in those belonging to the catego class of neurotic or retarded depression.

In conclusion, the paucity of information relating specifically to functioning in the adjustment disorders and the neuroses is a cause for concern. Investigation of these disorders is essential if our understanding of and therapeutic input into them is to be complete. Moreover the traditional view that these disorders are mild and less deserving of medical time is surely one which every clinician knows to be at best erroneous and a gross underestimation of the incapacity of patients with these disorders and of the impact on their families.

REFERENCES

Bille-Brahe, U. and Wang, A.G. (1985). Attempted suicide in Denmark. 11. Social Integration. *Social Psychiatry*, **20**, 163–170.

Bille-Brahe, U., Hansen, W., Kolmos, L. and Wang, A.G. (1985). Attempted suicide in Denmark. 1. Some basic social characteristics. *Acta Psychiatrica Scandinavica*, **71**, 217–226.

Bland, R.C. and Orn, H. (1979). Schizophrenia: diagnostic criteria and outcome. *British Journal of Psychiatry*, **134**, 34–38.

Breier, A., Schreiber, J.L., Dyer, J. and Pickar, D. (1991). NIMH longitudinal study of chronic schizophrenia: prognosis and predictors of outcome. *Archives of General Psychiatry*, **48**, 239–246.

Brennan, P.L. and Moos, R.H. (1991). Functioning, life-context and help-seeking among late-onset problem drinkers: comparisons with non-problem and early-onset problem drinkers. *British Journal of Addiction*, **86**, 1139–1150.

Casey, P.R. (1989). Personality disorder and suicide intent. *Acta Psychiatrica Scandinavica*, **79**, 290–295.

Casey, P.R. and Butler, E. (1993). Social functioning and recovery from severe depressive illness. *Journal of Affective Disorders*, submitted.

Casey, P.R. and Tyrer, P. (1986). Personality, functioning and symptomatology. *Journal of Psychiatric Research*, **20**, 353–374.

Casey, P.R., Tyrer, P. and Platt, S. (1985). The relationship between social functioning and psychiatric symptomatology in primary care. *Social Psychiatry*, **20**, 5–9.

Cheadle, A.J., Freeman, H.L. and Korer, J. (1978). Chronic schizophrenic patients in the community. *British Journal of Psychiatry*, **132**, 221–227.

Depue, R.A. (1976). An activity-withdrawal distinction in schizophrenia: behavioural, clinical, brain damage and neurophysiological correlates. *Journal of Abnormal Psychology*, **55**, 174–185.

Dohrenwend, B.S., Cook, D. and Dohrenwend, B.P. (1981). Measurement of social functioning in community populations, pp. 183–201. In: Wing, J.K., Bebbington, P. and Robins, L.N. (Eds), *What is a Case?* Grant McIntyre, London.

Dohrenwend, B.S., Dohrenwend, B.P., Link, B. and Levav, I. (1983). Social functioning of psychiatric patients in contrast with community cases in the general population. *Archives of General Psychiatry*, **40**, 1174–1182.

Durkheim, E. (1951). *Suicide: A study in Sociology (translated by Spalding, J. and Simpson, G.)*. Free Press, New York.

Edwards, G. and Gross, M.M. (1976). Alcohol dependence: provisional description of a clinical syndrome. *British Medical Journal*, **1**, 1058–1061.

Ennis, J., Barnes, R.A., Kennedy, S. and Trachtenberg, D.D. (1989). Depression in self-harm patients. *British Journal of Psychiatry*, **154**, 41–47.

Frank, J.D. (1961). *Persuasion and Healing*. Johns Hopkins Press, Baltimore.

Gibbons, J.S. and Butler, J.P. (1987). Quality of life for 'new' long-stay psychiatric in-patients: the effects of moving to a hostel. *British Journal of Psychiatry*, **151**, 347–354.

Johnstone, E.C., Frith, C.D., Gold, A. and Stevens, M. (1979). The outcome of severe acute schizophrenic illness after one year. *British Journal of Psychiatry*, **134**, 28–33.

Keitner, G.I. and Miller, I.W. (1990). Family functioning and major depression: an overview. *American Journal of Psychiatry*, **147**, 1128–1137.

Keitner, G.I., Miller, I.W. and Epstein, N.B. (1987). Family functioning and the course of major depression. *Comprehensive Psychiatry*, **28**, 54–64.

Lehman, A.F., Ward, N.C. and Linn, L.S. (1982). Chronic mental patients: the quality of life issue. *American Journal of Psychiatry*, **139**, 1271–1276.

McLeavy, B., Daly, R.J., Murray, C.M., O'Riordan, J. and Taylor, M. (1987). Interpersonal problem solving deficits in self-poisoning patients. *Suicide and Life-threatening Behaviour*, **17**, 33–49.

Mange-Ingvar, U., Ojehagen, A. and Traskman-Bendz, L. (1992). *Acta Psychiatrica Scandinavica*, **86**, 153–158.

Mann, A.H., Jenkins, R. and Belsey, E. (1981). The twelve month outcome of patients with neurotic illness in general practice. *Psychological Medicine*, **11**, 535–550.

Morgan, G.H., Burns-Cox, C.J., Pocock, H. and Pottle, S. (1975). Deliberate self-harm: Clinical and socio-economic characteristics of 368 patients. *British Journal of Psychiatry*, **127**, 564–574.

Murphy, G.E., Armstrong, J.W., Hermele, S.L., Fischer, J.R. and Glendenin, W.W. (1979). Suicide and Alcoholism. Interpersonal loss confirmed as a predictor. *Archives of General Psychiatry*, **36**, 65–69.

Ni Bhrolchain, M., Brown, G.W. and Harris, T.O. (1979). Psychotic and neurotic depression: 2. Clinical characteristics. *British Journal of Psychiatry*, **134**, 94–107.

Oldridge, M.L. and Hughes, I.T.C. (1992). Psychological well-being in families with a member suffering from schizophrenia. An investigation into long-standing problems. *British Journal of Psychiatry*, **161**, 249–251.

Paykel, E.S. and Weissman, M.M. (1973). Social adjustment and depression. A longitudinal study. *Archives of General Psychiatry*, **28**, 659–663.

Paykel, E.S., DiMascio, A., Haskell, D. and Prusoff, B.A. (1975). The effects of maintenance amitryptiline and psychotherapy on symptoms of depression. *Psychological Medicine*, **5**, 67–73.

Paykel, E.S., Weissman, M.M. and Prusoff, B.A. (1978). Social maladjustment and severity of depression. *Comprehensive Psychiatry*, **19**, 121–128.

Platt, S. and Kreitman, N. (1985). Parasuicide and unemployment among men in Edinburgh, 1968–82. *Psychological Medicine*, **15**, 113–123.

Platt, S.D., Hirsch, S.R. and Knights, A.C. (1981). Effects of brief hospitalization on psychiatric patients' behaviour and social functioning. *Acta Psychiatrica Scandinavica*, **63**, 117–128.

Platt, S., Hawton, K., Kreitman, N., Fagg, J. and Foster, J. (1988). Recent clinical and epidemiological trends in parasuicide in Edinburgh and Oxford: a tale of two cities. *Psychological Medicine*, **18**, 405–418.

Remington and Tyrer, P. (1979). The social functioning schedule — a brief semi-structured interview. *Social Psychiatry*, **40**, 151–157.

Rounsaville, B.J., Prusoff, B.A. and Weissman, M.M. (1980). The course of marital disputes in depressed women: a 48 month follow-up study. *Comprehensive Psychiatry*, **21**, 111–118.

Salkovskis, P.M., Atha, C. and Storer, D. (1990). Cognitive–behavioural problem solving in the treatment of patients who repeatedly attempt suicide. *British Journal of Psychiatry*, **157**, 871–876.

Scottish Schizophrenia Research Group (1992). The Scottish First Episode Schizophrenia Study. VIII. Five-year follow-up: clinical and psychosocial findings. *British Journal of Psychiatry*, **161**, 496–500.

Strauss, J.S. and Carpenter, W.T. (1974). The prediction of outcome in schizophrenia. *Archives of General Psychiatry*, **31**, 155–160.

Tanner, J., Weissman, M.M. and Prusoff, B. (1975). Social adjustment and clinical relapse in depressed outpatients. *Comprehensive Psychiatry*, **16**, 547–556.

Tyrer, P. (1990). Personality disorder and social functioning. In: Peck, D.F. and Shapiro, C.M. (Eds), *Measuring Human Problems: A Practical Guide*. Wiley, Chichester, pp. 119–142.

Tyrer, P., Merson, S., Harrison-Read, P., Lynch, S., Birkett, P. and Onyett, S. (1990). A pilot study of the effects of early intervention on clinical symptoms and social functioning in psychiatric emergencies. *Irish Journal of Psychological Medicine*, **7**, 132–134.

Venables, P.H. (1957). A short scale for rating 'Activity–Withdrawal' in schizophrenics. *Journal of Mental Science*, **103**, 197–199.

Williams, A.D., Reveley, M.A., Kolakowska, T., Arden, M. and Mandlebrote, B.M. (1985). Schizophrenia with good and poor outcome, II: cerebral ventricular size and its clinical significance. *British Journal of Psychiatry*, **146**, 239–246.

Wittenborn, J.R., McDonald, D.C. and Maurer, H.S. (1977). Persisting symptoms in schizophrenia predicted by background factor. *Archives of General Psychiatry*, **34**, 1057–1061.

World Health Organisation (1992). *The ICD-10 Classification of Mental and Behavioural Disorders, Clinical Descriptions and Diagnostic Guidelines*. WHO, Geneva.

Social Function in Psychiatry: The Hidden Axis of Classification
Edited by Peter Tyrer and Patricia Casey
©1993 Wrightson Biomedical Publishing Ltd

6

Social Function and Personality Disorder

PATRICIA CASEY

It has long been recognised that personality disorder has an impact on social function, indeed the diagnosis is dependent upon the presence of social incapacity. This is recognised formally by both the DSM-IIIR and the ICD-10 definitions of personality disorder. Since both axis I and axis II disorders have an impact on social function it is pertinent to consider the nature and relative magnitude of this effect in the psychiatric population and in the variety of treatment settings to which patients are exposed in current psychiatric practice. The importance of the distinction between the effect of axis I and axis II lies in the approach to the management of social incapacity — that which is secondary to mental state disorders generally responding to the appropriate biological interventions, whilst that due to personality disorder will be more protracted and require either a largely psychotherapeutic or behavioural approach, a point emphasised by Frank (1961) in his book *Persuasion and Healing* although recently contradicted by formal evidence (Tyrer *et al.*, 1993). Whilst the effect of personality on functioning is accepted in clinical practice, and may even be argued from the opposite viewpoint that because a person displays social dysfunction personality disorder also exists, it is important to examine the empirical evidence for this and to assess the relative contribution of personality and illness to this.

CONTRIBUTION OF PERSONALITY TO SOCIAL IMPAIRMENT

The contribution of personality to social dysfunction is perhaps best studied by examining cohorts derived from the community. A study by Casey and Tyrer (1986) selected at random 200 persons from the electoral register. These were divided equally between an urban and a rural group. Each person was assessed using the Social Functioning Schedule (SFS) (Remington and Tyrer, 1979) (see Chapter 3), the Personality Assessment Schedule (Tyrer

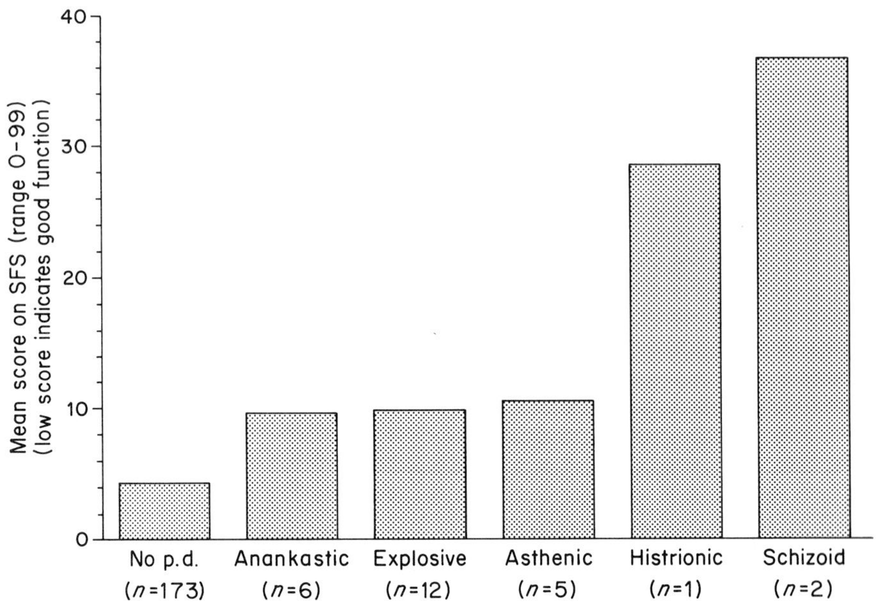

Figure 6.1. Social function in 199 subjects chosen at random from urban and rural communities measured by the Social Functioning Schedule (SFS) in a sample separated by personality status. Reproduced with permission, from Casey and Tyrer (1986).

et al., 1979) and the Present State Examination (Wing *et al.*, 1974). In addition demographic information was recorded. This enabled a categorical diagnosis of personality disorder to be made, where applicable, as well as an index of definition (I/D) and a mean social function score for each subject interviewed. Those which were related to social function were examined using regression analysis and only personality disorder ($F=6.2$, $p<0.01$) and I/D ($F=53.8$, $p<0.0001$) reached significance (Casey and Tyrer, 1986) (Figure 6.1). It is clear from these figures that I/D makes a greater contribution to the overall social function score than does personality. This is of particular interest in view of the relatively low level of caseness (8%) when compared with personality disorder (13%) in this community population and shows that mental state disturbance has a major impact on social function.

In a general practice study designed to examine the prevalence and nature of conspicuous psychiatric morbidity in that setting (Casey *et al.*, 1985), using the same interview schedules, personality disorder did not make any significant contribution to the degree of social impairment. Indeed I/D level ($F=29.061$, $p<0.001$) was the only variable which contributed significantly to the independent variable. The surprising finding that personality did not make a significant contribution confirms that symptom severity overshadowed personality. It is therefore likely that as symptoms increase in severity, as for example in passing from out-patient to in-patient status, the effect of personality and social factors on functioning will diminish at the peak of illness only to become apparent again as symptoms subside after treatment. This has indeed been described by Paykel and Weissman (1973) who showed that when assessed longitudinally there is a dissociation between social function and symptoms explicable by the emergence of personality effects during follow-up. He wrote 'much of the social impairment appears symptom related, subsiding with symptom reduction ... A small but definite portion reflects underlying personality disturbance'. The effect of personality on social outcome will be discussed later in this chapter.

SOCIAL FUNCTION IN DIFFERENT PERSONALITY DISORDER CATEGORIES

The categorical approach to personality assessment and disorder has many critics but despite this has remained the mainstay of the clinical approach. The criticisms are multiple and substantial and include such concerns as the arbitrariness of the categories used (Tyrer, 1988) as evinced by the seemingly *ad hoc* addition or removal of categories with each new edition of the ICD or DSM system of classification. A further criticism is the overlap which has been demonstrated between categories (Frances and Widiger, 1986) and the failure to validate any category except perhaps the antisocial category. Moreover the absence of any relationship between the category of personality disorder and the outcome of axis I disorders as well as the paucity of evidence for a link between category and symptom pattern (with the possible exception of the anankastic group and obsessional symptoms) adds further weight to the anti-categorist lobby.

A further question which has not so far been explored is whether the individual categories represent qualitative or quantitative differences between each other. It is generally assumed that at least some of the categories can be distinguished from each other on the basis of quantitative differences — in other words they represent degrees of severity on the basis of some external measure. A viable measure of this severity could be the extent to which social function is impaired. There are few studies of this so far but one by Casey *et al.* (1985) in a general practice population with conspicuous psychiatric morbidity failed to find any difference in degree of social dysfunction between the categories of personality disorder. There was however a significant difference in social function score between those with normal personality when compared with all the categories of abnormal personality combined. The results are shown in Table 6.1.

Table 6.1. Mean social function score for categories of personality disorder.[a]

Personality disorder	n	Score	SD	t-test
Normal	105	21.47	16.55	
Schizoid		33.12	13.87	
Explosive		30.13	23.25	$t=-3.21$
Anankastic		33.69	13.95	d.f.$=161$
Hysterical	58	29.45	11.10	$p<0.002$
Asthenic		33.57	17.44	
Sociopathic		19.80	—	
Other		20.17	6.82	

[a]Numbers within brace were analysed together.

The difference between those with and without personality disorder serves to provide construct validation for the concept of personality disorder — a notion challenged by some, who argue for the abandonment of this axis (Lewis and Appleby, 1988). A similar result was found in a community sample chosen at random from the electoral register: no difference was found between the categories of personality (see Figure 6.1) although the distinction between those with and without personality disorder, as found in the earlier study, remained (Casey and Tyrer, 1986).

The failure to find any important difference in the degree of social dysfunction among the categories of personality disorder lends further weight to the arguments of those who feel that there are too many categories and that they could be reduced to one or two major groups (Rutter, 1987). Further studies using larger samples are needed if this view is to be supported although there are other aspects apart from social dysfunction which are important in personality disorder. The possibility that personality disorder is best represented as dimensions rather than categories needs to be examined further and again investigation of specific areas of social function may throw some light on possible qualitative differences.

FUNCTIONAL OUTCOME OF PERSONALITY DISORDERS

Follow-up studies of the functional outcome of the categories of personality disorder are scarce. The Chestnut Lodge study by McGlashan (1986) is the best known and found that those with an initial diagnosis of borderline personality were functioning well in their work and in their relationships in the long term despite at least moderate impairment in social function at the index admission. Many did however have axis I symptomatology. When compared with those with a diagnosis of schizotypal personality the functional outcome was much better. Moreover functioning continued to improve even two decades after the initial assessment. Follow-up studies of those with antisocial personality disorder also show an improvement in relationships and a decrease in unacceptable behaviour as adulthood progresses (Maddocks, 1970). Surprisingly those categories which are most common but also least intrusive (i.e. passive–dependent, anankastic and anxious) have no literature relating to their natural history or their social prognosis with treatment. This is most likely to be due to the fact that treatments for these are in their infancy (Casey, 1992) and that it is only recently that adequate measures for their assessment have been developed.

PERSONALITY AND SOCIAL OUTCOME IN AXIS I DISORDERS

In view of the recognition that functioning as well as symptoms is an important manifestation of disorder, more researchers have begun to examine the outcome of psychiatric disorders in terms of social function as well as symptoms. This has been described in Chapter 5. In view of the complexity of the factors which contribute to social function and to differences between demographic groups which have been outlined in Chapter 2, it is pertinent to investigate the interplay between personality and mental state in relation to social outcome.

The recognition that personality contributes to the outcome of psychiatric disorders has a long and venerable history (Sargant and Slater, 1944). More recently it has been shown that in-patients with co-occurring depressive illness and personality disorder have a poorer response to antidepressant drugs (Black *et al.*, 1988) and have higher readmission rates following ECT than their counterparts with an axis I diagnosis only (Zimmerman *et al.*, 1986; Black *et al.*, 1988). For all diagnoses those with both axis I and II disorders have greater service utilisation than those with axis I disorders only (Tyrer and Seivewright, 1988). Interestingly there are few studies which have measured outcome in terms of social function having instead used the more usual indices of symptom severity and readmission to hospital.

A recent investigation by the author examined the social outcome of depressive illness following ECT and the contribution which personality along with symptomatic and demographic variables made to that.

Methods

Forty patients with a diagnosis of major depression all requiring in-patient treatment with ECT entered this study and were followed up for six months following discharge. The present results relate to the assessment of the patients' social function at the time of discharge from hospital.

Table 6.2. Variables in regression analysis.

Dependent variable	Social function at discharge
Independent variables	Hamilton depression score at outset
	Social functioning at outset
	Normal personality/personality disorder
	Antisocial dimension
	Anankastic dimension
	Passive–dependent dimension
	Schizoid dimension
	Age
	Marital status
	Past history
Contributing variables	Normal personality/Personality disorder 31%
	Hamilton depression score at outset 50%
	Schizoid dimension 56%
	Anankastic dimension 62%

Each patient was assessed at the outset using the Hamilton Rating Scale for depression and the Social Functioning Schedule (SFS) (Remington and Tyrer, 1979). In addition demographic data were gathered. At discharge from hospital the above measures were again applied and personality was assessed using the Personality Assessment Schedule (PAS) (Tyrer *et al.*, 1979). This schedule uses both subject and an informant to obtain information relating to 24 enduring traits of personality present since adolescence. Only if the trait impinges negatively upon other people is it regarded as abnormal and using a cluster analytic technique a categorical diagnosis based on ICD-10 can be made. In addition, this schedule has the advantage of providing four-dimensional measures on each patient irrespective of whether a personality disorder is present or not. This has the advantage of increasing the instrument's flexibility and subtlety — a response to the justified criticisms of the traditional categorical approach.

Results

There were significant differences in the mean social function score at the time of discharge between those with combined axis I and II disorders and those with an axis I diagnosis alone (35.8 and 11.2, respectively; $t=4.30$, d.f.$=35$, $p<0.001$). In order to assess the magnitude of the variance contributed by a number of variables to the social outcome at discharge a regression analysis was carried out. The variables entered in the analysis and those contributing significantly are listed in Table 6.2.

From this it can be seen that 62% of the variance was explained and the bulk of this was due to personality variables, with severity of depression at outset making a smaller contribution. This suggests that social recovery from depressive illness, at least in the short term, is related more to personality than to the severity of symptoms.

CONCLUSIONS

Research to date has been scanty in examining the specific aspects of social function and personality disorder. There are no differences in social function between the traditional categories of personality disorder but outcome studies suggest that borderline has a better social outcome than schizotypal personality. There are no studies of the social outcome of the more common categories such as passive–dependent, anxious or anankastic. The social outcome of severe depressive illness is determined more by personality than by symptomatic severity.

REFERENCES

Black, D.W., Bell, S., Hulbert, J. and Nasarallah, A. (1988). The importance of axis-II in patients with major depression. A controlled study. *Journal of Affective Disorders*, **14**, 115–122.

Casey, P.R. (1992). Personality disorders: do psychological treatments help? In: Hawton, K. and Cowen, P. (Eds), *Practical Problems in Clinical Psychiatry*. Oxford University Press, Oxford.

Casey, P.R. and Tyrer, P.J. (1986). Personality, functioning and symptomatology. *Journal of Psychiatric Research*, **20**, 363–374.

Casey, P.R., Tyrer, P.J. and Platt, S. (1985). The relationship between social functioning and psychiatric symptomatology in primary care. *Social Psychiatry*, **20**, 5–9.

Frances, A.J. and Widiger, T. (1986). The classification of personality disorders; an overview of problems and solutions. In: Frances, A.J. and Hales, R.E. (Eds), *American Psychiatric Association Annual Review. Vol. 5*. American Psychiatric Press, Washington DC.

Frank, J.D. (1961). *Persuasion and Healing*. Johns Hopkins Press, Baltimore.

Lewis, G. and Appleby, L. (1988). Personality disorders: the patients psychiatrists dislike. *British Journal of Psychiatry*, **153**, 44–49.

McGlashan, T.H. (1986). The Chestnut Lodge follow-up study III. Long term outcome of borderline personalities. *Archives of General Psychiatry*, **43**, 20–30.

Maddocks, P.D. (1970). A five year follow-up of untreated psychopaths. *British Journal of Psychiatry*, **116**, 510–515.

Paykel, E.S. and Weissman, M.M. (1973). Social adjustment and depression. A longitudinal study. *Archives of General Psychiatry*, **28**, 659–663.

Remington, M. and Tyrer, P. (1979). The Social Functioning Schedule — a brief semi-structured interview. *Social Psychiatry*, **40**, 151–157.

Rutter, J. (1987). Temperament, personality and personality disorder. *British Journal of Psychiatry*, **150**, 443–458.

Sargant, W. and Slater, E. (1944). *Physical Methods of Treatment in Psychiatry*. Churchill-Livingstone, Edinburgh.

Tyrer, P. (1988). What's wrong with DSM-III-R personality disorders? *Journal of Personality Disorders*, **2**, 281–291.

Tyrer, P. and Seivewright, H. (1988). Studies of outcome. In: Tyrer, P. (Ed.), *Personality Disorders. Diagnosis, Management and Course*. Wright, Bristol.

Tyrer, P., Alexander, M.S., Cicchetti, D., Cohen, M.S. and Remington, M. (1979). Reliability of a schedule for rating personality disorders. *British Journal of Psychiatry*, **135**, 168–174.

Tyrer, P., Seivewright, N., Ferguson, B., Murphy, S. and Johnson, A.L. (1993). The Nottingham study of neurotic disorder. Effect of personality status on response to drug treatment, cognitive therapy and self-help over two years. *British Journal of Psychiatry*, **162**, 219–229.

Wing, J.K., Cooper, J.E. and Sartorius, N. (1974). *The Measurement and Classification of Psychiatric Symptoms*. Cambridge University Press, Cambridge.

Zimmerman, M., Coryell, W., Pfohl, B., Corenthal, C. and Stangl, D. (1986). ECT response in depressed patients with and without a DSM-III personality disorder. *American Journal of Psychiatry*, **143**, 1030–1032.

Social Function in Psychiatry: The Hidden Axis of Classification
Edited by Peter Tyrer and Patricia Casey
©1993 Wrightson Biomedical Publishing Ltd

7

Social Function in People with Learning Difficulties

MARK RAPLEY

INTRODUCTION

The first chapter of this volume has discussed the difficulty of defining 'social function' as a global construct and some of the problems inherent in attempting to disentangle social roles, social performance and social networks. In the context of mental handicap these difficulties are compounded by the circularity of prevailing definitions of mental impairment in respect of the concept of social competence, by which the ascription of 'mental impairment' is dependent, at least in part, upon *a priori* judgements of inadequate social function. A further impediment to clarity in this field is the fact that the construct of 'social competence' has become virtually isomorphic with that of 'adaptive behaviour', neither of which has precisely the same sense that 'unimpaired social function' might connote in other areas.

This chapter will consider these definitional issues, discuss the nature of impaired social performance in people with learning difficulties and examine the relationship between social competence and social context in this population. Throughout this chapter the terms 'mental handicap'/'learning difficulties' and 'social competence'/'social function' are used interchangeably.

CONCEPTUAL ISSUES

As noted above, a conceptual difficulty arises in addressing the issue of social competence in people with a mental handicap. The distinction between those 'with' and those 'without' a mental impairment is inherently circular. All of the major classification systems define 'mental impairment' or 'mental retardation' on the grounds of poor performance on IQ tests and co-presenting inadequacies of social function. For example the American Psychiatric Association's *Diagnostic and Statistical Manual (3rd Edition — Revised)* defines 'the essential features' of mental retardation as:

'significantly subaverage general intellectual functioning accompanied by (2) significant deficits or impairments in adaptive functioning, with (3) onset before the age of 18. Treating the IQ with some flexibility permits inclusion in the...category [of mental retardation] of people with IQs somewhat higher than 70 who exhibit significant deficits in adaptive behaviour...Adaptive functioning refers to the person's effectiveness in areas such as social skills, communication, and daily living skills, and how well the person meets the standards of personal independence and social responsibility expected of his or her age by his...cultural group. Adaptive functioning is influenced by personality characteristics, motivation, education, and social and vocational opportunities.'
(American Psychiatric Association, 1987).

Whilst both transient and more permanent impairments in social performance may be displayed by people at all levels of intellectual ability, for a wide range of reasons, it is explicit in current taxonomic systems that people with impaired intellectual abilities (i.e. below IQ 70) are *de facto* also socially incompetent. As Landesman-Dwyer and Berkson (1984) put it: 'by definition mentally retarded individuals lack the adaptive behaviour skills demonstrated by non-retarded agemates in their culture'. Furthermore, implied by the conjunction of apparently 'hard' descriptors, in the form of IQ scores, with 'soft data' (Tyrer, 1990) in judgements of social function, are the notions of stasis and individual pathology. Despite the APA's genuflection towards the possible influence of personality characteristics, motivation and social factors, 'mental impairment' remains a once-and-for-all diagnosis of a condition possessed by the individual.

The existence of discrete diagnostic categories, whilst perhaps administratively convenient, obscures the fact that no universally acknowledged manner of defining social impairment objectively yet exists (Clements, 1987), but rather suggests that clear, unambiguous criteria are available for making such judgements. This is not the case: as Clarke and Clarke pointed out as long ago as 1974; 'while no doubt boundaries do exist in nature, these are seldom as sharply defined or as rigid as we seek to make them...intellectual abilities, and also social competence, form graded continua, so that any dividing line must, in effect be arbitrary.'

The definition of persons as 'mentally impaired' thus rests on performance below an administratively selected cut-off (two standard deviations below the mean, itself arbitrarily set at the figure of 100) and subjective, possibly 'flexible', assessments by individual clinicians of social incompetence, as demonstrated by 'significant deficits' in, for example, social skills or 'social responsibility'. Inasmuch as social impairment has yet to be adequately defined, there is even less sign of agreement as to what might constitute adequate social performance, an appropriate level of social responsibility, or a normative inventory of social skills against which to calibrate a 'deficit'. As Tyrer (1990) and many others have suggested, the assessment of social function, or the impairment thereof, may be particularly prone to contamination by value judgements; in the case of persons with learning difficulties the pre-existence of known intellectual impairment can only increase the likelihood of this outcome. A cursory examination of the changes in criteria employed for inferring mental impairment over the course of the last century provides ample evidence that, in the case of 'moral deficiency' for instance, the violation of cultural values has been sufficient to warrant such an attribution. More recently, experimental studies have suggested that clinical judgements of the severity of psychopathology (as rated from therapy transcripts) may be significantly swayed merely by the information that the 'patient' is 'mentally retarded' (Alford and Locke, 1984). It is also apparent that the type and degree of contamination by value judgements may vary as a function of professional training and the expectations of individuals with learning disabilities inculcated during professional enculturation. Wolraich and Siperstein (1986), for example, demonstrated that physicians — as opposed to social workers, psychologists and educationalists — had significantly lower expectations of the abilities of persons with learning difficulties and made gloomier prognoses about their future capabilities. 'Retardation' is, as Belmont (1978) notes, 'a complicated social judgement embodied in a single word'.

The implication, conveyed by established classification systems, that the characteristics employed as indices of mental handicap are fixed properties of individuals, also serves to distract attention from the essentially interactive nature, and contextual dependence, of the social behaviour of all persons, regardless of their measured IQ. Studies specifically examining the relationship between the social environment and the behaviour of people with learning difficulties will be discussed in further detail below.

The existence of diagnostic systems thus creates a misleading impression of uniformity. Whilst it is clear that there appears to be an unambiguous relationship between severe mental handicap and pronounced impairments in many areas of motor and social performance, as yet — perhaps partly as a result of some of the definitional difficulties referred to above — that literature which exists is in the main descriptive and rarely specifically addresses the nature of the relationship between intellectual disability and impairments of social performance. It is difficult to better Clements' (1987) observation that 'social impairments can certainly be found at all levels of ability, it is just that they are more common among those with marked intellectual difficulties, which suggests some relationship between the two areas'. Even given this apparent relationship caution is warranted: discussing the subjects of an earlier study, Berg and Wacker (1991) observed that 'individuals who are diagnosed as severely/profoundly mentally handicapped represent an extremely heterogeneous group of people...the participants in these investigations were all persons diagnosed with severe handicaps, from those who were non-verbal, non-ambulatory, had seizure disorders, cerebral palsy...and who were completely dependent in all basic self-care tasks, to those who were ambulatory, had no sensory or motor impairments, and routinely performed multiple functional skills'.

As is indicated by Berg and Wacker (1991), and by the considerations outlined above, the predictive utility of the attribution of mental handicap is likely to be extremely limited in specific cases. Knowledge of an individual's IQ score provides only a broad indication of their likely performance in everyday situations, precisely because many items in IQ tests are selected against a criterion of relative novelty (Sternberg and Spear, 1985), and a number of studies have now shown that IQ *per se* is either unrelated to, or at best a poor predictor of, community adjustment (for example, see Flynn, 1989; Heal *et al.*, 1980). The difficulty with the incautious or unqualified use of IQ scores may be illustrated by Bronfenbrenner's account of the consequences of the erroneous admission of 'normal' children to an institution: in the space of the few weeks it took to arrange a discharge 'their scores on the intelligence tests administered as a compulsory part of the discharge process proved them mentally deficient' (Bronfenbrenner, 1979, cited in Howe, 1991).

The result of definitional inexactitude, the circularity of diagnostic criteria, the high probability of assessments contaminated by value judgements, and the tendency noted by Goode (1983) for clinical judgements to fail to take adequate account of social context of the individual, is that people with learning difficulties constitute a diverse and heterogeneous population. Given this state of affairs broad generalisations are not only difficult to make, but must also, when made, be treated with caution.

SOCIAL IMPAIRMENTS IN PEOPLE WITH LEARNING DIFFICULTIES

With due regard to these considerations, it is unarguable that many people with a mental handicap can be described as experiencing considerable difficulties in social function. It is also the case that many persons with learning difficulties can and do enjoy reciprocally satisfying social relationships with peers who would not be described as intellectually impaired (Atkinson and Ward, 1986). Edgerton, in his classic and well-known series of studies of ex-inmates of American institutions, has documented how some people who were diagnosed as 'retarded' were not only well aware of inadequacies of their abilities, but also were able to recruit long-term 'benefactors' to assist them with many of the tasks of daily living with which they experienced difficulty (Edgerton, 1967; Edgerton and Bercovici, 1976).

In order to avoid, as much as is possible, the conceptual muddles described above, the nature of impaired or dysfunctional social performance in people with learning difficulties is most usefully considered from two perspectives. On the one hand there are difficulties at the individual level: as Clements (1987) pointed out, marked intellectual impairment does tend to co-occur with increasing difficulties in all areas of functioning. It is also the case, however, that for many people with learning difficulties, the nature of the social environments within which they spend their time is at considerable variance from that within which the majority of their peers operate. Social behaviour that may be judged dysfunctional or impaired in 'normal' social environments may have significant adaptive function in social environments such as mental handicap hospitals, hostels and day centres, where the patterns and norms of social interaction may be both qualitatively and quantitatively different (Felce, 1991; Mayhew *et al.*, 1978). Durand (1991), discussing the severe problem behaviours that are displayed by some persons with mental handicaps, articulates this view unambiguously: 'such behavior problems are not abnormalities...these responses are reasonable behavioral adaptations necessitated by the abilities of our students and the limitations of their environments'.

In order to gain a clear picture of the social function of people with learning difficulties it is, therefore, necessary to consider deficits in social function arising from both individually and situationally mediated factors. These factors are discussed in the sections below.

INDIVIDUAL FACTORS IN SOCIAL FUNCTION

Adequate social function demands the deployment and co-ordination of a wide array of skills and behaviours: such a wide array, indeed, that some writers have despaired of ever defining the concept except by exclusion (Spreat *et al.*, 1983). For the purpose of this chapter, rather than provide yet another definition of a 'construct which is only definable in terms of other constructs whose own definitions are vague' (Zigler and Trickett, 1978), consideration will be given to the behaviour of people with learning difficulties in relation to the notion of 'social skilfulness' elaborated by Christoff and Kelly (1983). They propose that:

'...social skilfulness can be defined functionally, in terms of effectiveness. In any situation, a response can be termed skilful if it serves to elicit a desired response from the environment. The critical defining factor of socially skilful behaviour

is the effectiveness of the behaviour in social interactions. Determinations of effectiveness will necessarily vary with the context of the interaction and with the parameters of the specific situation. Skilful behaviour will always involve the co-ordination of appropriate verbal and non-verbal responses.'

Factors affecting the abilities of people with learning difficulties to demonstrate such effective social function are discussed below.

Associated impairments

In addition to the fact that, in comparison with people without a marked intellectual impairment, many 'mentally retarded persons often appear to exhibit relatively generalised, striking social skill impairment' (Christoff and Kelly, 1983), it is also the case that many people with a mental handicap also display associated difficulties with the prerequisite skills of social competence. Here, perhaps more clearly than anywhere else, is the relationship between increasing degrees of intellectual impairment and the increasing likelihood of associated impairment of the physical and structural underpinnings of social behaviour demonstrated. For example, Ager (1985) observes that 'difficulties of speech are a characteristic feature of mental handicap', and goes on to note that the degree and incidence of speech impairment or absence covaries in a linear fashion with the degree of intellectual impairment. Jacobson and Janicki (1983) found that the prevalence of epilepsy and cerebral palsy also increases with more pronounced intellectual impairment. There are a number of methodological difficulties in arriving at unequivocal estimates of the prevalence of impairments associated with different degrees of intellectual impairment (see Hogg and Sebba, 1986, Chapter 1, for a fuller discussion) but a number of surveys have found that, for those classified as severely (IQ<35–40) or profoundly (IQ<20–25) intellectually retarded, (both figures from Hogg and Sebba's (1986) adaptation of the AAMD classification (Grossman, 1983)), the likelihood of associated physical or sensory impairments is relatively high.

Cerebral palsy has been reported to occur in between 17% (Dupont, 1981) and 29% (Preddy and Mittler, 1981) of individuals described as being severely handicapped. Up to 50% of children with profound retardation have been reported as being unable to walk independently (Wald and Zdzienicka, 1981). The level of visual and auditory impairments reported vary widely, but there is some evidence to suggest that, again, there is a relationship between lower levels of intellectual functioning and increased likelihood of, for example, auditory impairment (Kropka, 1983). The literature provides contradictory assessments of the relationship between levels of intellectual impairment and visual problems but Hogg and Sebba (1988) conclude that it 'is clear that people who are retarded are especially susceptible to eye problems...and that the more profoundly retarded they are the more difficulties are associated with the assessment of their vision.' To give an example of what these rather dry figures might mean in practice, it is helpful to consider the total population survey of a long-stay mental handicap institution in the North of England conducted by Kiernan and Moss (1990). These authors found 7.1% of the population to be blind, 6.9% deaf, 24.9% to have a physical disability, with 20.6% described as non-ambulant, and 3.2% having both a sensory and a physical disability.

If social function is reconstrued as behavioural effectiveness in interpersonal interactions, with effectiveness being mediated by the co-ordination of appropriate verbal and non-verbal responses, as suggested by Christoff and Kelly (1983), then given the wide range of physical and sensory impairments which may be superimposed on an extant intellectual impairment it becomes apparent that the social function of many persons with a mental handicap is in double jeopardy. It is also apparent that the effects of physical impairments may be overlooked: in the author's experience it is not uncommon for difficulties in the social behaviour of people with learning difficulties (for instance repetitive questioning and apparent inability to respond to simple requests) attributable to an auditory disability, for example, to be exclusively and erroneously ascribed to intellectual impairment.

Intellectual ability

Psychological studies of mental handicap have, historically, tended to focus on attempts to delineate specific problems or deficits in the cognitive processes of people who achieve low scores on IQ tests. An array of competing deficits has been advanced to explain poor performance on measures of intellectual functioning: problems with encoding information (Nettlebeck and Lally, 1979), inefficient attentional strategies (Zeaman and House, 1963; Borkowski *et al.*, 1983), stimulus over-selectivity (Bailey, 1981) and memory storage, processing and retrieval difficulties (Ellis, 1970; Glidden, 1985; Detterman, 1979). Synthesis has also been sought, in the work of Sternberg and Spear (1985) for example, with attempts to develop metatheories encompassing the diversity of the experimental literature.

Whilst there is no doubt that some or all of these factors may play a role in the difficulties experienced by some people with learning difficulties in social situations, the experimental literature has yet to unequivocally establish the nature of the relationship(s) between impaired performance in experimental tasks and behaviour in the natural environment. It is likely that these relationships are complex and a full discussion of this area is beyond the scope of this chapter.

As was noted above, however, detailed studies of the social behaviour of people with learning difficulties in natural settings have found no clear relationship between IQ and various aspects of social behaviour. Gollay and colleagues' (1978) study of 440 people discharged from institutional care found that although problems in interpersonal relationships were more often reported by the more intellectually able members of the cohort, the frequency of friendships reported did not vary as a function of intellectual level. Similarly, another American deinstitutionalisation study, conducted by Bell *et al.* (1981) found that numbers of friends and frequency of visits were independent of IQ and adaptive behaviour. Romer and Heller (1983), in a review of studies concerned with the social networks of adults with a mental handicap in community settings, argue that level of intellectual ability is related to neither the extensity nor the intensity of learning-disabled persons' social networks: the correlation previously reported in the literature between IQ and sociability is, they suggest, 'illusory' and the result of a confound introduced by the frequent service practice of grouping people by ability levels. Of perhaps greater significance, however, is Romer and Berkson's (1980) finding that in their study, unlike IQ which was of no predictive utility, the desire for affiliation expressed by learning-disabled people themselves was a robust predictor of their social behaviour. Of all possible individual predictors of social behaviour it is perhaps those such as motivation and relationship history which have, until recently, received the least attention. Recognition has now started to grow of the influence of these 'personality' factors in social behaviour and any assessment of the social function of individuals with learning difficulties should be careful to take them into account.

Social cognition

Although now an expanding research area — for example Baron-Cohen's (1990) work on the 'theory of mind' of children described as 'autistic' — the literature on social cognition is presently relatively poorly developed (Clements, 1992). It is in this area, however, that a fuller understanding of the nature of impaired social function in people with learning difficulties must be sought. Only a brief overview of this area will be presented here: Clements (1987) provides good coverage of the experimental literature; Firth and Rapley (1990) offer a more detailed discussion of approaches to assisting people in this area of functioning.

It has been noted above that in order to be effective in interpersonal interactions or to function socially in a manner that achieves desired goals, it is necessary for individuals to master the co-ordination of culturally appropriate verbal and non-verbal responses. It has also been noted that for many people with learning difficulties associated impairments may make this level of performance extremely difficult, if not impossible, to reach. In addition to the performance problems posed by sensory, linguistic or motor impairments, however, it appears that people with a mental handicap often have problems of knowledge, as well as production, of those verbal and non-verbal responses which are appropriate in social situations. The research literature suggests a number of possible causes for this impairment.

Baron-Cohen's (1990) work has already been mentioned. In brief it would appear that people who are diagnosed as 'autistic' may have a particular problem with taking the place of the other in social interactions. In experimental situations these children find it extremely difficult to assess the extent to which others share their knowledge of the world: they appear to operate as if their 'theory of mind' does not apply to persons other than themselves. The implications of this in social situations are clear: effective interaction with others demands prediction of their intentions and the production of behaviour, in response to that of the other and estimations of their intentions, that achieves desired social goals. As Clements (1987) observes 'lack of such insight [into the intentions of others] would make it extremely difficult to predict accurately how others will behave. This would render the social world a very frightening place with people appearing to act quite "arbitrarily" (i.e. unexpectedly)'. In circumstances such as this, or in situations where communication problems hinder the achievement of the individuals' goals in social interactions, it becomes apparent that people may adopt behaviours, possibly considered socially inappropriate, which are in fact effective (functional) in producing desired responses from others. Although work on the theory of mind has concentrated on children diagnosed as 'autistic', it is suggestive insofar that many people with learning difficulties also appear to have problems with 'decoding' information about others in social interactions (Kernan et al., 1981).

Other cognitive skills essential to effective social function appear to pose difficulties for people with mental handicaps. As well as the need to accurately assess the nature of the social situation, which the inability to predict the behaviour of others or difficulty with comprehension of verbal and non-verbal cues will compromise, production of behaviour may also be impaired. Kernan et al. (1981) itemise a number of the impairments commonly displayed by people with learning difficulties in social interactions: interactions may be poorly structured with no clear beginning, middle or end, appropriate greeting and/or terminating behaviours may not be displayed, information may be inappropriately organised, events may be presented in incorrect temporal order, referents may be unclear, much information may be situationally irrelevant, misunderstandings may not be noticed or, if they are, may go uncorrected. These authors suggest that many of these impairments may be a consequence of lack of sensitivity to the social cues that indicate which forms of language and which behavioural repertoires are appropriate in given situations, cognitively mediated inability to learn the rules of speech (or interaction more generally) that govern different social situations or difficulty in adapting to new situations where different rules of conduct apply.

From the perspective of social cognition, difficulty with a number of key skills appears to underlie these deficits. First, people with a mental handicap may be lacking in the ability to think about social relationships; secondly, in the ability to assess interactions accurately; thirdly, in the knowledge of the social rules of the interaction in question; and, finally, in the selection of behaviours from the individual's repertoire which are appropriate in the situation. Failure in any of these areas will result in social behaviour that is situationally incongruous. It is apparent, however, that in the case of knowledge of social rules for example, there is here an interaction between the individual's intellectual impairment and the nature of the learning opportunities to which, historically, they have been exposed. People with a mental handicap, as Kernan *et al.* (1981) note, do often show an impairment in their ability to adapt flexibly to new situations such that those cognitive strategies, with associated behavioural repertoires, that are functional in one environment may well be out of place in another. The nature of the learning experiences offered to people with a mental handicap, is addressed below.

Despite progress in this area however, unfortunately it is not easy to contest Landesman-Dwyer and Berkson's (1984) conclusion that we do not yet really know 'to what degree the ability (1) to think about social relationships and (2) to solve social problems...relates to a given subject's observable social behaviour and friendship patterns'.

Experiential deficits

Landesman-Dwyer and Berkson (1984) concluded their chapter on the friendships and social behaviour of people with a mental handicap with the statement that 'we know of no principles about social behaviour that appear unique to retarded individuals, nor are there any theoretical reasons that affiliative patterns should be guided by different factors in this population'. It might appear that this conclusion is in some tension with Christoff and Kelly's (1983) observation that 'mentally retarded persons often appear to exhibit relatively generalised, striking social skill impairment', which would seem to suggest that there may be some factor, peculiar to mental handicap, that underpins all such difficulty in social function. From the discussion above, however, it appears beyond doubt that the most obvious such candidate — intellectual impairment — is not in itself sufficient to explain observed differences in social behaviour, whereas other factors, with no intrinsic relation to mental impairment, such as motivation, may have a high degree of predictive utility. If supposedly 'fixed' individual attributes (in the form of IQ scores) are unsatisfactory indices of social function and those, such as the desire to affiliate, which are more readily modified by interaction with the environment, provide a better criterion of social behaviour, then this suggests that the examination of factors commonly associated with, but extrinsic to, mental handicap may offer further insights into the nature and origins of impaired social abilities. The influence of the immediate social environment is examined below, but first consideration is given to social features in the lives of people with learning difficulties which have become central to the experience of learning disability.

Social behaviour is learned behaviour. As Flynn (1989) observes, 'nobody is born with an understanding of appropriate behaviour. This is culturally determined and passed on. People with mental handicap are denied many of the socialising experiences to which non mentally handicapped people are exposed.'. This denial of normative socialising experiences begins very early in life: despite recent advances the majority of children with learning difficulties attend segregated special schools. This, as Firth and Rapley (1987) point out, has two important effects. First, children with learning difficulties in special schools do not have more capable classmates available as models for appropriate social behaviour, which the literature increasingly suggests, with structured support where necessary, they can successfully imitate (Cooke *et al.*, 1977; Peterson *et al.*, 1977) and from which they can derive social benefits (Mittler and Farrell, 1987). Having said this, the caution of writers such as Stobart (1986), who points out that it is not merely enough to place disabled children in ordinary settings, but that the systematic provision of support to both children and teachers is necessary, must be acknowledged. Secondly, because of different catchment areas 'it is much more difficult for children attending special schools to meet their school friends outside of the school situation. This problem compounds that which they already have in that children locally [sic] to them will go to a different school. They are handicapped both ways.' (Firth and Rapley, 1987).

Unlike their non-disabled peers the 'childhood' of people with learning difficulties is lengthened both by statute and by opportunity. Again, Flynn's observations trenchantly describe the common experience of many, if not most, people with learning difficulties: 'people with mental handicap are not brought up to believe that they will take their place in adult society. Many people are infantilised, experiencing extended parenting long after this has ceased to be appropriate' (Flynn, 1989). This may result, as Firth and Rapley (1990) suggest, in a situation whereby 'parents' natural protectiveness and lack of clear expectations can combine to bring up children who are, with the best of intentions, discouraged from exploration and experiment: who learn to stay close to parents, and hence fail to learn many of the basic skills of social interaction'.

Access to models of normative social behaviour continues to be denied to people with mental handicaps after school-leaving age. Adult residential and day time occupational services are segregated such that a number of studies have documented the striking paucity of contact that many people with learning difficulties have with non-disabled people. (Bercovici, 1981; McConkey *et al.*, 1983; Richardson and Ritchie, 1989; Gollay *et al.*, 1978; Reiter and Levi, 1980). This is as true of people living 'in the community' as it is for those in traditional long-stay institutional provision. In addition to an absolute absence of normative socialising experiences, there is also evidence that the 'extended parenting' that people experience is often continued well into adulthood by staff in the service settings in which people live or spend their days. In many settings it is staff who control the social opportunities open to the people who use them: Firth and Rapley (1990) note, in discussing small homes, that 'management philosophy and staff attitudes [which] are likely to be critical in influencing the social opportunities of the residents'. Gollay and his co-workers (1978) observed what this might mean in practice in the lives of some of the people they studied following their discharge into the community: 'They had few friends, even fewer romantic relationships, and often lived in residences which did not permit or encourage social independence.'.

Although the focus of their study was on friendship, the conclusions that Richardson and Ritchie (1989) drew with regard to the difficulty that many people with mental handicap have in developing and sustaining such relationships are equally applicable to all areas of social function. They note that 'people with learning difficulties are...victims of their own lack of experience...Lack of experience leads to inappropriate behaviour, as well as inappropriate interpretations of others' behaviour...they...may not learn, as other people do, how to make the right sense of other people'. In sum, the impaired social function of many people with a mental handicap owes perhaps as much, if not more, to a combination of lack of normative experiences, near exclusive availability of impaired behavioural models and their occupation of restrictive environments, interacting with a pre-existing intellectual impairment, as it does to any inherent deficit in the individual.

Medication

Space precludes anything more than a passing mention of the need to take medication into account when considering the social function of people with learning difficulties. The prescription of high doses of antipsychotic medication is extremely widespread with people with learning difficulties (Sprague, 1977; Lynch, 1989), in many instances for the sole purpose of establishing behavioural control (Hubert, 1992), often in the absence of any diagnosed psychiatric disorder (Kiernan, 1991), and frequently for extended periods of time (Reynolds, 1980). Polypharmacy is common and adequate monitoring of the effects of medication is often problematic (Aman *et al.*, 1986). With the comparatively high incidence of seizure disorders in people with learning difficulties, the use of anticonvulsant medication is also common. A growing literature is now starting to document the deleterious effects of this use on the functioning, in all areas of performance, of people with mental handicaps (Russell, 1985; Hubert, 1992). It is perhaps unnecessary to point out that heavy sedation is unlikely to be conducive to the learning of socially appropriate behaviours in any setting, particularly if the learner is intellectually impaired at the outset.

SITUATIONAL FACTORS IN SOCIAL FUNCTION

Competent social function, as has been intimated in the introduction to this chapter, is perhaps easier to recognise *in absentia* than to define from first principles. 'Social competence' as an attribute represents more than the sum of its parts: it is more than the possession of a selection of adaptive behaviours or social skills. Competent social function may, as has been discussed above, depend to a greater or lesser extent, upon individual knowledge of the prevailing social rules that govern which behaviours are appropriate in which circumstances. It should not, however, be forgotten that a major lesson of the social psychology of the twentieth century, as Milgram (1974) has observed, is that 'it is not so much the kind of person a man is, as the kind of situation in which he finds himself [that] determines how he will act'. The negative influence of experiential deprivation on the behavioural repertoires available to many people with learning difficulties has been briefly explored above. Immediate environmental and situational factors which impinge on the social function of people with learning difficulties — the 'kinds of situations' in which they find themselves — will now be examined.

The nature of the environment and staff activity

In their review of the literature on the social relationships of people with learning difficulties Firth and Rapley (1990) noted that 'many people with learning disabilities do have very limited personal relationships, that frequently lack of opportunity for social contact is a major barrier to friendship and companionship, and that lack of appropriate teaching and learning opportunities contribute significantly to this'. These authors also observed that whilst many people with learning difficulties do have significant problems in various areas of social performance, they are also to a significant degree dependent upon others in terms both of the provision of opportunities for social contact and of skills teaching, for the amelioration of those problems in social function that they experience.

Arguably the most salient mediators of social function of people with learning difficulties, after parents and siblings, are the paid staff of human services with whom they interact. A large, and growing, body of literature now suggests that much of the social behaviour of people with learning difficulties is directly mediated both by the social structures of the settings they occupy and by the behaviour of the staff with whom they are in daily contact.

Since Goffman's pioneering work in the 1960s, the effects of total institutions on the behaviour of their inmates has been well-known (Goffman, 1961). Later work related the size of institutions to the practice orientation of the staff working within them (e.g. McCormick *et al.*, 1975) and began to examine the behaviour of residents in relation to that of staff. Warren and Mondy (1971) observed that appropriate social behaviour may attract no response from staff for up to 80% of the time. McGarry and West (1975) noted that people without well-developed communication skills received even fewer staff-initiated interactions than did their more able peers who, as pointed out by Gardner and Giampa (1971), were receiving very little anyway. In their 1978 study Mayhew *et al.*, demonstrated that the social behaviour of their subjects (severely and profoundly handicapped institutionalised adolescents) could be increased or decreased under systematically varied social reinforcement–non-reinforcement conditions. They concluded that 'it would appear that the deficits seen in the social behaviour of retarded persons may be due, in part, to the failure of their environment to maintain and increase existing social behaviour'.

A further study to address this issue is reported by Bray *et al.*, (1983). Noting that many people with learning difficulties have communication difficulties, and that one specific social behaviour, making requests, may pose serious difficulties particularly for more severely handicapped people, an experimental task was employed to assess the effect of situational demand upon request making. The findings of this study suggest that, given environmental conditions in which the situational demand for a specific social behaviour is increased, then the likelihood that the behaviour will be emitted is consequentially raised.

Similar studies in natural settings have confirmed this effect (e.g. VanBiervliet *et al.*, 1981). Mansell and Beasley's (1989) study of a residential service for people with 'severe and profound mental handicaps who also have very severe problem behaviour' furthermore suggests that 'even though problem behaviour persists, adaptive behaviour can continue to develop if services provide the occasion for it to do so.' Disappointingly often, it would seem, services fail to provide the occasion, failing particularly the older, more institutionalised, less physically attractive and less able people who rely on them. In general terms the literature would seem to illustrate the operation of the 'inverse care law': the greater the level of need, the less will be offered to meet it (Felce, 1991).

Since the early 1980s much more interest has focused upon the examination of residents' social behaviour as a function of the social interactions between staff and residents in a variety of residential services. The results of much of this work have confirmed the general trends identified in the early studies, such as that of Tizard (1964) which demonstrated that gains in the verbal mental age of moderately and severely handicapped children were differentially affected by institutional, nursing-oriented versus small home, education-oriented placements.

A series of studies by Felce and co-workers, (Felce *et al.*, 1986; Saxby *et al.*, 1986; Thomas *et al.*, 1986; Mansell *et al.*, 1984) compared, like Tizard (1964), small group homes with institutional settings. With well matched subjects, they found that residents in the small homes received 'markedly higher rates and longer durations of staff interactions...in comparison, the institutional settings were characterised by an almost total absence of staff attempts to either encourage or discourage any form of client behaviour'. Other studies have confirmed these findings (e.g. Rawlings, 1985), if disagreeing with the policy implications of them. In a small-scale study, using the same observational methodology as Felce *et al.* (1986), the author found that the residents of a long-stay mental handicap hospital ward were not engaged in any purposeful activity for 71% of their time. Clear social behaviour — operationally defined as 'recognisable attempt[s] by the client to engage in a form of communication with someone else (e.g. a staff member or another client)...[including] attempts to speak, vocalise, attend to, sign or gesture' (Beasley *et al.*, 1989) — was only observed to occur 6.5% of the time (Rapley, 1993). For these people, as in the studies discussed above, 'time passed with little meaningful interaction with the material or social world' (Felce, 1991). Of further interest in this study was the fact that clear differences in the amount and nature of social interaction between staff and residents varied systematically as a function of the staff group on duty. This finding suggests that the current direction of research in this area, which has clearly indicated both quantitative and qualitative differences *between* settings (Felce, 1991), might profitably move on to focus much more detailed attention on identifying and altering differences *within* them.

The effects of both the higher rates of staff interaction, and the opportunities afforded by the domestic style and location of group homes are reflected in the developing social competence of the residents. In Felce's studies measures were taken of mental age, language age, and of adaptive behaviour. In all of these areas residents of the small group homes, all with mental ages below 48 months, demonstrated significantly more progress than matched groups living in their parental home — who made what is described as 'moderate progress' (Felce, 1991). Persons resident in the institutional setting showed no change in their scores. The correlation obtained between the level of staff support given to residents and the level of their engagement in activities was of the order of 0.97 (Spearman's *r*). That progress which was observed in the small home group 'was mainly found in the domains of independent functioning, domestic activity and self-direction as defined by the Adaptive Behaviour Scale' (Felce, 1991). Firth (1986), in a study of the move of five people with severe or profound learning difficulties from an institution to a community setting showed that there were consistent increases in scores on the Adaptive Behaviour Scale (Nihira *et al.*, 1974), that contact with friends and family had increased and that the range of activities that people were engaged in had widened greatly. It was, however, also noted that 'many of the benefits of living in the community are dependent...upon the staff employed'. Clearly, then, the abilities of people with learning difficulties are not static. They are not fixed, determined exclusively by an IQ score or mental age quotient. Like the rest of us, their behaviour is, to a large extent, dependent upon the circumstances in which they find themselves and the expectations and demands made of them.

ASSESSMENT OF SOCIAL FUNCTION

The assessment of social function in people with a mental handicap is a topic which itself justifies book length coverage and which cannot be done adequate justice in the space available here. Full descriptions, and evaluation of, the range of assessment tools and procedures frequently used with this population can be found in Hogg and Raynes (1987), Matson and Breuning (1983), Cullen and Dickens (1991) and Spreat *et al.* (1983).

CONCLUSIONS

Impaired social function is commonly observed in people with learning difficulties. It has been seen that the reasons for this are far from simple: as Clements (1987) notes 'there is no need to believe in a single dysfunction'. People described as having an intellectual impairment represent a broad and extremely heterogeneous population, and the causes of impaired abilities — or lessened effectiveness in social situations, to employ Christoff and Kelly's (1983) conceptualisation — are equally diverse.

Whilst severe intellectual impairment will, by definition, make learning the skills and rules of social interaction difficult, for many people with learning disabilities it is simply not convincing to attribute impaired social function solely to intellectual handicap. Impaired social performance is a multifaceted problem, resulting from an interaction between attributes of the individual, both current and historically determined, and the qualities of their environment. The environments in which most learning-disabled people pass their time, as has been seen, are by and large antithetical to the development of the level of social competence expected of members of mainstream society.

This need not be so. Although space has precluded consideration of issues to do with intervention in this chapter, recent research has begun to demonstrate that the provision of assistance to people that takes account of their individual difficulties in social function, for example the training of cognitive problem-solving skills as well as traditional social skills training, enabling individuals, particularly those described as displaying 'challenging behaviour', to develop functional communicative alternatives to behavioural excesses, the provision of well designed and aggressively developmental supported housing services and the development of supported open employment, can result in dramatic increases in the social competence of severely intellectually impaired people. For many people with learning difficulties, then, it is probably true to say that they are only as socially impaired as services are prepared to let them be.

ACKNOWLEDGEMENTS

I should like to thank John Clements and Chris Lawes for their valuable criticisms of an earlier draft of this chapter.

REFERENCES

Ager, A. (1985). Alternatives to speech for the mentally handicapped. In: Watts, F.N. (Ed.), *New Developments in Clinical Psychology*. British Psychological Society and Wiley, Chichester, pp. 96–110.

Alford, J.D. and Locke, B.J. (1984). Clinical responses to psychopathology of mentally retarded persons. *American Journal of Mental Deficiency*, **89**, 195–197.

Aman, M.G., Paxton, J.W., Field, C.J. and Foote, S.E. (1986). Prevalence of toxic anticonvulsant drug concentrations in mentally retarded persons with epilepsy. *American Journal of Mental Deficiency*, **90**, 643–650.

American Psychiatric Association (1987). *Diagnostic and Statistical Manual of Mental Disorders (3rd edn –Revised)*, American Psychiatric Association, Washington DC.

Atkinson, D. and Ward, L. (1986). *A Part of the Community: Social Integration and Neighbourhood Networks*. Talking Points, No. 3, CMH, London.

Bailey, S.L. (1981). Stimulus over-selectivity in learning disabled children. *Journal of Applied Behavior Analysis*, **14**, 239–249.

Baron-Cohen, S. (1990). Autism: A specific cognitive disorder of 'Mind-Blindness'. *International Review of Psychiatry*, **2**, 81–90.

Beasley, F., Hewson, S. and Mansell, J. (1989). *MTS: Handbook for Observers (3rd edn)*. Centre for the Applied Psychology of Social Care, University of Kent, Canterbury.

Bell, N.J., Schoenrock, C.J. and Bensberg, G.J. (1981). Change over time in the community: Findings of a longitudinal study. In: Bruininks, R., Meyers, C.E., Sigford, B.B. and Lakin, K.C. (Eds), *Deinstitutionalisation and Community Adjustment of Mentally Retarded People*. Monograph No. 4, American Association on Mental Deficiency, Washington DC, pp. 195–206.

Belmont, J.M. (1978). Individual differences in memory: the cases of normal and retarded development. In: Gruneberg, M.M. and Morris, P.E. (Eds), *Aspects of Memory*. Methuen, London.

Bercovici, S.M. (1981). Qualitative methods and cultural perspectives in the study of deinstitutionalisation. In: Bruininks, R., Meyers, C.E., Sigford, B.B. and Lakin, K.C. (Eds), *Deinstitutionalisation and Community Adjustment of Mentally Regarded People*. Monograph No. 4, American Association on Mental Deficiency, Washington DC, pp. 133–144.

Berg, W.K. and Wacker, D.P. (1991). The assessment and evaluation of reinforcers for individuals with severe mental handicap. In: Remington, B. (Ed.), *The Challenge of Severe Mental Handicap: A Behaviour Analytic Approach*. Wiley, Chichester, pp. 25–47.

Borkowski, J.G., Peck, V.A. and Damberg, P.R. (1983). Attention, memory and cognition. In: Matson, J.L. and Mulick, J.A. (Eds), *Handbook of Mental Retardation*. Pergamon, New York.

Bray, N.W., Biasini, F.J. and Thrasher, K.A. (1983). The effect of communicative demands on request-making in the moderately and severely mentally retarded. *Applied Research in Mental Retardation*, **4**, 13–27.

Bronfenbrenner, V. (1979). *The Ecology of Human Development*. Harvard University Press, Cambridge, Mass.

Christoff, K.A. and Kelly, J.A. (1983). Social skills. In: Matson, J.L. and Breuning, S.E. (Eds), *Assessing the Mentally Retarded*. Grune & Stratton, New York, pp. 181–209.

Clarke, A.M. and Clarke, A.B.D. (Eds) (1974). *Mental Deficiency: The Changing Outlook*. Methuen, London.

Clements, J. (1987). *Severe Learning Disability and Psychological Handicap*. Wiley, Chichester.

Clements, J. (1992). I can't explain: Challenging behaviour, towards a shared conceptual framework. *Clinical Psychology Forum*, **39**, 29–38.

Cooke, T., Appolone, T. and Cooke, S. (1977). Normal pre-school children as behaviour models for retarded peers. *Exceptional Children*, **43**, 531–532.

Cullen, C. and Dickens, P. (1991). People with mental handicaps. In: Peck, D.F. and Shapiro, C.M. (Eds), *Measuring Human Problems*. Wiley, Chichester, pp. 303–317.

Detterman, D.K. (1979). Memory in the mentally retarded. In: Ellis, N.R. (Ed.), *Handbook of Mental Deficiency. Psychological Theory and Research*. Laurence Erlbaum Associates, New Jersey, pp. 727–755.

Dupont, A. (1981). Epidemiological studies in mental retardation: methodology and results.*International Journal of Mental Health*, **10**, 56–63.

Durand, V.M. (1991). *Severe Behavior Problems: A Functional Communication Training Approach*. The Guilford Press, New York.

Edgerton, R.B. (1967). *The Cloak of Competence: Stigma in the Lives of the Mentally Retarded*. University of California Press, Berkeley.

Edgerton, R.B. and Bercovici, S.M. (1976). The cloak of competence — years later. *American Journal of Mental Deficiency*, **80**, 485–497.

Ellis, N.R. (1970). Memory processes in retardates and normals. In: Ellis, N.R. (Ed.), *International Review of Research in Mental Retardation, Vol. 4*, Academic Press, New York, pp. 1–32.

Felce, D. (1991). Using behavioural principles in the development of effective housing services for adults with severe or profound mental handicap. In: Remington, B. (Ed.), *The Challenge of Severe Mental Handicap: A Behaviour Analytic Approach*, Wiley, Chichester, pp. 285–317.

Felce, D. de Kock, U. and Repp, A. (1986). An eco-behavioural analysis of small community-based houses and traditional large hospitals for severely and profoundly mentally handicapped adults. *Applied Research in Mental Retardation*, **7**, 393–408.

Firth, H. (1986). *A Move to Community: Social Contacts and Behaviour.* Northumberland Health Authority, Morpeth.

Firth, H. and Rapley, M. (1987). *Making Acquaintance.* Northumberland Health Authority, District Psychology Service, Morpeth.

Firth, H. and Rapley, M. (1990). *From Acquaintance to Friendship: Issues for People with Learning Disabilities.* British Institute of Mental Handicap, Kidderminster.

Flynn, M.C. (1989). *Independent Living for Adults with Mental Handicap: 'A Place of My Own'.* Cassell Educational, London.

Gardner, J.M. and Giampa, F.L. (1971). The Attendant Behavior Checklist: Measuring on-the-ward behavior of institutional attendants. *American Journal of Mental Deficiency*, **75**, 617–622.

Glidden, L.M. (1979). Training of learning and memory in retarded persons: Strategies, techniques and teaching tools. In: Ellis, N.R. (Ed.), *Handbook of Mental Deficiency. Psychological Theory and Research.* Laurence Erlbaum Associates, New Jersey, pp. 619–658.

Goffman, E. (1961). *Asylums: Essays on the Social Situations of Mental Patients and Other Inmates.* Penguin, London.

Gollay, E., Freedman, R., Wyngaarden, M. and Kurtz, N.R. (1978). *Coming Back — The Community Experiences of Institutionalised Mentally Retarded People.* Abt Books, Cambridge, Mass.

Goode, D.A. (1983). Who is Bobby? Ideology and method in the discovery of a Down's syndrome person's competence. In: Kielhofner, G. (Ed.), *Health through Occupation.* F.A. Davis, Philadelphia, pp. 237–255.

Grossman, H.J. (Ed.) (1983). *Classification in Mental Retardation.* American Association on Mental Deficiency, Washington DC.

Heal, L.W., Sigelman, C.K. and Switzky, H.N. (1980). Research on community residential alternatives for the mentally retarded. In: Flynn, R.J. and Nitsch, K.E. (Eds), *Normalization, Integration and Community Services.* University Park Press, Baltimore, pp. 215–259.

Hogg, J. and Raynes, N.V. (1987). *Assessment in Mental Handicap: A Guide to Assessment Practices, Tests and Checklists.* Croom Helm, London.

Hogg, J. and Sebba, J. (1986). *Profound Retardation and Multiple Impairment: Volume 1: Development and Learning.* Croom Helm, London.

Howe, M.J.A. (1991). *Fragments of Genius: The Strange Feats of Idiot Savants.* Routledge, New York.

Hubert, J. (1992). *Too Many Drugs: Too Little Care.* VIA, London.

Jacobson, J.W. and Janicki, M.P. (1983). Observed prevalence of multiple developmental disabilities. *Mental Retardation*, **21**, 87–94.

Kernan, K.T., Turner, J.L., Langness, L.L. and Edgerton, R.B. (1981). Issues in the community adaptation of mildly retarded adults. In: Haywood, H.C. and Newbrough, J.R. (Eds), *Living Environments for Developmentally Retarded Persons.* University Park Press, Baltimore, pp. 125–154.

Kiernan, C. (1991). Personal communication.

Kiernan, C. and Moss, S. (1990). Behaviour disorders and other characteristics of the population of a mental handicap hospital, *Mental Handicap Research*, **3**, 3–20.

Kropka, B. (1983). A summary of the results of the questionnaire into hearing impairment in the mentally handicapped in NHS hospitals and hostels in England and Wales. Unpublished Report, BIMH, South West Division, Exeter.

Landesman-Dwyer, S. and Berkson, G. (1984). Friendships and social behaviour. In: Wortis, J. (Ed.), *Mental Retardation and Developmental Disabilities, Vol. 13*. Plenum Press, London, pp. 129–154.

Lynch, S.P.J. (1989). Prescribing practice in a mental handicap hospital — 2: Psychotropic medication from 1978–1987. *Mental Handicap*, **17**, 123–128.

McConkey, R., Naughton, M. and Nugent, U. (1983). Have we met? Community contacts of adults who are mentally handicapped. *Mental Handicap*, **11**, 57–59.

McCormick M., Balla, D. and Zigler, E. (1975). Resident care-practices in institutions for retarded persons: A cross-institutional, cross-cultural study. *American Journal of Mental Deficiency*, **80**, 1–17.

McGarry, M.S. and West, S.G. (1975). Stigma among the stigmatised: resident mobility, communication ability and physical appearance as predictors of staff-resident interactions. *Journal of Abnormal Psychology*, **84**, 399–405.

Mansell, J. and Beasley, F. (1989). Small staffed homes for the severely mentally handicapped: strengths and weaknesses. In: Cowie, V. and Harten-Ash, B.J. (Eds), *Current Approaches: Mental Retardation*. Duphar Medical Relations, Southampton, pp. 26–35.

Mansell, J., Jenkins, J., Felce, D. and de Kock, U. (1984). Measuring the activities of severely and profoundly mentally handicapped adults in ordinary housing. *Behaviour Research and Therapy*, **22**, 23–29.

Matson, J.L. and Breuning, S.E. (Eds) (1983). *Assessing the Mentally Retarded*. Grune & Stratton, New York.

Mayhew, G.L., Enyart, P. and Anderson, J. (1978). Social reinforcement and the naturally occurring social responses of severely and profoundly retarded adolescents. *American Journal of Mental Deficiency*, **83**, 164–170.

Milgram, S. (1974). *Obedience to Authority*. Tavistock, London.

Mittler, P. and Farrell, P. (1987). Can children with severe learning difficulties be educated in ordinary schools? *European Journal of Special Needs Education*, **2**, 221–236.

Nettlebeck, T. and Lally, M. (1979). Age, intelligence and inspection time. *American Journal of Mental Deficiency*, **83**, 398–401.

Nihira, K., Foster, R., Shellhaus, M. and Leland, H. (1974). *AAMD Adaptive Behaviour Scale*, American Association on Mental Deficiency, Washington, DC.

Peterson, C., Peterson, J. and Scriven, C. (1977). Peer imitation by non-handicapped pre-schoolers. *Exceptional Children*, **43**, 223–225.

Preddy, D. and Mittler, P. (1981). *Children with Severe Learning Difficulties: A Survey in North West England*. Final Report to the Department of Education and Science, University of Manchester, Manchester.

Rapley, M. (1993). A multi-level analysis of client and staff behaviour on a long-stay hospital ward, in preparation.

Rawlings, S. (1985). Behaviour and skills of severely retarded adults in hospitals and small residential homes. *British Journal of Psychiatry*, **146**, 358–366.

Reiter, S. and Levi, A.M. (1980). Factors affecting social integration of non-institutionalised mentally retarded adults. *American Journal of Mental Deficiency*, **85**, 25–30.

Reynolds, E.H. (1980). Clinical application of the monitoring of anti-convulsant drug levels. *Drug Concentrations in Neuropsychiatry*, CIBA Foundation Symposium 74: pp. 199–214.

Richardson, A. and Ritchie, J. (1989). *Developing Friendships: Enabling People with Learning Difficulties to Make and Maintain Friends*. Policy Studies Institute/Social and Community Planning and Research, London.

Romer, D. and Berkson, G. (1980). Social ecology of supervised communal facilities for mentally disabled adults: II. Predictors of affiliation. *American Journal of Mental Deficiency*, **85**, 229–242.

Romer, D. and Heller, T. (1983). Social adaptation of mentally retarded adults in community settings: A social-ecological approach. *Applied Research in Mental Retardation*, **4**, 303–314.

Russell, O. (1985). *Mental Handicap*. Churchill-Livingstone, London.

Saxby, H., Thomas, M., Felce, D. and de Kock, U. (1986). The use of shops, cafes and public houses by severely and profoundly mentally handicapped adults. *British Journal of Mental Subnormality*, **32**, 69–81.

Sprague, R.L. (1977). Overview of psychopharmacology for the retarded in the United States. In: Mittler, P. (Ed.), *Research to Practice in Mental Retardation, Vol. 3*. University Park Press, Baltimore, pp. 199–203.

Spreat, S., Roszkowski, M.J. and Isett, R.D. (1983). Assessment of adaptive behaviour in the mentally retarded. In: Breuning, S.E., Matson, J.L. and Barrett, R.P. (Eds), *Advances in Mental Retardation and Developmental Disabilities: Vol. 1*. Jai Press, Greenwich, Conn., pp. 45–97.

Sternberg, R.J. and Spear, L.C. (1985). A triarchic theory of mental retardation. In: Ellis, N.R. and Bray, N.W. (Eds), *International Review of Research in Mental Retardation, Vol. 13*. Academic Press, Orlando, Fla., pp. 301–327.

Stobart, G. (1986). Is integrating the handicapped psychologically defensible? *Bulletin of the British Psychological Society*, **39**, 1–4.

Thomas, M., Felce, D., de Kock, U., Saxby, H. and Repp, A. (1986). The activity of staff and of severely and profoundly mentally handicapped adults in residential settings of different sizes. *British Journal of Mental Subnormality*, **32**, 82–92.

Tizard, J. (1964). *Community Services for the Mentally Handicapped*. Oxford University Press, Oxford.

Tyrer, P. (1990). Personality disorder and social functioning. In: Peck, D.F. and Shapiro, C.M. (Eds), *Measuring Human Problems*. London, Wiley, pp. 119–143.

VanBiervliet, A., Spangler, P.F. and Marshall, A.M. (1981). An ecobehavioral examination of a simple strategy for increasing mealtime language in residential facilities. *Journal of Applied Behavior Analysis*, **4**, 295–305.

Wald, I. and Zdzienicka, E. (1981). Simple neurological and clinical means of diagnosing severe mental retardation: Studies in Poland. *International Journal of Mental Health*, **10**, 47–55.

Warren, S.A. and Mondy, L.W. (1971). To what behaviors do attending adults respond?, *American Journal of Mental Deficiency*, **75**, 449–455.

Wolraich, M.L. and Siperstein, G.N. (1986). Physicians' and other professionals' expectations and prognoses for mentally retarded individuals. *American Journal of Mental Deficiency*, **91**, 244–249.

Zeaman, D. and House, B.J. (1963). The role of attention in retardate discrimination learning. In: Ellis, N.R. (Ed.), *Handbook of Mental Deficiency*. McGraw-Hill, New York, pp. 159–222.

Zigler, E. and Trickett, P.K. (1978). IQ, Social competence and evaluation of early childhood intervention programs. *American Psychologist*, **33**, 789–798.

Social Function in Psychiatry: The Hidden Axis of Classification
Edited by Peter Tyrer and Patricia Casey
©1993 Wrightson Biomedical Publishing Ltd

8

Social Function in Child Psychiatry and its Relationship to Mental State and Outcome

MATTHEW HODES and ELENA GARRALDA

SOCIAL DEVELOPMENT

Disturbance in social function is often a feature of the psychiatric disorders of children as it is in adults. Social function in adults refers as much to the individual's ability to perform his social duties adequately, for example being able to keep a job, maintain a home and provide for a family, indulge in social activities, as to the ability to form and maintain relationships with others, whether they are intimate relationships within the family or with close friends, or more superficial relationships with colleagues and acquaintances.

In childhood the range of social duties is different to that of adults, but from infancy there are already expectations about appropriate communication and behaviours. Later on more active ways of participating in and contributing to family life become important, and attendance at school is expected. While school adjustment is strongly influenced by the child's intellectual and learning skills, it is also determined by the child's ability to form and maintain both superficial and close relationships. In all contexts, there are expectations for children and young people to follow social norms, although infractions are common, and offending and aggressive behaviours may be related to a variety of psychiatric disorders. Thus, social function in children, analogous to that of adults, needs to be considered in the context of the family, peer relations and relationships with other adults. In addition, school adjustment, analogous to adjustment at work for adults, is highly relevant.

Social function in childhood

To understand social adjustment in children it is essential to take account of the marked developmental changes that occur throughout childhood and adolescence, and the nature of human relationships. Anomalies in social function will manifest themselves differently depending on developmental stages. For example, the young pre-school child's environment is predominantly family based and centred around the specially close relationship with the main care-taker, usually the mother in the 'attachment' phase, and the establishment of sibling relationships. Social adjustment in mid-childhood whilst retaining the primacy of family relationships is strongly influenced by the need to learn to negotiate peer group interactions and in adolescence by the ability to make close friendships outside the family. Social dysfunction as a manifestation of childhood psychiatric disturbance will accordingly affect these areas of function differentially.

Another feature of social function in childhood is the fact that although children from early in their development are active players in social relationships they are also heavily dependent on adults, on the way others react to them. Problems in child–mother relationships might reflect as much behavioural peculiarities in the child as poor ways of relating in a mother who, for example, may be suffering from a major psychiatric disorder herself.

A final consideration relates to children's understanding of social relationships. Children's ability to sympathise and empathise with others progresses throughout childhood from the experience of just sadness about other people's predicaments to a desire to help and eventually the capacity to become preoccupied about others in distress (Szagun, 1992). Pre-schoolers are adept at attributing simple emotions to themselves and others but emotional terms requiring more complex understanding of social and inter-personal situations, such as pride and embarrassment, develop later in childhood (Capps et al., 1992). There are individual variations in young children's ability to understand the feelings of others and their ability to explain human actions in terms of beliefs, and these variations are related to the degree of the child's participation in family communications on issues such as feelings and causality, as well as to the verbal fluency of the mother towards the child (Dunn et al., 1991).

This chapter will examine (1) the relevance of social function for childhood psychiatric disturbance, (2) aspects of the nature and measurement of social relationships within a developmental framework, and in relation to the dysfunctional patterns that occur in psychiatric disorders and (3) it will detail the nature of social dysfunction in specific disorders.

THE RELEVANCE OF SOCIAL FUNCTION FOR CHILDHOOD PSYCHIATRIC DISORDER

Disturbance in relationships with parents, sibs, peers and/or teachers can occur and be prominent in any psychiatric disorder in childhood but it is the main symptom of a number of conditions. In many of these the problems are present since early childhood and tend to persist, suggesting the presence of enduring psychological or personality characteristics in the child. The conditions are classified in current classificatory systems, such as ICD-10, and involve different aspects of social dysfunction:

- autism and autistic-related conditions such as Asperger syndrome or Schizoid personality disorder of childhood: a core symptom is the profound inability to engage in social relationships, due to deficits in the ability to empathise with others;
- attachment disorders: difficulties in making selective, stable and close relationships;
- elective mutism: inability to relate sufficiently to communicate verbally with individuals outside the close family circle;
- separation anxiety: difficulties in tolerating child/mother separations consequent on anxiety/emotional insecurity in the child;
- relationship disorders of childhood where difficulties in the child's relationships — usually with parents or siblings (for example in severe sibling jealousy), but sometimes also with peers or teachers — is the most prominent and handicapping symptom;
- conduct disorder: the key symptoms are socially deviant or 'antisocial' behaviours, and frequently aggression.

Discordant relationships with parents, siblings and peers can occur as an associated feature in other emotional disorders, in the hyperkinetic syndrome, in neurotic and somatization disorders and in virtually any psychiatric disorder of childhood.

The assessment of social function as part of the evaluation of any psychiatric disorder is particularly crucial because disturbances in the child's relationships with others have been found to be linked to the aetiology of disorder. A good example of this is the association between a high level of aggressive and coercive interchanges and antisocial behaviour or conduct disorder in the child (Rutter and Quinton, 1984; Patterson *et al.*, 1989). Hostile and rejecting attitudes of parents, as well as threats and actual violence are important factors in the aetiology of the conduct disorder. The child's aggressive and antisocial behaviour may be seen as a learned response to the relationship style initiated by the parents (Patterson and Dishion, 1988). In addition, disturbances in relationships may also be related to the persistence of disorder (Wolff, 1985; Richman *et al.*, 1982). Aggressive behaviour in the child may induce coercive and negative interactions with parents which act as maintaining factors for the disorder. It may also indicate enduring deviations in personality function which may in themselves contribute to the development of childhood psychiatric disorder.

There are indications that the presence of interpersonal problems in the child is a relevant factor for the referral of schoolchildren to specialist services. In a study of children referred by their general practitioners to child psychiatric clinics, disturbed referred children differed from disturbed but non-referred children by having significantly more problems in their relationships with parents, siblings, peers and teachers (Garralda and Bailey, 1988). This study moreover showed that discord in the parent–child relationship was related to referral to child psychiatrists even in the absence of definite psychiatric disorder in the child, since difficulties in this area were recorded in the small group of referred children who were judged to have only minor and not definite anomalies in psychiatric adjustment.

THE NATURE, VARIATIONS AND MEASUREMENT OF SOCIAL RELATIONSHIPS IN CHILDREN

Effective social behaviour in children requires:

1. Pro-social behaviour: aimed at establishing communication and contact with others. There is individual variation since early childhood and anomalies in this area are characterised by
   (i) social inhibition or withdrawal;
   (ii) pro-social behaviour which is excessive or insufficiently discriminatory.
2. Co-operation/mutuality: the ability to develop mutually complementary relationships that are friendly, affectionate, and where effective communication and sharing takes place. There are individual variations from early childhood and anomalies characterised by:
   (i) insufficient co-operation, friendliness and sharing leading to oppositional behaviour, hostility/aggression;
   (ii) excessive mutuality and insufficient differentiation leading to anxious–clingy or attention-seeking over-dependent behaviour in the child.

Both pro-social behaviour and co-operation/mutuality determine the relationships between children and others, be it parents, siblings or peers.

Child relationships: Measurement

Observations of parent/child relationships identify pro-social behaviour directed towards the mother in the first few months of the baby's life. Infants older than seven weeks frequently spend long periods of time looking at and scanning the mother's face and by three months the infant is already able to recognise his mother as different from other adults as shown by differential heart rate, pupillary responses, smiling, visual attention and changes in behaviour (Rutter, 1980).

Over the course of the second half of the first year selective attachments take place by the child to his parents, particularly the mother or main caretaker. Attachment has been defined as 'a regulatory system hypothesised to exist within a person. The goal is to regulate behaviours that maintain proximity to and contact with a discriminated person, referred to as the attachment figure. From the psychological vantage point of the attached person, however, the system's set goal is felt security.' (Mussen *et al.*, 1990). As elaborated by Bowlby (1978), attachment is a complex two-way process in which the child becomes emotionally linked to members of his family and it forms the basis for the child's later capacity to develop social relationships. Ainsworth *et al.* (1978) developed an experimental situation to assess the security or quality of the child's attachment to the mother. This procedure has been widely used and is regarded as a valid, reliable measure of this aspect of the mother/child relationship.

Other aspects of the mother/child relationships are assessed through direct observations (for example by studying the nature of interactions between depressed mothers and their babies or toddlers) (Cox, 1988) and include pro-social behaviour as well as co-operativeness/mutuality.

For older children commonly used instruments such as interviews or questionnaires are aimed at assessing the child's temperament, behaviour or the presence or absence of psychiatric disturbance. Often they have questions that explore the child's relationships with parents, with other adults such as teachers, and with sibs and peers. A frequently used method to assess a child's popularity with peers is through sociometric ratings (see later). More recently, semi-structured interviews have been developed to examine the child's own perception of peer relationships and measure features such as developmental appropriateness, social skills and self-esteem (Kernberg *et al.*, 1992). Questionnaires are available to measure other aspects such as pro-social behaviour (Weir and Duveen, 1981). The usefulness of these semi-structured interviews and questionnaires has still to be established.

As will be discussed later, the use of these instruments identifies associations between anomalous/conflictive relationships and psychiatric disorder in the child. However, it is important to point out that the social anomalies identified either through temperamental, behavioural or interactive and attachment measures cannot be equated with psychiatric disturbance in the child. A number of children with problems in social relations fail to have psychiatric disorders and conversely, disturbed children may enjoy adequate, harmonious and rewarding parent–child relationships.

Peer relationships: siblings, groups, friends

Peer relationships may be subdivided into those involving groups, friendships and siblings (Dunn and McGuire, 1992). Interactions with peers involve a wide range of different kinds of exchanges, such as negotiating conflict, dealing with teasing, hostility and group situations, and in close relationships also the sharing of fantasy and intimacy. Children's relationships with their peers range from intense, intimate friendships to passing acquaintances. Friendships differ from group peer relationships because of the dyadic, affectionate and intimate nature of the relationship. Processes central to friendship are shared fantasy, intimate gossip, teasing and self-disclosure.

Sibling relationships, like friendships, are close dyadic relationships, but whereas the children in a friendship are committed to a degree of mutual trust, affection and support, many sibling relationships do not involve such affection and trust even though they are intimate in the sense that the children know each other well and are uninhibited in their communication with one another.

Peer relationships become increasingly important as the child's attachment to the main care-taker decreases. At about one year of age the child tends to engage in solitary play but by two years he plays alongside other children and by three he indulges in co-operative play. Co-operation, reciprocity and the ability to keep friends are already present in the pre-school years.

The junior school years are a time when group activities are consolidated, sex-linked behaviour and same sex groups common as is peer group identification and changing patterns of friendships. At this age there is striving for achievement so that educational progress becomes an important part of the child's view of himself and his popularity. Peer popularity and conformism are particularly important and 'feeling different' because of handicap, illness, disfigurement or being teased is particularly difficult.

In adolescence there may be a qualitative change in social relationships with increased distancing from family activities, the development of close friendships, groups and cliques. More than in earlier childhood, changing friendships can give rise to marked psychological distress and are one of the reasons youngsters give for despair reactions such as taking overdoses. Parent–child alienation is not common but some adolescents resist parental discipline and reject parental values and social norms. Peer influences are very important and are related to socialised health-risk behaviours such as experimenting with drugs. Persistent drug use however is usually associated in this age group with personal instability and/or psychiatric disturbance.

Popularity

The most common way of assessing peer group interactions is through the use of sociometric ratings. Children are asked to rate other children in their class or group in a hierarchical way in order of popularity. Group acceptance is indicated by positive nominations by peers and rejection by negative nominations.

Co-operativeness and pro-social behaviour are associated with popularity at any age and conversely rejection by peers is linked to a combination of limitations in pro-social/co-operative behaviour and aggressiveness/submissiveness (Dunn and Mcguire, 1992).

Popularity status in early childhood is linked to behaviour problems in later childhood. Early poor peer acceptance, social isolation and perceptions of social incompetence, have been found to be associated with fearfulness, anxiety and withdrawal later in childhood, and early peer rejection and aggression with subsequent aggressive and oppositional behaviours (Hymel *et al.*, 1990). However, problems in peer acceptance do not necessarily predict the development of psychiatric disorders. Dunn and McGuire (1992) have recently summarised the evidence from retrospective studies showing associations between poor peer acceptance in school and aggressiveness, and later dropping out of school, delinquency and criminality. These features are better predictors of later adjustment problems than shyness or withdrawal. However, prospective studies give inconsistent findings, and little is known about the predictive value of lack of peer support and friendships in childhood for the ability to make friends in adulthood, marital adjustment, the ability to work with others and to maintain good work attendance.

Influences on peer relationships: temperament and environmental factors

The kinds of factors that have been found to be related to the presence of unsatisfactory relationships in children are factors also linked to childhood psychiatric disturbance. They include child temperamental features and environmental distress, for example family discord and break-up, maternal depression, lack of adequate parental discipline and monitoring (Dunn and McGuire, 1992).

Of special relevance for sibling relationships are *parental attitudes*. The birth of a sib commonly leads to an increase in diverse problems such as dependency and anxiety, disturbances of bodily functions, and withdrawal and aggression. There are individual variations and in families in which mothers discuss the feelings and needs of the baby with their pre-school age firstborn the children tend to be friendly to each other. Furthermore, there is consensus that the greater the differential maternal behaviour is towards siblings, the more conflict and negative behaviour the siblings show to each other. This link may be especially strong for families under stress. In some cases sibling jealousy is of such severity that it constitutes a handicapping psychiatric disorder in itself leading to considerable suffering.

Parental attitudes are also of relevance for the child's peer relationships. Attachment status in toddlers, for example, is related to positive responsiveness to peers and social competence (Lewis *et al.*, 1984) although whether this is a causal connection is debatable. Styles of maternal discipline, emotional expressiveness and responsiveness and maternal depression are linked to popularity and success in peer interactions (Dunn and McGuire, 1992). They are also linked to the strategies used by children in their responses to peers. For example, daughters of depressed women are less likely than other children to recommend aggressive solutions to peer conflict but the opposite is true of sons of depressed mothers, who are more likely than others to advocate aggression (Hay *et al.*, 1992).

Temperament refers to individual variations in physical, emotional, social behavioural styles, present from early childhood and showing some consistency over the years. Nine temperamental characteristics were described by Thomas and Chess (1977) in their longitudinal study of babies: activity level, regularity of sleeping, hunger and elimination patterns, adaptability to altered circumstances, tendency to approach or withdraw from new situations or people, threshold of emotional responsiveness, quality of mood, intensity of emotional expression, distractibility and attention span. Other authors have emphasised different behavioural styles as indicative of child temperament, but they all include characteristics relevant to social behaviour (i.e. sociability or approach or withdrawal from new situations), and sociability is a stable behavioural pattern through childhood (Prior, 1992). Division of children into easy or difficult temperament predicts the development of later difficulties (Berger, 1985).It is unclear whether temperamental features are important for the development of secure attachments as measured by the Ainsworth experimental situation (Sroufe, 1985) but the significance of temperament for sibling conflict has been repeatedly highlighted. Children who are active, intense, hostile or unadaptable, for example, have more frequently conflicting relationships with their siblings (Dunn and McGuire, 1992).

Shyness and ill-temper

Two adverse specific temperamental styles, shyness and ill-temper, constitute the two major components of social behaviour (pro-social behaviour and co-operativeness) that predict later social adjustment. Kagan and colleagues (1987) followed up toddlers described as being extremely cautious and shy (inhibited) to unfamiliar events and people and compared them with uninhibited children. Like other authors (Broberg *et al.*, 1990) they have shown preservation of this characteristic into later childhood and they have demonstrated an increased risk for developing anxiety disorders, although it is worth highlighting that many of the children do not develop psychiatric disorders. Because of moderate correlations between inhibited behaviour and indices of norepinephrine activity the authors have postulated a lower threshold for limbic-hypothalamic arousal to unexpected changes in the environment or to challenge.

Children may also be differentiated already in early childhood in terms of aggressive behaviour shown at home and at school. Disobedience, fighting, destructiveness are all more common in boys than in girls (Rutter *et al.*, 1970). Aggression in young pre-school children is associated with delays in inter-personal awareness and perspective-taking ability (Minde, 1992).

Caspi *et al.* (1990) have followed up ill-tempered, shy or dependent children into adulthood and demonstrated considerable continuity. Ill-tempered children continue to experience difficulty in their reactions to frustration and controlling authority in adulthood and shy children tend to be delayed in developmental transitions.

There are close associations between temperamental features in the child and parental attitudes and their psychological functioning. Behavioural inhibition is found in excess in the children with parents with anxiety disorder (Biederman *et al.*, 1990) and aggressive children tend to have cold, harsh, disharmonious, poorly supervising and criminal parents (Farrington, 1978).

Peer relationships and chronic physical illness

Whereas social difficulties are often an intrinsic manifestation of psychiatric disorders, also important is the effect on social relationships of having a chronic physical condition, with the implication that any social anomaly will be a consequence of the physical problem. Having a severe physical condition often involves limitations in opportunities for social contact with peers although this will vary with the type or severity of illness. In a study of children with end-stage chronic renal failure for example, opportunities for intimate friendships (i.e. having a special friend: Mannarino, 1978) were reduced in the more severely affected and handicapped children on hospital haemodialysis when compared with matched healthy controls. However, following transplantation considerably more children reported having a special friend and this applied also to children at earlier stages in their condition not having reached the stage of needing dialysis or transplantation (Reynolds *et al.*, 1991).

This study moreover suggested that although opportunities for friendships varied during the course of the illness, the childhood experience of illness as a whole affected the survivor's ability to make close relationships in adulthood. Fewer children with severe end-stage chronic renal failure followed up into early adulthood than healthy matched controls were involved in intimate relationships and they expressed more feelings of stress in this area (Reynolds *et al.*, 1993).

SOCIAL ADJUSTMENT IN CHILD AND ADOLESCENT PSYCHIATRIC DISORDERS

The developmental and social processes that have been described will now be related more to specific psychiatric disorders encountered in childhood.

The disorders selected are those which have been shown to be meaningful and valid (Werry, 1992), and which are the basis for a substantial body of research.

The accounts of social adjustment in each disorder take a similar form. First, salient characteristics of the disorders and their social aetiology are described. Then, social adjustment is considered in the context of both family and school, which includes peer relationships and performance in class. Thirdly, antisocial behaviour, offending and substance and alcohol abuse are described where relevant. The changes in social adjustment that may be brought about by treatment are mentioned. Finally, there is discussion of the outcome of the disorders, especially in relation to social adjustment stressing the continuities into adulthood.

Conduct disorder

Conduct disorder (CD) is manifested by antisocial behaviour. These behaviours may include disobedience, defiant and oppositional behaviour, as well as disruptive and aggressive behaviour such as bullying, and destruction of property. Older children with conduct disorders may indulge in offending, such as theft, truanting from school and consumption of illicit drugs and alcohol. Thus, there is an overlap between conduct disorder, a clinical diagnosis, and delinquency, a legal definition which refers to adolescent offending. Many studies have investigated the epidemiology of CD, and a number of factors have consistently been found to be associated with the disorder. These include male sex, lower intellectual functioning, reading difficulties, recurrent physical illness and hospitalisation, disrupted parenting and harsh but inconsistent discipline, parental criminality, growing up in large poor families, and living in urban rather than rural areas (Robins, 1991).

Many studies have investigated the role of the family in the development and maintenance of CD. Very influential is the social-interactional perspective, which takes the view that family members directly train the child to perform antisocial behaviour (Forehand et al., 1975; Patterson, 1982; Snyder, 1977). Parents do not appropriately reward desirable behaviour and punish deviant behaviours. The effect is that the child and parents are involved in frequent interactions daily in which the coercive child behaviours are reinforced. The child's aversive behaviours make it possible to survive in a highly aversive social system. It is further postulated that the level of coercion escalates and leads to physical attacks by the child who is resorting to a behaviour that gives some control over other family members (Patterson et al., 1989). These coercive interactions in families may be mediated by cognitive processes which include the regulation of self-esteem. For example, children may feel better about themselves if they 'deliver' more negative behaviour to their siblings than they receive (Dunn and McGuire, 1992).

Outside the family context the child has considerable social difficulties. As far as school adjustment is concerned, there is often poor academic achievement. This may be related to spending less time on appropriate tasks as compared to their non-deviant peers. This may arise for a variety of reasons such as poor motivation and frustration because of learning or reading difficulties, defiance of the teacher's instructions, or associated attention deficits. There may also be truanting from school which leads to falling behind academically and subsequent lowering of self-esteem when later unsuccessful attempts are made to perform tasks. Such behaviours may lead to conflict with teachers, who in their exasperation may become critical and rejecting. This may culminate in exclusion from school which in turn may have an exacerbating effect on the children's behaviour (Rutter and Giller, 1983).

There are also difficulties in peer relations. Aggressive children are more likely to be rejected by their peer group, a consistent finding from both sociometric studies, teacher ratings and independent observations (Coie *et al.*, 1990). It seems that the combination of rejection and aggression more than the presence of aggression alone is found in the more severe and diverse conduct problems (Dunn and McGuire, 1992). There is greater difficulty in initiating contact with peers and greater chance of responding in a hostile way. In part this is mediated by their attributional style, in which they perceive the world as a more hostile place and are more likely to attribute aggressive meaning to peers (Dodge and Feldman, 1990).

As a consequence of rejection by a well adjusted peer group, antisocial children are more likely to associate with other deviant children. It has been suggested that the peer group has a powerful influence on the maintenance and increase in antisocial behaviours (Snyder *et al.*, 1986). Consistent with this view is the finding that offending frequently takes place with peer involvement (Emler *et al.*, 1987). Delinquency rates are higher in schools with a higher proportion of behaviourally deviant boys (Rutter *et al.*, 1979). Also, choosing to give up a delinquent peer group is associated with reduction in offending (Knight and West, 1975). Long-term studies of CD indicate that the rate of persistence is higher than was thought previously. About half the children with CD in middle childhood have the disorder in adolescence (Rutter *et al.*, 1970; Esser *et al.*, 1990). Conduct problems predict later offending (Farrington *et al.*, 1990). They are also associated with later relationship difficulties, and a higher risk of drug and alcohol abuse (Robins, 1978). Retrospective studies of adults with antisocial personality disorder show that their aggressive, antisocial and relationship difficulties always started in childhood (Robins, 1966).

Hyperkinetic or attention deficit disorder

The key features of hyperkinesis or 'hyperactivity' are developmentally inappropriate overactivity, inattentiveness and impulsiveness. In practice emphasis is placed on symptoms of inattention and overactivity, rather than on impulsiveness (Schachar, 1991). The disorder is most commonly recognised in children, typically boys, aged 6–10 years, although the disorder has antecedents manifesting in infancy (Taylor, 1986). Although hyperactivity is generally considered to be a distinct disorder, it frequently occurs in the presence of conduct disorder. The causes of hyperactivity are diverse, although there seem to be some differences from the causes of CD (Taylor, 1986), so validating the distinction between the two disorders. For example, many studies indicate that hyperactivity is not especially associated with psychosocial adversity such as poor parental coping and inter-parental inconsistency (Schachar, 1991). However, other investigators suggest that such family factors are marital discord, parental separation, critical parents and periods spent in institutions are associated with hyperactivity (Taylor, 1986; Haddad and Garralda, 1992). These different views may be partly explained by the overlap between the two disorders. Nevertheless, in considering psychosocial adjustment it is important to consider, in so far as this is possible, impairment that may be associated with the hyperactivity or the co-existing CD.

Most studies of hyperactive children in the family have considered their relationship with the mother rather than the father. Some studies have found important aspects of the relationship with the mother to be context dependent. Mothers may become more critical of their hyperactive children during a task period, than the mothers of normal children. This is distinct from the findings during an unstructured play period (Befera and Barkley, 1985). As might be expected the greater the number of contexts in which the hyperactivity is present, the greater the level of stress on the mother (Beck *et al.*, 1990). Treatment with stimulants, which produces symptomatic change, improves the relationships between mothers and their hyperactive children (Barkley *et al.*, 1985).

It is also clear that hyperactive children are disadvantaged in school. They show academic underachievement related in part to poor attention and task performance. Hyperactivity may also affect motivation, and this in turn has a further detrimental effect on learning (Schachar, 1991). Naturally inattention and impulsivity are likely to lead to conflict with the teachers especially when they are associated with conduct disorder. There are also difficulties in peer relations. Hyperactive children have more difficulty adjusting behaviour according to contextual demands, and they initiate more negative and aggressive interactions than normal peers. Hyperactive children have deficits in knowledge about how to maintain relationships. Peers evaluate hyperactive children negatively (Grenell *et al.*, 1987). Peer relations, like other difficulties associated with hyperactivity are improved with stimulants (Cunningham *et al.*, 1991).

The long-term outcome of hyperactivity is similar overall to that of CD. This finding is perhaps because of the co-morbidity between the two disorders. There are high rates of persistence of hyperactivity, delinquency, adult criminality, substance abuse and antisocial personality disorders (Klein and Mannuzza, 1991). Despite the overall similarity in outcome, longitudinal studies indicate that hyperactivity predicts early convictions, while CD is more predictive of adult convictions. Hyperactivity has an additive effect in predicting criminality with CD (Farrington *et al.*, 1990).

Autism and Asperger Syndrome

Autism is a serious disorder, manifesting before the age of 30 months, in which there are deficits in three main areas (Rutter and Schopler, 1988). There is a basic deficit in the capacity to form relationships. Children with the disorder do not show the appropriate, and normal, attachment to primary care-givers or any other person. They appear to lack understanding of socio-emotional cues and fail to use gaze, facial expression and body posture to regulate social interaction. Secondly, they show deviance, and often delay in speech, failing to use language for social purposes. Thirdly, they show restricted, repetitive and stereotyped patterns of behaviour. This may be shown in fascination with mechanical objects, repetitive body movements and difficulties in changing routines. Many children with autism show generally low intellectual function, only 25% having IQ scores in the normal range. It is becoming increasingly apparent that autism is associated with varied genetic and neurobiological disturbances (Gillberg, 1990, 1992). Despite this aetiological heterogeneity, there is more uniformity in the underlying psychological deficits, which makes the diagnosis meaningful.

Within the family, the autistic child's ways of interacting are frequently evident within the first year of life. Abnormalities may include no real preference for primary care-giver over other adults, failure to seek out parents when hurt, and the absence of enjoyment of physical affection. The difficulties in communication include absence of normal eye contact and gesture, and restricted speech and reduced understanding of language. Play is also restricted, and rather than it involving other family members is likely to be solitary, repetitive, mechanical and lacking in imagination. For example, young children may endlessly line up toys or collect curious objects. These features may result in other family members feeling the autistic child is remote and not part of the family, and induce considerable guilt and anxiety.

Difficulties with peers are profound. The autistic child's lack of prosocial behaviour, lack of empathy and difficulty in understanding emotional expression will all contribute to isolation. The child plays in a solitary unimaginative way, all characteristics which fail to engage peers. However, it has been shown that the introduction of non-handicapped playmates into the autistic children's classroom results in increases in the amount and quality of play (Lord, 1984). Nevertheless social initiations do not generalise to less structured interactions, and they tend to centre around object-oriented interaction, e.g. responsiveness or attention. The association of relationship difficulties, intellectual impairment and rigid, stereotyped interests means that most children with autism will require education in special schools.

The nature of the underlying psychological deficits has been the subject of interesting research and theorizing in recent years. This has aimed to explain the specificity of the social and pragmatic deficits in autism (summarised in Baron-Cohen, 1988a). There are two contemporary theories. The Affective theory argues that autistic individuals lack the innate capacity to interact emotionally with others. This underlies the ability to recognise other people's mental states, as manifested by their emotional expressions (Hobson, 1986a,b), and the ability to symbolise, a prerequisite for play (Hobson, 1989). A rather different approach, called the Cognitive theory has been postulated (Baron-Cohen, 1988a). This is similar to the Affective theory in regarding as central the autistic child's difficulty in understanding other people's mental states. However unlike the Affective theory it starts from the premise that mental states are not directly observable but have to be inferred. Cognitive theory places more emphasis on the inference of belief rather than emotion. The cognitive theory postulates that beliefs about other people's mental states, which are representations of representations, i.e. meta-representations, are impaired in autism (Baron-Cohen, 1989). This view regards the difficulty in understanding others' mental states as underlying the social skills deficits, pragmatic deficits and capacity to play.

Typically there are improvements in autistic children's adjustment, especially in relationships during middle childhood (Gillberg, 1991). During adolescence, a substantial proportion, perhaps half, have a deterioration. This may be associated with the onset of epilepsy. A small proportion, probably less than 10%, do well, in the sense of having a job and living independently as adults. However about 60% of children with typical autism will grow up to be completely dependent on adults in all aspects of life.

It has been argued by many investigators in the field of autism that the disorder exists as the extreme end of a continuum from those who are normal (Gillberg, 1992). Moderate degrees of disturbance of the autistic type have been called Asperger syndrome (Wing, 1981; Tantam, 1988; Gillberg, 1990). This disorder is regarded as high-functioning autism, with deficits in similar areas to autism, specifically failure of two-way social interaction, limited communication and play but normal IQ. Although such children may be regarded as having high functioning autism, and receive a diagnosis of Asperger syndrome in adulthood, this group typically has continuing difficulties. Social isolation, difficulties in living independently including difficulties in sustaining employment are usual (Tantam, 1988). Occasionally violence is carried out by people with Asperger syndrome, related to their rigidity and lack of empathy (Baron-Cohen, 1988b; Tantam, 1988).

A mild form of Asperger syndrome may be schizoid personality, conceptualised as being closer to the normal end of the autism continuum (Wolff, 1991; Gillberg, 1992). These children show solitariness, impaired empathy, rigidity in their interests, increased sensitivity and paranoid ideas, and odd styles of communication (Wolff and Chick, 1980). As compared with psychiatric controls, these children are more likely to have developmental delays of language, and difficulties in reading and spelling. However they are not more likely to have used special educational services. They are significantly more solitary than the children with conduct disorders. Their adjustment when adults shows more solitariness, fewer having developed close or sexual relationships, and less empathy. Those with schizoid personalities have more contact with psychiatric services than the controls.

Depression

In recent years considerable attention has been given to the topic of childhood depression (Kazdin, 1990). While previous commentators sometimes denied that depression could exist in children, this view is no longer tenable. However, most epidemiological studies do indicate that depression in early and middle childhood is rare. The disorder becomes more common in adolescence, especially in girls (Rutter, 1986). Depression may occur with anxiety and conduct disorders (Kovacs and Gatsonis, 1989; Ollendick *et al.*, 1991). It is clear that depression is associated with poor adjustment in many areas.

Within the family context, childhood depression is associated with high levels of hostility and low levels of warmth from parents, and difficulties in communicating. There may be less cohesion and expressiveness (Billings and Moos, 1983). There are also difficulties with sibling relationships (Puig-Antich *et al.*, 1985). Family relationships generally are less satisfying than those of non-depressed children. These difficulties improve but do not disappear after the depression has been treated (Puig-Antich *et al.*, 1985).

There are also difficulties at school. Peer relationships suffer, depressed children reporting lower assertion and greater submissiveness, and tending to be perceived less favourably than their classmates (Kennedy *et al.*, 1989). They are less likely to have special friends and have less peer contact (Puig-Antich *et al.*, 1985). There are also more difficulties in academic achievement and relationships with teachers are worse. This may lower self-esteem further and exacerbate depression. Depression is associated with school non-attendance and social isolation (Berney *et al.*, 1991). When recovery occurs, the children improve at school (Puig-Antich *et al.*, 1985).

Most children with depressive disorders will make a full symptomatic recovery. However, children who have experienced one depressive disorder are at increased risk of further episodes, and at increased risk for bipolar disorder (Zeitlin, 1986; Kovacs and Gatsonis, 1989). There may also be an increased risk of suicide (Harrington *et al.*, 1990). Outcome is likely to be related to intrinsic and extrinsic factors such as a family processes. For example, it has been shown that there is a close temporal relationship between maternal depression and depression in the child (Hammen *et al.*, 1991).

Fears, Phobias, Somatisation and Obsessive–Compulsive Disorder

Understanding *fears and anxiety* in children requires a developmental perspective. The fears experienced in humans, like those in primates, vary according to age (Marks, 1987). Thus all neonates show a startle response to stimuli such as loud noises and bright lights. Infants of 12–36 months show fear of strangers, and anxiety about separation, especially in threatening circumstances. Older children of 4–6 years commonly experience fear of the dark, animals and imaginary creatures. Older children are more likely to show fear of failure (Ollendick *et al.*, 1991). These fears may be manifested in extreme forms and become handicapping, and then will be considered to be symptoms of psychiatric disorder. Thus, excessive anxiety about separation is the essential feature of separation anxiety disorder. Similarly, excessive fear of animals may be handicapping to the extent that social function is restricted.

Fears and phobias may affect social function. In terms of ICD-10, three disorders are especially relevant. These are separation anxiety disorder, social anxiety disorder of childhood (a persistent wariness of strangers in children over 6 years of age), and phobic anxiety disorder of childhood, which consists of an exaggeration of developmentally appropriate fears. In early childhood, separation anxiety disorder may be associated with school refusal, whereas in later childhood it is more likely to be associated with social or phobic anxiety disorder (Berg, 1992). Outside of the family these disorders may be associated with stranger avoidance, poor school attendance and poor peer group relations. Many of the phobias and anxiety disorders persist into adulthood. It has been shown that many children who had school refusal later develop neurotic disorders such as anxiety states, depression and agoraphobia (Tyrer and Tyrer, 1974; Berg and Jackson, 1985).

These symptoms of fearfulness, and anxiety symptoms can frequently be seen in children presenting with *functional somatic symptoms* (Garralda, 1992). Family members may also have experienced such physical symptoms, which become an important aspect of family life, for example frequently being the subject of conversation, the focus of attention and reason for help seeking (Benjamin and Eminson, 1992). These qualities of symptom sharing and the preoccupation by parents with their children's health may be seen in association with other features of the 'psychosomatic family' described by Minuchin and his colleagues (Minuchin *et al.*, 1978). This constellation is identified by enmeshment (a high level of responsiveness), over-protective-ness, rigidity and avoidance of conflict or lack of conflict resolution. Somatic symptoms may intensify following stressful events such as school attendance and examinations, or even peer contact. In severe cases, there may be social isolation and intractable school non-attendance.

The phenomenology of *obsessive–compulsive disorder* (OCD) in children and adolescents is similar to that in adults, with rituals usually involving washing or cleaning, and obsessional thoughts usually involve fears of harm or illness, of doing wrong, or fear of contamination (Swedo *et al.*, 1989). The OCD is likely to interfere substantially with functioning in all social spheres. The need to carry out rituals may take a long time, and there may also be interference because of associated fears, frequently of contamination and dirt, that lead to a restricted life-style. Family members are typically expected to participate in the OCD, and indeed the psychopathology may be closely linked to the pattern of family organisation. The child may become very angry when others do not comply, and adolescents may tyrannise the family. Levels of discord may be high despite parents taking a surprisingly placatory stance (Hibbs *et al.*, 1991). Often there is a restriction in peer relations. It has been suggested that OCD is related to a restriction of emotional reper-toire, and a lack of empathy (Gillberg, 1992). There may also be social impairment because of associated psychiatric disorders such as tics and Tourette syndrome, depression and anorexia nervosa (Rastam, 1992). Longitudinal studies, using cases that have come to treatment, show a high level of continuity into adulthood, with associated social adjustment difficul-ties (Zeitlin, 1986; Flament *et al.*, 1990).

Eating disorders

Anorexia nervosa in children and young adolescents has many of the charac-teristics of adult onset anorexia nervosa. Sufferers are more likely to have had early feeding difficulties, perfectionist personality, and to have experi-enced more loss through death of first degree relatives or parental divorce (Jacobs and Isaacs, 1986; Rastam and Gillberg, 1992). It has been argued that the anorexia nervosa is a response to the intolerable demands of psychosex-ual maturation (Crisp, 1980). Another influential theory is the family systems view. This claims that the disorder is associated with disturbed family dynam-ics, in which the sufferer fails to develop appropriate autonomy because of the parents' ongoing, but covert discord that involves the sufferer (Minuchin *et al.*, 1978; Selvini Palazzoli *et al.*, 1978). As would be expected from these perspectives, social adjustment is impaired in many ways in anorexia nervosa.

During the period of starvation, there may be increased concern in families. Community studies, in which many cases may not be receiving treat-ment suggest a high level of confiding from the anorectic to her mother and a low level of discord between parents (Monck *et al.*, 1990). In clinic populations, family members indicate that the disorder is associated with some degree of tension, and there may be an air of crisis, although to the outsider the level of discord may appear low. Good response to treatment, including return of weight to normal, is associated with improvement in family relationships (Le Grange *et al.*, 1992).

There may also be disturbances in peer relationships. This may occur premorbidly, or friends may have been lost as the illness developed (Jacobs and Isaacs, 1986; Rastam and Gillberg, 1992). There are delays in psychosexual development, manifesting sometimes as delayed pubertal development, and indifference or anxiety associated with sexual relationships. This may also affect same-sex peer relationships, as a considerable amount of peer conversation and activity may be concerned with heterosexual relationships and the area of sexual relations. Young women who have anorexia nervosa lose their interest in sex, are less likely to marry and have children as compared with their normal peers (Ratnasuriya *et al.*, 1991; Walford and McCune, 1991).

It has been suggested that people with anorexia nervosa have a restricted emotional repertoire, and also that they are not very expressive in their communication style (Bruch, 1973; Rastam and Gillberg, 1992; Hodes and Le Grange, 1993). Consistent with this is the finding from one of the best population studies that has been carried out of a high rate of Asperger syndrome or obsessive–compulsive disorder amongst the adolescents with anorexia nervosa (Rastam and Gillberg, 1992). These findings have led to the suggestion that anorexia nervosa is a disturbance of empathy and so is related to the autism spectrum (Gillberg, 1992).

The long-term outcome of anorexia nervosa with onset in childhood and early adolescence has been the subject of many studies in recent years. While most sufferers will make good recoveries from their first episodes, there is the risk of recurrence. There is a high level of peer relationship difficulties, especially associated with difficulties in the development of sexual relationships, leaving home and marriage (Walford and McCune, 1991). Those patients who do not recover from the first episode may become chronic sufferers and have a mortality of 15% at 20 year follow-up (Ratnasuriya *et al.*, 1991). Pre-pubertal and very early onset may be associated with worse prognosis (Bryant-Waugh *et al.*, 1988; Walford and McCune, 1991).

Bulimia nervosa is rare in children and young adolescents (Hoek, 1991; Kent *et al.*, 1992). It is associated with unsettled family relationships, such as family discord, parental neglect and abuse (Strober and Humphrey, 1987; Schmidt *et al.*, 1992; Waller, 1991, 1992). Early onset bulimia nervosa, like that of more typical onset, is associated with conduct problems such as school non-attendance and stealing. However the early onset bulimics show more emotional disturbance with higher rates of attempted suicide (Schmidt *et al.*, 1992).

Psychoses

Psychoses are rare in children and adolescents, but their detection is important because of the extent of the social impairment and need for special management. Psychoses may be drug induced, and the characteristics are similar to that of adults with such reactions. Specifically there may be sudden onset of the psychotic disorder, with severe impairment of social function in all contexts, with fairly rapid return to normal. In young children drug-induced psychoses are likely to be the result of accidental ingestion of the drugs, whereas in adolescents they may be associated with recreational use of drugs. For adolescents, substance abuse is frequently associated with conduct disorder (Robins and McEvoy, 1990).

The adult type psychoses, bipolar affective and schizophrenic disorders, may occur in children and adolescence. Distinguishing between the psychoses at presentation may be difficult, and frequently the diagnosis is changed from one psychosis to the other as the children pass into adulthood (Zeitlin, 1986). Social impairments are likely to be very considerable, relationships with family and peers being affected, and school attendance may be impossible. A high level of negative symptoms is associated with social impairment and lower IQ (Bettes and Walker, 1987). Recovery from the psychosis will also be associated with improvement in functioning in all contexts. However, outcome studies suggest that those with schizophrenia have worse social adjustment, with fewer in employment or education, and living independently (Werry *et al.*, 1991). Although some investigators report that child and adolescent onset of bipolar or schizophrenic psychosis is associated with worse outcome, others have questioned this (McGlashan, 1988; Werry and McClellan, 1992).

Much attention has been given to the investigation of childhood antecedents of adult schizophrenia. There appears to be consensus that the antecedents include deficits in social function. Typically the children who later develop schizophrenia show odd, unpredictable behaviour, they are socially isolated, and tend to be rejected by peers. Some have conduct problems, especially male adolescents (Zeitlin, 1986; Kupersmidt *et al.*, 1990). There may be also learning difficulties, associated with lower IQ, language difficulties, attention deficits and neurodevelopmental immaturities, which make progress in school difficult.

CONCLUSIONS

There is a complicated relationship between development, child psychiatric disorders and social function. In general, it can be said that children with good relationships with their parents, and normal attachment patterns, are likely to develop healthy relationships with their peers. This is especially the case in the presence of an easy, adaptable temperament, and in the absence of physical illness. This cluster of characteristics also places the child at substantially lower risk of developing psychiatric disorders. There are some childhood psychiatric disorders, such as CD and bulimia nervosa, which in terms of their onset and persistence are causally related to the quality of relationships, especially in the family. On the other hand in some conditions such as anorexia nervosa and bipolar affective disorder social dysfunction occurs more as a consequence of the disorder. When the disorder is treated effectively, the social function improves and frequently returns to normal. There are many continuities from childhood into adulthood, in terms of both the quality of social adjustment and the persistence of psychiatric disorder. However, the extent of this, and the degree of discontinuity requires careful consideration, and prediction in individual cases may be difficult.

REFERENCES

Ainsworth, M.D.S., Blehar, M.C., Waters, E. and Wall, S. (1978). *Patterns of Attachment*, Lawrence Erlbaum, Hillsdale, New Jersey.

Barkley, R.A., Karlsson, J., Pollard, S. and Murphy, J.V. (1985). Developmental changes in the mother–child interactions of hyperactive boys: effects of two dose levels of Ritalin. *Journal of Child Psychology and Psychiatry*, **26**, 705–715.

Baron-Cohen, S. (1988a). Social and pragmatic deficits in Autism: cognitive or affective? *Journal of Autism & Developmental Disorders*, **18**, 379–402.

Baron-Cohen, S. (1988b). An assessment of violence in a young man with Asperger's syndrome. *Journal of Child Psychology and Psychiatry*, **28**, 351–360.

Baron-Cohen, S. (1989). The autistic child's theory of mind: a case of specific developmental delay. *Journal of Child Psychology and Psychiatry*, **30**, 285–288.

Beck, S.J., Young, G.H. and Tarnowski, K.J. (1990). Maternal characteristics and perceptions of pervasive and situational hyperactivity and normal controls. *Journal of The American Academy of Child and Adolescent Psychiatry*, **29**, 558–565.

Befera, M.S. and Barkley, R.A. (1985). Hyperactive and normal girls and boys, parent psychiatric status and child psychopathology. *Journal of Child Psychology and Psychiatry*, **26**, 439–452.

Benjamin, S. and Eminson, D.M. (1992). Abnormal illness behaviour: childhood experiences and long-term consequences. *International Review of Psychiatry*, **4**, 55–70.

Berg, I. (1992). Absence from school and mental health. *British Journal of Psychiatry*, **161**, 154–166.

Berg, I. and Jackson, A. (1985). Teenage school refusers grown up: follow-up study of 168 subjects ten years on average after inpatient treatment. *British Journal of Psychiatry*, **147**, 366–370.

Berger, M. (1985). Temperament and Individual Differences. In: Rutter, M. and Hersov, L. (Eds), *Child and Adolescent Psychiatry: Modern Approaches. 2nd edn.* Blackwell Scientific, Oxford.

Berney, T.P., Bhate, S.R., Kolvin, I., Famuyiwa, O.O., Barrett, M.L., Fundadis, T. and Tyrer, S. (1991). The context of childhood depression. The Newcastle Childhood Depression Project. *British Journal of Psychiatry*, **159** (Suppl. 11), 28–35.

Bettes, B.A. and Walker, E. (1987). Positive and negative symptoms in psychotic and other psychiatrically disturbed children. *Journal of Child Psychology and Psychiatry*, **28**, 555–568.

Biederman, J., Rosenbaum, J.F., Hirshfeld, D.R., Faraone, S.V., Bolduc, E.A., Gersten, M. *et al.* (1990). Psychiatric correlates of behavioural inhibition in young children of parents with and without psychiatric disorders. *Archives of General Psychiatry*, **47**, 21–26.

Billings, A.G. and Moos, R.H. (1983). Comparisons of children of depressed and non-depressed parents: a socio-environmental perspective. *Journal of Abnormal Child Psychology*, **11**, 463–486.

Bowlby, J. (1978). *Attachment*. Penguin, Harmonsworth.

Broberg, A., Lamb, M.E. and Hwang, P. (1990). Inhibition: Its stability and correlates in sixteen-to-forty-month-old children. *Child Development*, **61**, 1153–1163.

Bruch, H. (1973). *Eating Disorders: Obesity, Anorexia Nervosa and the Person Within*. Basic Books, New York.

Bryant-Waugh, R., Knibbs, J., Fosson, A., Kaminski, Z. and Lask, B. (1988). Long term follow-up of patients with early onset anorexia nervosa. *Archives of Disease in Childhood*, **63**, 5–9.

Capps, L., Yirmiya, N. and Sigman, M. (1992). Understanding of simple and complex emotions in non-retarded children with autism. *Journal of Child Psychology and Psychiatry*, **33**, 1169–1182.

Caspi, A., Elder, G.H. and Herbiner, E.S. (1990). Childhood personality and the prediction of life-course patterns. In: Robbins, L. and Rutter, M. (Eds), *Straight and Devious Pathways from Childhood to Adulthood*. Cambridge University Press, Cambridge, pp. 13–35.

Coie, J.D., Dodge, K.A. and Kupersmidt, J.B. (1990). Peer group behavior and social status. In: Asher, S.R. and Coie, J.D. (Eds), *Peer Rejection in Childhood*. Cambridge University Press, Cambridge, pp. 17–59.

Cox, A. (1988). Maternal depression and impact on child development. *Archives of Disease in Childhood*, **63**, 90–95.

Crisp, A. (1980). *Anorexia Nervosa: Let Me Be*. Kegan Paul, London.

Cunningham, C.E., Siegel, L.S. and Offord, D.R. (1991). A dose-responsive analysis of the effects of methylphenidate on the peer interactions and simulated classroom performance of ADD children with and without conduct problems. *Journal of Child Psychology and Psychiatry*, **32**, 439–452.

Dodge, K.A. and Feldman, E. (1990). Issues in social cognition and sociometric status. In: Asher, S.R. and Coie, J.D. (Eds), *Peer Rejection in Childhood*. Cambridge University Press, Cambridge, pp. 119–155.

Dunn, J. and McGuire, S. (1992). Sibling and peer relationships in childhood. *Journal of Child Psychology and Psychiatry*, **33**, 67–105.

Dunn, J., Brown, J., Slomkowski, C., Tesla, C. and Youngblade, L. (1991). Young children's understanding of other people's feelings and beliefs: Individual differences and their antecedents. *Child Development*, **62**, 1352–1366.

Emler, N., Reicher, S. and Ross, A. (1987). The social context of delinquent conduct. *Journal of Child Psychology and Psychiatry*, **28**, 99–109.

Esser, G., Schmidt, M. and Woerner, W. (1990). Epidemiology and course of psychiatric disorders in school-age children — results of a longitudinal study. *Journal of Child Psychology and Psychiatry*, **31**, 243–264.

Farrington, D.P. (1978). The family backgrounds of aggressive youths. In: Hersov, L.A., Berger, M. and Shaffer, D. (Eds), *Aggression and Antisocial Behaviour in Childhood and Adolescence*. Pergamon, Oxford, pp. 73–93.

Farrington, D., Loeber, R., Van Kammen, W.B> (1990). Long term criminal outcomes of hyperactivity — impulsivity — attention deficit and conduct problems in childhood. In: Robins, L. and Rutter, M. (Eds), *Straight and Devious Pathways from Childhood to Adulthood*. Cambridge University Press, Cambridge, pp. 62–81.

Flament, M.F., Koby, E., Rapoport, J.L., Berg, C.J., Zahn, T., Cox, C., Denckla, M. and Lenane, M. (1990). Childhood obsessive–compulsive disorder: a prospective follow-up study. *Journal of Child Psychology and Psychiatry*, **31**, 363–380.

Forehand, R., King, H.E., Peed, S. and Yoder, P. (1975). Mother–child interactions: Comparison of a non-compliant clinic group and a non-clinic group. *Behaviour Research and Therapy*, **13**, 79–85.

Garralda, M.E. (1992). A selective review of child psychiatric syndromes with a somatic presentation. *British Journal of Psychiatry*, **161**, 759–773.

Garralda, M.E. and Bailey, D. (1988). Child and parental factors related to the referral of children to child psychiatry. *British Journal of Psychiatry*, **153**, 81–89.

Gillberg, C. (1990). Autism and pervasive developmental disorders. *Journal of Child Psychology and Psychiatry*, **31**, 99–119.

Gillberg, C. (1991). Outcome in autism and autistic-like conditions. *Journal of the American Academy of Child and Adolescent Psychiatry*, **30**, 375–382.

Gillberg, C.L. (1992). The Emanuel Miller Memorial Lecture 1991. Autism and autistic-like conditions: subclasses among disorders of empathy. *Journal of Child Psychology and Psychiatry*, **33**, 813–842.

Grenell, M.M., Glas, C.R. and Katz, K.S. (1987). Hyperactive children and peer interaction: knowledge and performance of social skills. *Journal of Abnormal Child Psychology*, **15**, 1–13.

Haddad, P. and Garralda, M.E. (1992). Hyperkinetic syndrome and disruptive early experiences. *British Journal of Psychiatry*, **161**, 700–703.

Hammen, C., Burge, D. and Adrian, C. (1991). Timing of mother and child depression in a longitudinal study of children at risk. *Journal of Consulting and Clinical Psychology*, **59**, 341–345.

Harrington, R., Fudge, M., Rutter, M., Pickles, A. and Hill, J. (1990). Adult outcomes of childhood and adolescent depression: I. Psychiatric status. *Archives of General Psychiatry*, **47**, 465–473.

Hay, D.F., Zahn-Waxler, C., Cummings, E.M. and Iannotte, R.J. (1992). Young children's views about conflict with peers: a comparison of the daughters and sons of depressed and well women. *Journal of Child Psychology and Psychiatry*, **33**, 669–683.

Hibbs, E.D., Hamburger, S.D., Lenane, M., Rapoport, J.L., Kreusi, M.J.P., Keysor, C.S. and Goldstein, M.J. (1991). Determinants of expressed emotion in families of disturbed and normal children. *Journal of Child Psychology and Psychiatry*, **32**, 757–770.

Hobson, R.P. (1986a). The autistic child's appraisal of expressions of emotion. *Journal of Child Psychology and Psychiatry*, **27**, 321–342.

Hobson, R.P. (1986b). The autistic child's appraisal of expressions of emotion: a further study. *Journal of Child Psychology and Psychiatry*, **27**, 671–680.

Hobson, R.P. (1989). Beyond cognition. A theory of autism. In: Dawson, G. (Ed.), *Autism: Nature, Diagnosis and Treatment*. Guilford Press, New York/London, pp. 22–48.

Hodes, M. and Le Grange, D. (1993). Expressed Emotion in the investigation of eating disorders: a review. *International Journal of Eating Disorders*, **13**, 279–288.

Hoek, H.W. (1991). The incidence and prevalence of anorexia nervosa and bulimia nervosa in primary care. *Psychological Medicine*, **21**, 455–460.

Hymel, S., Rubin, K.H., Rowden, L. and LeMare, L. (1990). Children's peer relationships: Longitudinal prediction of internalizing and externalizing problems from middle to late childhood. *Child Development*, **61**, 2004–2021.

Jacobs, B.W. and Isaacs, S. (1986). Pre-pubertal anorexia nervosa: a retrospective controlled study. *Journal of Child Psychology and Psychiatry*, **27**, 237–250.

Kagan, J., Reznick, J.S. and Snidman, N. (1987). The physiology and psychology of behavioural inhibition in children. *Child Development*, **58**, 1459–1473.

Kazdin, A.E. (1990). Childhood depression. *Journal of Child Psychology and Psychiatry*, **31**, 121–160.

Kennedy, E., Spence, S.H. and Hensley, R. (1989). An examination of the relationship between childhood depression and social competence amongst primary schoolchildren. *Journal of Child Psychology and Psychiatry*, **30**, 561–573.

Kernberg, P.F., Clarkin, A.J., Greenblatt, E. and Cohen, J. (1992). The Cornell Interview of Peers and Friends: Development and Validation. *Journal of the American Academy of Child and Adolescent Psychiatry*, **31**, 483–489.

Kent, A., Hubert Lacey, J. and McCluskey, S.E. (1992). Pre-menarchal bulimia nervosa. *Journal of Psychosomatic Research*, **36**, 205–210.

Klein, R.G. and Mannuza, S. (1991). Long-term outcome of hyperactive children: a review. *Journal of the American Academy of Child and Adolescent Psychiatry*, **30**, 383–387.

Knight, B.J. and West, D.J. (1975). Temporary and continuing delinquency. *British Journal of Criminology*, **15**, 43–50.

Kovacs, M. and Gatsonis, C. (1989). Stability and change in childhood — onset depressive disorders: longitudinal course as a diagnostic validator. In: Robins, L.N. and Barrett, J.E. (Eds), *The Validity of Psychiatric Diagnosis*. Raven, New York, pp. 57–73.

Kupersmidt, J.T., Coie, J.D. and Dodge, K.A. (1990). The role of poor peer relationships in the development of disorder. In: Asher, S.R. and Coie, J.D. (Eds), *Peer Rejection in Childhood*. Cambridge University Press, Cambridge, pp. 274–305.

Le Grange, D., Eisler, I., Dare, C. and Hodes, M. (1992). Family criticism and self-starvation: a study of expressed emotion. *Journal of Family Therapy*, **14**, 177–192.

Lewis, M., Feiring, C., McGuffog, C. and Jaskir, J. (1984). Predicting psychopathology in six-year-olds from early social relations. *Child Development*, **55**, 123–136.

Lord, C. (1984). Development of peer relations in children with autism. In: Morrison, F., Lord, C. and Keating, D. (Eds), *Applied Developmental Psychology (Vol. 1)*, Academic Press, New York.

McGlashan, T.H. (1988). Adolescent versus adult onset mania. *American Journal of Psychiatry*, **145**, 221–223.

Mannarino, A.P. (1978). The interactional process in preadolescent friendships. *Psychiatry*, **41**, 308–312.

Marks, I. (1987). The development of normal fear: a review. *Journal of Child Psychology and Psychiatry*, **28**, 667-697.

Minde, K. (1992). Aggression in preschoolers: Its relation to somatization. *Journal of the American Academy of Adolescent Psychiatry*, **31**, 853–9462.

Minuchin, S., Rosman, B.L. and Baker, B.L. (1978). *Psychosomatic Families: Anorexia Nervosa in Context*. Harvard University Press, Cambridge, Mass.

Monck, E., Graham, P., Richman, N. and Dobbs, R. (1990). Eating and weight-control problems in a community population of adolescent girls aged 15–20 years. In: Remschmidt. H. and Schmidt, M.H. (Eds), *Anorexia Nervosa*. Hogrefe and Huber Publishers, Toronto, pp. 1–12.

Mussen, P.H., Conger, J.J., Kagan, J. and Huston, A.C. (1990). *Child Development and Personality*. Harper & Row, New York.

Ollendick, T.H., Yule, W. and Ollier, K. (1991). Fears in British children and their relationship to manifest anxiety and depression. *Journal of Child Psychology and Psychiatry*, **32**, 321–331.

Patterson, G.R. (1982). *A Social Learning Approach: 3. Coercive Family Process*. Eugene OR, Castalia.

Patterson, G.R. and Dishion, T.J. (1988). Multilevel family process models: traits, interactions and relationships. In: Hinde, R.A. and Stevenson-Hinde, J. (Eds), *Relationships within Families*. Clarendon Press, Oxford, pp. 283–310.

Patterson, G.R., De Baryshe, B.D. and Ramsey, E. (1989). A developmental perspective on antisocial behaviour. *American Psychology*, **44**, 329–335.

Prior, M. (1992). Childhood temperament. *Journal of Child Psychology and Psychiatry*, **33**, 249–280.

Puig-Antich, J., Lukens, E., Davies, M., Goetz, D., Brennan-Quatrack, J. and Todak, G. (1985). Psychosocial functioning in prepubertal major depressive disorders. *Archives of General Psychiatry*, **42**, 500–507.

Rastam, M. (1992). Anorexia nervosa in 51 Swedish adolescents: premorbid problems and comorbidity. *Journal of the American Academy of Child and Adolescent Psychiatry*, **31**, 819–829.

Rastam, M. and Gillberg, C. (1992). Background factors in anorexia nervosa. *European Child and Adolescent Psychiatry*, **1**, 54–65.

Rastam, M., Gillberg, C. and Garton, M. (1989). Anorexia nervosa in a Swedish urban region. A population-based study. *British Journal of Psychiatry*, **155**, 642–646.

Ratnasuriya, R.H., Eisler, I., Szmukler, G.I. and Russell, G.F.M. (1991). Anorexia nervosa: outcome and prognostic factors after 20 years. *British Journal of Psychiatry*, **158**, 495–502.

Reynolds, J.M., Garralda, M.E., Postlethwaite, R. and Goh, D. (1991). Changes in psychosocial adjustment following renal transplantation. *Archives of Disease in Childhood*, **66**, 508–513.

Reynolds, J.M., Morton, M.J.S., Garralda, M.E., Postlethwaite, R.J. and Goh, D. (1993). Psychological adjustment of adult survivors of a paediatric dialysis or transplant programme. *Archives of Disease in Childhood*, **68**, 104–110.

Richman, N., Stevenson, J. and Graham, P.J. (1982). *Preschool to School: A Behavioural Study*. Academic Press, London.

Robins, L.N. (1966). *Deviant Children Grown Up: A Sociological and Psychiatric Study of Sociopathic Personality*. Williams & Wilkins, Baltimore.

Robins, L.N. (1978). Sturdy childhood predictors of adult outcomes: replications from longitudinal studies. *Psychological Medicine*, **8**, 611–622.

Robins, L.N. (1991). Conduct Disorder. *Journal of Child Psychology and Psychiatry*, **32**, 193–212.

Robins, L.N. and McEvoy, L. (1990). Conduct problems as predictors of substance abuse. In: Robins, L. and Rutter, M. (Eds), *Straight and Devious Pathways from Childhood to Adulthood*. Cambridge University Press, Cambridge, pp. 182–204.

Rutter, M. (1980). Attachment and the development of social relationships. In: Rutter, M. (Ed.), *Scientific Foundation of Developmental Psychiatry*. William Heinemann, London, pp. 267–279.

Rutter, M. (1986). The developmental psychopathology of depression: issues and perspectives. In: Rutter, M., Izard, C.E. and Read, P.B. (Eds), *Depression in Young People: Developmental and Clinical Perspectives*. Guilford Press, New York, pp. 3–30.

Rutter, M. and Giller, H. (1983). *Juvenile Delinquency*. Penguin, Harmondsworth.

Rutter, M. and Schopler, E. (1988). Autism and pervasive developmental disorders. Concepts and Diagnostic Issues. In: Schopler, E. and Mesibov, G.B. (Eds), *Diagnosis and Assessment in Autism*. Plenum Press, New York/London, pp. 15–36.

Rutter, M. and Quinton, D. (1984). Parental psychiatric disorder: effects on children. *Psychological Medicine*, **14**, 853–880.

Rutter, M., Tizard, J. and Whitmore, K. (Eds) (1970). *Education, Health and Behaviour*. Longman, London.

Rutter, M., Maughan, B., Mortimore, P. and Ouston, J. (1979). *Fifteen Thousand Hours*. Open Books, London.

Schachar, R. (1991). Childhood hyperactivity. *Journal of Child Psychology and Psychiatry*, **32**, 155–191.

Schmidt, U., Hodes, M. and Treasure, J. (1992). Early onset bulimia nervosa: who is at risk? A retrospective case-control study. *Psychological Medicine*, **22**, 623–628.

Selvini-Palazzoli, M., Boscolo, L., Cechin, G. and Prata, G. (1978). *Paradox and Counterparadox: A New Model in the Therapy of the Family in Schizophrenic Transactions*. Jason Aronson, New York.

Snyder, J.J. (1977). Reinforcement analysis of interaction in problem and nonproblem families. *Journal of Abnormal Psychology*, **86**, 528–535.

Snyder, J.J., Dishion, T.J. and Patterson, G.R. (1986). Determinants and consequences of association with deviant peers during preadolescence and adolescence. *Journal of Early Adolescence*, **6**, 20–43.

Sroufe, L.A. (1985). Attachment classification from the perspective of infant–caregiver relationships and infant temperament. *Child Development*, **56**, 1–14.

Strober, M. and Humphreys, L.L. (1987). Familial contributions to the etiology and course of anorexia nervosa and bulimia. *Journal of Consulting and Clinical Psychology*, **55**, 654–659.

Swedo, S.E., Leonard, H.L., Rapoport, J.L., Lenane, M.C., Goldberger, E.L. and Cheslow, D.L. (1989). A double-blind comparison of clomipramine and desipramine in the treatment of trichotillomania (hair pulling). *New England Journal of Medicine*, **321**, 497–501.

Szagun, G. (1992). Children's understanding of the feeling experience and causes of sympathy. *Journal of Child Psychology and Psychiatry*, **33**, 1183–1191.

Tantam, D. (1988). Asperger's syndrome. *British Journal of Psychiatry*, **29**, 245–255.

Taylor, E.A. (1986). *The Overactive Child. Clinics in Development Medicine No. 97*. Blackwell Scientific, Oxford.

Thomas, A. and Chess, S. (1977). *Temperament and Development*. Brunner Mazel, New York.

Tyrer, P. and Tyrer, S. (1974). School refusal, truancy and adult neurotic illness. *Psychological Medicine*, **4**, 416–421.

Walford, G. and McCune, N. (1991). Long term outcome of early onset anorexia nervosa. *British Journal of Psychiatry*, **159**, 383–389.

Waller, G. (1991). Sexual abuse as a factor in eating disorders. *British Journal of Psychiatry*, **159**, 664–671.

Waller, G. (1992). Sexual abuse and the severity of bulimic symptoms. *British Journal of Psychiatry*, **161**, 90–93.

Weir, K. and Duveen, G. (1981). Further development and validation of the prosocial behaviour questionnaire for use by teachers. *Journal of Child Psychology and Psychiatry*, **22**, 357–374.

Werry, J.S. (1992). Child psychiatric disorders: are they classifiable? *British Journal of Psychiatry*, **161**, 472–480.

Werry, J.S. and McClellan, J.M. (1992). Predicting outcome in child and adolescent (early onset) schizophrenia and bipolar disorder. *Journal of the American Academy of Child and Adolescent Psychiatry*, **31**, 147–150.

Werry, J.S., McClellan, J.M. and Chard, L. (1991). Childhood and adolescent schizophrenic, bipolar, and schizoaffective disorders: a clinical outcome study. *Journal of the American Academy of Child and Adolescent Psychiatry*, **30**, 457–465.

Wing, L. (1981). Asperger's syndrome: a clinical account. *Psychological Medicine*, **11**, 115–129.

Wolff, S. (1985). Non-delinquent disturbances of conduct. In: Rutter, M. and Hersov, L. (Eds), *Child and Adolescent Psychiatry: Modern Approaches. 2nd edn.* Blackwell Scientific, Oxford.

Wolff, S. (1991). Schizoid personality in childhood and adult life. I: The vagaries of diagnostic labelling. *British Journal of Psychiatry*, **159**, 615–620.

Wolff, S. and Chick, J. (1980). Schizoid personality in childhood: controlled follow-up study. *Psychological Medicine*, **10**, 85–100.

World Health Organisation (1992). *ICD-10: International Classification of Disease — 10. Mental Disorders: Glossary and Guide to the Classification in accordance with the 10th Revision of the International Classification of Diseases*, WHO, Geneva.

Zeitlin (1986). *The Natural History of Psychiatric Disorder in Children. Maudsley Monograph 29.* Oxford University Press, Oxford.

9

Quality of Life and Social Function

JOHN GREEN and FIONA HENDERSON

This chapter examines the links between the concepts of quality of life and social function. Quality of life is an area of investigation in which many of the key theoretical issues are routinely ducked. We have tried to examine some of these issues to see to what extent they can be resolved, to identify what needs to be further elucidated and to try to see what conclusions we can draw about the practical conduct of research studies in the quality of life and social functioning area.

The concept of quality of life (QOL) has become widely used within general medicine over the past 20 years. A computer search by the authors located 124 treatment studies using QOL measures published in the first six months of 1990. Given that it is very likely that some were missed in the search and many studies may have remained unpublished for one reason or another, the volume of research using QOL measures is high. However these are only the studies which actually sought to measure QOL (or claimed to do so). Many more studies mention QOL or make unsupported assertions about it. Indeed perhaps as many as seven times as many papers mention QOL as actually seek to measure it (Bowling, 1991).

The volume of research might suggest that most of the problems in measuring QOL have been sorted out. However this is far from the case. Amongst the 124 studies there was little consistency in the measures used and almost half the studies used at least one measure not used by more than one other study, often a scale developed specifically for a particular study.

Few authors addressed one of the key issues in QOL, the definition of what 'quality of life' actually means. This reflects the fact that the field is largely atheoretical. For most authors QOL is what they are measuring. Given that situation, the lack of consistency in measures and even in approach is hardly surprising.

The reason for the upsurge in popularity of QOL measures in general medicine is simple, for many treatments used in medicine today it is difficult to specify an obvious outcome.

Two sorts of outcome are very clear in medicine, death (or its avoidance or postponement) or cure. If I am involved in a car crash and am taken to hospital haemorrhaging heavily, operated on to stop the bleeding and then recover, the outcome is clear. My life has been saved. Similarly, if I get pneumonia, attend my GP and, after a course of antibiotics, no longer have pneumonia then I have, to all intents and purposes, been cured. Whether you think either of these procedures was worthwhile, or whether you would rather have given some other person some other treatment with the same resources is a different matter. There is a clear outcome.

Unfortunately most of medicine neither has a clear impact on death rates nor provides a complete cure. Most of the resources of a modern health service are likely to be aimed at chronic or incurable conditions, often those associated with ageing. Or they may be aimed at conditions which are capable of control only. This concentration of resources on the incurable in highly developed medical systems is not surprising. After all, cured patients don't keep coming back.

Over the past decade the main treatments for gastric ulcers have been drugs which kept the ulcer at bay. When these drugs are stopped, and often when they are still being taken, recurrence is common. Lives have been saved through prevention of the complications of gastric ulcers but for most patients the main outcome of taking them is a considerable improvement in their well-being. It is when you try to specify in what way their lives are improved that problems arise.

An ulcer patient obviously gets relief from pain. However, they may also gain weight and have more energy, they may have less time off work and so not lose their job, they may be able to enjoy eating in a way that they were not able to do previously. They may be able to go out socially more and feel less irritable and distressed. So the outcome of treatment, for most ulcer sufferers, is neither avoidance of death nor cure but a whole range of possible gains. The question for the clinician or researcher trying to assess the outcome of treatment is which of the many possible areas of improvement should be measured to assess the outcome of treatment?

Similar problems attach to outcomes in much of modern medicine. The issue of palliative care of the dying is another clear example. Here there is neither cure nor delay of death. Indeed, in some cases more aggressive treatment might have kept a patient alive longer. So in some way length of life has been potentially traded off against an idea that it matters fundamentally not just how long life is, but how good it is.

Even in conditions where a treatment has a clear outcome in terms of preventing death, it often has this effect only for a proportion of patients. If death rates are the only measure, the impact of treatment on other patients in a population may be missed.

Even where there is a clear prolongation of life or a 'cure' almost all treatments have some side-effects. A clear case is antihypertensive medication. This reduces the mortality amongst hypertensives in the long term (Smith, 1990). However, in a large proportion of hypertensive patients the condition itself causes the patient no obvious symptoms, at least in its early stages. Most antihypertensive drugs on the other hand have unpleasant side-effects and can make a patient who was otherwise healthy feel unwell. It is not surprising that patient compliance is a real problem (Kong *et al.*, 1990).

It is not just drug treatments which can have side-effects. The admission of a patient into a psychiatric hospital for a moderate period can cause them to lose their job. It can put a strain on their families or cause the patient to lose contact with them. It can lead to the patient losing what remaining confidence they have in coping in the outside world. Of course this is not the case for every admission, but it happens to some patients. There needs to be some way to enter the side-effects of treatment into the outcome equation even where life may be prolonged or where there may be an eventual cure.

These considerations have led to the development of the field of QOL. The central concept is that there is a second dimension in medicine, life has not just length but has some element which can be seen as 'quality'.

However anyone looking at the range of QOL measures used in different studies would be hard-pressed to see any common ground. Quite disparate measures are called QOL measures. There are at least five different dimensions which are commonly used as QOL measures.

Probably the most commonly used QOL measures are measures of functioning, most commonly physical functioning, but quite often including ability to carry out activities of daily living. One of the most widely used measures of functioning is the Karnofsky Scale (Karnofsky *et al.*, 1948). Originally developed to measure levels of dependency in cancer patients, it is a 100 point scale — confusingly with only 10 defined levels of discrimination — which sets a patient on a point from 100 (normal, no evidence of disease) through to 0 (dead). Doubts have been cast on its reliability and on its statistical properties (Slevin *et al.*, 1988).

However, the main criticism about it is that the results from it do not make intuitive sense. Because the scale relies on the physical functioning of the patient it would rate the world wheelchair javelin champion as having a much lower quality of life (40 'requires considerable assistance and frequent medical care') than many chronically depressed but physically well patients (80 'normal activity with effort').

There are a large number of other measures of functioning in use. Many of these are rather better than the Karnofsky in their statistical properties, but most are aimed at particular populations, especially activity and self-care in the elderly. However all share at least some of the underlying problems of the Karnofsky Scale. Examples are Katz's Activities of Daily Living Scale (Katz *et al.*, 1963) and variants on it and the Crichton Royal Behavioural Rating Scale (Wilkin and Jolley, 1979). Many other scales use measures of physical functioning as part of a composite score, for instance the Quality of Well-being Scale (Kaplan *et al.*, 1976) and the McMaster Health Index Questionnaire (Chambers *et al.*, 1976).

While these scales offer a more sophisticated approach than the Karnofsky Scale they usually focus on capacity to carry out particular activities, whether it be playing golf or being continent. There is always the question as to whether the right activities are included in the ones being asked about and the question about the weighting of items. If double incontinence weights as four, how many is not being able to play golf worth? A lot of them would also fail the wheelchair test, our wheelchair javelin champion might well be both incontinent and unable to play golf but is he any less happy?

Another common element in QOL measures is the measurement of symptoms either as a single index or as part of a wider battery of QOL measures, as for instance in the Cornell Medical Index (Brodman *et al.*, 1949).

Most symptom inventories work in a fairly simple way. A list of common symptoms of a particular disease is developed, the patient is asked whether they have these, or how severe they are. A good example of this approach is the Rotterdam Symptom Inventory (De Haes *et al.*, 1983) and the approach is also used in psychiatry, for instance in the Hamilton Depression Scale (Hamilton, 1967). The scores, or number of symptoms, are added up to give a final score. One of the problems is that most scales do not seek to weight the items in any sensible way. In most diseases some symptoms are much more important than others. So in AIDS most patients feel that skin rashes are fairly trivial but going blind is extremely important (Green *et al.*, 1992). This is particularly important when considering treatment trials. A single side-effect might be much worse as far as the patient is concerned than 10 relieved symptoms put together. Finding out how patients view particular symptoms is crucial.

Again, there is a conceptual problem with calling a symptom checklist a quality of life measure. Can your quality of life be reduced to whether you have a skin rash or not?

Another commonly measured dimension is psychological distress. The sort of measures of anxiety and depression familiar in psychiatry are often used as QOL measures, the Beck (Beck *et al.*, 1961), the Spielberger anxiety scale (Spielberger *et al.*, 1970) and the Hospital Anxiety and Depression Scale (HADS) (Zigmond and Snaith, 1983) being commonly used. There are limitations to the usefulness of these measures. One obvious limitation is that they can only measure how distressed someone is, not how happy they are. This is most easily seen from an example. Suppose we were to embark on a treatment trial in AIDS. Probably about 35–40% of patients would be classified as depressed or anxious (Green *et al.*, 1992). Therefore two-thirds of the patients would not. Suppose that the trial was a roaring success and we found a cure for AIDS, the two-thirds of patients who were not depressed or anxious would probably be exultant, yet on our measures they could only get less depressed or anxious, symptoms which they did not have in the first place. Psychological distress is only one possible direction for mood, it is important not to ingore the other direction or to miss the fact that it is perfectly possible to be miserable without being clinically depressed.

Another commonly measured dimension of QOL is the subject of this book, social function. This is particularly important in psychiatry. Many interventions in psychiatry do not produce symptomatic relief but increase physical functioning or improve ability to carry out activities of daily living. For instance if we measure the symptoms of a chronic psychiatric patient transferred from a long-stay hospital to a group home or hostel before and after transfer it is unlikely that we would detect a difference in symptomatology. Indeed symptom control may well be worse. Similarly the ability of patients to carry out basic self-care skills may be unchanged or, in an unfamiliar environment with reduced supervision, actually reduced. However for many patients we might expect that their social function would be improved by the opportunities offered by a more 'normal' environment.

In the sense that man is a social animal it is easy to see why social function should be seen as a measure of some aspect of QOL. However it is more doubtful if social function can be seen as the sole criterion of quality of life. A round-the-world sailor presumably has few social contacts (one of the important elements of social function) other than seagulls and those provided by the radio, but would they set off if they did not feel that, in some way, the trip would make their life better?

The final dimension which is measured in QOL studies is life satisfaction. A variety of approaches has been taken to measuring life satisfaction. Different authors have applied different terms to what they are measuring: happiness, satisfaction, morale, well-being. There have been complicated and sometimes rather arcane arguments about the differences between these different terms which have tended to obscure rather than clarify the issue (Gurin *et al.*, 1960; Campbell, 1976; Stones and Kozma, 1980). However all of these approaches have centred on the idea that there is some element of subjective well-being in people which can be measured and that this is affected by a whole range of different influences. These dimensions are measured in various ways by authors in different studies. However there are also a whole range of 'omnibus' scales of QOL which take different dimensions and combine them in different ways so that a final score may be made up, for instance, of psychological distress and physical functioning as in the Rosser–Kind index (Rosser and Kind, 1978). This raises an issue in itself.

How can you add together inability to go to the shops and how distressed a person is and come up with a single index figure?

On a broader front, in what sense are the Karnofsky Scale, the Beck, the Rotterdam symptom inventory, the faces scale and a social function measure all measuring a single entity which can be called 'quality of life'. At this stage it is tempting simply to assume that there is no common ground between the different scales and that quality of life is simply a convenient term for any measure in medicine other than death rates. However this is probably unduly pessimistic. A clue to what the core of QOL is can be found by looking beyond medicine at uses of the term outside medicine.

'According to a report today from Regional Railways, a division of BR, and the Association of Metropolitan Authorities, the railways are increasingly easing congestion in towns and cities outside London, improving the quality of life for more than 13.5 million residents.'

(Guardian 7.11.92)

Governments, economists and a variety of public bodies use the term quality of life freely. For them quality of life is usually linked to objective indicators: whether people have decent housing, safe water, consumer goods such as televisions and refrigerators, and to issues like how long it takes them to get to work, how crowded their transport is and how good or bad the environment they live in is. Quality of life is measured by governments in terms of pre-set standards, although what those standards are varies from place to place and time to time. There are several implicit assumptions in the approaches that are used.

It is assumed, for instance, that life is better for a person with a car than one without a car or that a short journey to work on uncrowded public transport is better than a long one with too many people. Similarly it is assumed that people who do not have a safe water supply are likely to have worse lives than those who have access to clean drinking water. The concept as used by governments includes 'standard of living' but goes further than that and includes things which cannot be measured simply in terms of income and expenditure for the individual.

This way of looking at quality of life is interesting because it shows up particularly starkly many of the problems and compromises of all approaches to measuring quality of life. Who decides what things are included in the measures and on what basis? Are measures incremental, if one television increases your quality of life, will two televisions increase it twice as much? How should items be weighted, does one television plus one car equal having a safe water supply and a 15 minute journey to work? How much does this sort of group assessment relate to the individual; after all, many monks would have a pretty low quality of life on the basis of possession of consumer goods, but does that make their quality of life worse?

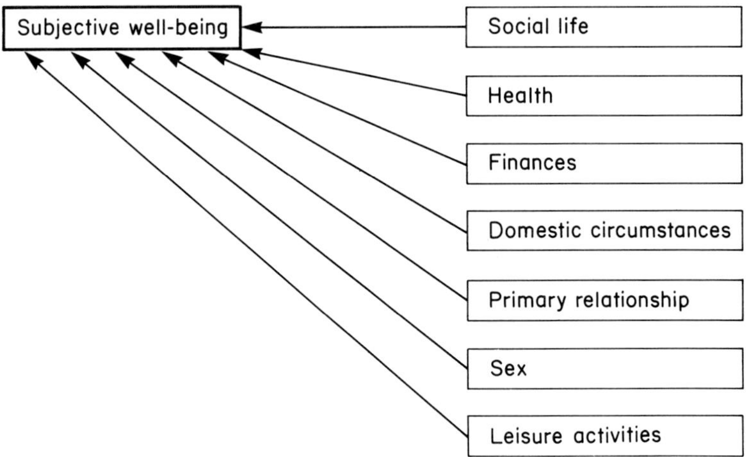

Figure 9.1. Proposed relationship between subjective well-being and influencing factors in quality of life. N.B. Only a selection of possible influencing factors is shown.

This usage of the term quality of life does, however, show up clearly one key issue about QOL which gets lost in most studies and most reviews. Governments measure refrigerators, water supplies and transport because these are the things which they can do something about. Governments cannot sort out people's marriages, although they sometimes try to legislate to do so. They cannot give people contentment or peace of mind. So the measures they use are linked to what they expect procedures available to them to achieve. *They do not measure what they do not expect to change.*

What links all the different uses of the term QOL in medicine with the use of the term by governments is the idea of subjective well-being. Having to travel every day for an hour standing in a crowded train is similar to having constant pain from a stomach ulcer only in so far as both are likely to make people's subjective well-being less.

People with poor Karnofsky scale scores, poor social function, bad housing, physical pain, long uncomfortable journeys to work, high Beck Depression Inventory scores and lots of physical symptoms are linked together in that we expect that these things reflect the fact that they have reduced subjective well-being. They are less likely to be happy or satisfied with their lives than they would be if they did not have these problems. It is not necessary to postulate some quite separate health-related type of quality of life as some authors have tried to do (e.g. Torrance, 1986).

Figure 9.1 suggests how these concepts might be linked together. In this formulation subjective well-being (SWB) is the core, it is a person's quality

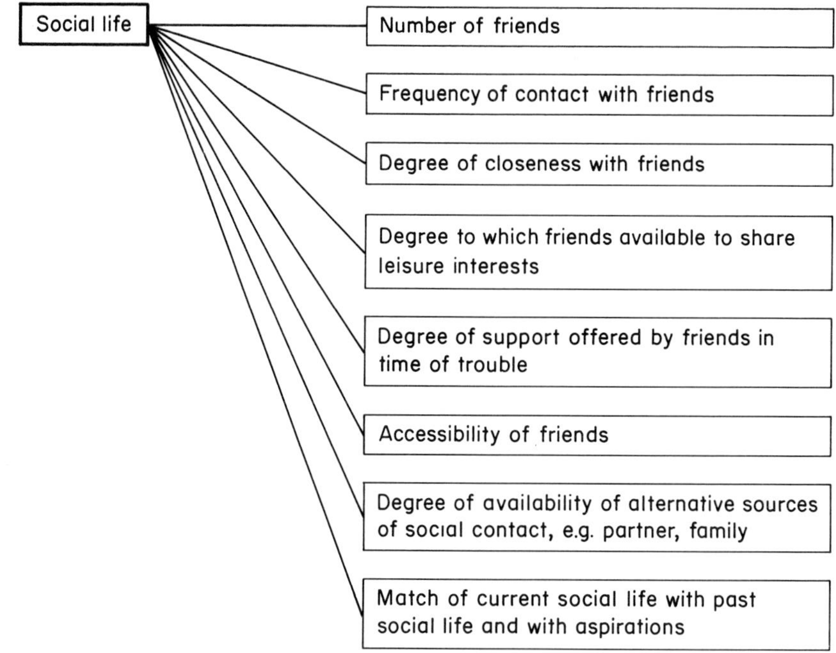

Figure 9.2. Some of the factors which may contribute to a person's satisfaction with their social life. N.B. Only a selection of possible elements is shown.

of life. Various other factors affect what an individual's SWB is likely to be. The list of influencing factors is intended as an example not as a definitive list.

Clearly different individuals may give different weights to different influencing factors. For a monk physical living conditions are unlikely to be as important as for a woman with a young family. The relative importance of different influencing factors in a person's life is likely to vary over time and with different circumstances. They are also likely to differ from person to person in an individual manner according to attitudes, cognitions, past experiences and so on.

It is also interesting that some influencing factors may be positive, some negative and some (potentially) both. In part it may depend how one looks at things. We would speculate that health is not likely to contribute to subjective well-being except where there are health problems. So that, for many people, being in good health is not something which increases their SWB, however having ill-health is likely to reduce it. In the same way winning a new car in a raffle is likely to increase SWB, if only transitorily, while not winning a new car is unlikely to reduce SWB.

Each of the influencing factors is, in itself, likely to be made up of different elements. Figure 9.2 shows a possible breakdown of some elements which might contribute to a person's social life.

If this formulation is correct it has some interesting implications. It should, in principle, be possible to combine quite disparate measures of QOL into single omnibus indices or to use a mix of different types of QOL measure. This is something which would not be possible if there is no underlying core element to QOL. However the weighting of the different elements would need to be related in some way to the importance of each element in contributing to SWB.

It is instructive to consider again the subject of the world wheelchair javelin champion and his Karnofsky score. Why should the Karnofsky score of an individual in a wheelchair be worse than that of an individual who is fully mobile? Clearly the answer is that it was the expectation of the developers of the scale (and of those who have used it subsequently) that people with restricted mobility have a worse QOL than those who are fully mobile. Applying the formulation outlined above one might translate that into the idea that such individuals have a lower SWB. However the expectation was that this was so *on average*. So a group of individuals with restricted mobility would be expected to have significantly less SWB than a group of individuals with full mobility. However it would not be reasonable to assume that that would necessarily apply to a single individual.

On average individuals with asthma are probably less likely to achieve sporting excellence but there are a number of asthmatics playing soccer professionally in the United Kingdom. In the same way there are likely to be some individuals with restricted mobility who enjoy much higher SWB than some individuals with full mobility. This is because physical functioning is only one of several influencing factors on an individual's SWB.

The formulation suggests that there are, potentially, two ways to approach the measurement of QOL. Which is adopted depends on what the objectives of the study are, on the numbers of individuals involved and on what else is known about the area of a person's life being measured.

The first approach is to identify, for the individual, what are important elements in their quality of life. Individuals are likely to differ in their priorities and in the weighting that they give to different aspects of their life. An individual may identify lack of a partner as the key issue for them. If they had a partner they might expect that their SWB would be greatly enhanced. Or they might identify anxiety attacks or lack of good housing as a key issue in reducing their SWB. This approach implies taking an essentially single-case approach to QOL, developing individual scales or measurement instruments for each individual. At an individual level this is likely to be the only approach to QOL which is practicable. It does however make the analysis of the outcome of a standardised treatment approach rather difficult if every patient is being rated on different scales.

The second approach is more suited to groups and depends on average responses. If it can be demonstrated, for example, that increasing the number of friends that people have increases their SWB then a scale measuring number of friends is an appropriate QOL outcome measure for a study of, say, social skills training. It is not necessary to establish that the SWB of all members of a population will be enhanced by increasing their number of friends, only that for the group as a whole it will be. Connections between SWB and the QOL outcome measure being used do not have to be established within the study, they can be established from separate studies, including from the available published literature. Where more than one outcome measure is being used, where outcome measures may show differential results or where an attempt is being made to establish or validate an omnibus QOL measure there needs to be a more direct attempt to find out the relative weightings of different scales or different parts of the omnibus, implying that there needs to be an attempt to measure the relative impact of each area being measured on SWB.

To some extent it may be possible to combine the two approaches by using standardised areas of enquiry but getting patients to make judgements about the relative importance of different areas in their lives. In other words, the assessor gets the patients to generate weightings for standardised scales.

It would seem an obvious question, if the formulation being put forward in this chapter is correct, to ask why not simply try to measure SWB directly? Why ask an individual how mobile they are if they can be asked how satisfied they are with their lives?

In fact there are very good reasons for taking a more indirect route. Our own research with patients with HIV infection (Green *et al.*, 1992) and a recently completed study of patients with terminal cancer suggests that there are a large number of influences on SWB for any individual. The effect of an intervention to, say, increase the number of friends someone has may require largish numbers of patients to get a significant effect on SWB given the variance from other influences on SWB.

It often happens that one will have only a limited number of patients in a study and it may be difficult or impossible with clinical samples to increase that population. However, providing the underlying assumption that number of friends is an influence on SWB is correct then a scale measuring number of friends might be reasonably regarded as a QOL measure. In other words it may not be necessary, though it is clearly most desirable, to show that a particular intervention has had an influence on SWB *within that study* where patient numbers are small.

The other consideration is the same as that which governments apply in their measures of QOL, measuring directly those things which one is trying to change is good policy.

Developing accurate measures of SWB in itself has proved a problem. These problems mean that existing measures of SWB are rather crude and that it is also likely to make getting change on SWB measures with low numbers of patients difficult. It is worth reviewing a few of the problems with SWB measurement.

First, there is a problem with terminology. There has been argument about whether terms like 'satisfaction', 'happiness' and 'morale' are referring to the same concepts. There have been many definitions put forward but most researchers have effectively ignored the fact that it is not the definition of the researcher which matters, but what someone answering a questionnaire or scale understands that they are being asked. However there are more difficult questions about the extent to which subjective well-being is a matter of cognition or affect or both. Trying to resolve these issues is beyond the scope of this chapter so we have made an assumption, which we believe to be reasonable, that satisfaction, happiness and morale, even if they are not identical concepts in the subject's mind are likely to be strongly inter-correlated and strongly related to some central core of subjective well-being.

Then there is the problem of selecting a measure of SWB. It is clear that individuals can give ratings for their overall level of happiness with their lives on a seven-point scale. These ratings are strongly correlated with other measures. In 180 individuals with HIV infection selected randomly from an HIV out-patients department and from infectious diseases wards patients ratings of overall happiness correlated 0.72 with the HAD depression scale, 0.72 with a measure of social function, the Social Functioning Questionnaire (Tyrer *et al.*, 1990, Table 3.3)), 0.77 with an aggregated score derived from patient ratings of satisfaction with 11 areas of life and 0.33 with the number and severity of symptoms they reported on an HIV symptom rating scale. On the other hand ratings of general happiness correlated 0.46 with ratings of satisfaction with their primary relationship, 0.56 with ratings of their social life and 0.52 with ratings of their sex life (Green *et al.*, 1992).

The study suggests that a simple measure of how happy people are is likely to be valid and worth including in an outcome study. Indeed we would argue that some measure of SWB should be included in all studies. A simple seven-point scale appears acceptable as a minimum, however it does provide extremely limited information. There are a number of more elaborate standardised measures of life satisfaction and happiness available which can be used although anyone using them needs to consider their properties, strengths and weaknesses carefully since all available measures are rather unsatisfactory in one way or another.

Development of more satisfactory and more detailed measures of SWB is partly hindered by a basic lack of understanding of how SWB works and how it is structured.

While people seem able to rate their general happiness on a global scale, there are a number of questions about how they arrive at that judgement which have important implications. They may be very satisfied with their marriage, satisfied with their living conditions but very dissatisfied with their job. Do they assess their level of satisfaction by adding these together? If so, do they weight them? Or is it perhaps the case that some things simply overshadow everything else so that the man in a very unhappy job may be miserable even though other areas of life are going well? If some important areas of life are influences largely in their absence, for instance health, how would this influence life satisfaction in a treatment trial.

In developing a Life Satisfaction Scale to investigate the area further we started by interviewing individuals about their life satisfaction. People reliably identify certain domains of satisfaction, such as sex life, primary relationship, leisure activities. Do these reflect actual discrete domains in people's thinking about their lives, or do they simply reflect conventional ways of identifying different domains in everyday speech? It was clear that people making judgements about life satisfaction in different areas of their life did so by comparison. They have at least three possible types of comparison, with their aspirations, with how they remember they were at some time in the past or with how satisfied they perceive other people to be. However there appeared to be no consistency between people in the approach they took unless this was specified by the interviewer.

There is a lack of clear theoretical understanding of the mental structures underlying subjective well-being which needs to be corrected. A better understanding of the issues might lead to a better understanding of how to measure SWB and, indeed, how to increase SWB in people. Even so, just because we do not fully understand something, it does not imply that it is not important to measure, however crudely we have to do so or however unsatisfactory the instruments that we have to hand.

Overall, then, this chapter argues that at the core of a person's quality of life is their subjective well-being. A QOL measure measures quality of life to the extent that it is measuring something which has an impact on subjective well-being. Social function is one influence on quality of life amongst others. Therefore valid social function measures are likely to be those which can be shown to be measuring real influences on subjective well-being. Finally, it is worth pointing out that there are other reasons for measuring social function than for its value in telling us something about an individual's QOL. An individual's social function has an effect on other people around them and so it may influence the QOL of others.

REFERENCES

Beck, A.T., Mendelson, M., Mock, J. *et al.* (1961). Inventory for measuring depression. *Archives of General Psychiatry*, **4**, 561–571.

Bowling, A. (1991). *Measuring Health: A Review of Quality of Life Measurement Scales*. Open University Press, Milton Keynes.

Brodman, K., Erdmann, A.J. and Wolff, H.G. (1949). *Cornell Medical Index Health Questionnaire*. Cornell University Medical College, New York.

Campbell, A. (1976). Subjective measures of well-being. *American Psychologist*, **31**, 117–124.

Chambers, L.W., Sackett, D.L., and Goldsmith, C.H. (1976) Development and application of an index of social functioning. *Health Services Research*, **11**, 430–441.

De Haes, J.C.J.M., Pruyn, J.F.A. and Knippenberg, F.C.E. (1983). Klachtenlijst voor Kanxerpatienten Eerste ervaringen. *Nederlands Tijdschrift voor de Psychologie*, **38**, 403–422.

Green, J., Henderson, F., Tyrer, P. and Hedge, B. (1992). Subjective quality of life in persons with HIV disease. Presented at VIIth International Conference on AIDS, Amsterdam. Abstract No: PoB 3565.

Gurin, G., Verloff, J. and Feld, S. (1960). *Americans View Their Mental Health*. Basic Books, New York.

Hamilton, M. (1967). Development of a rating scale for primary depressive illness. *British Journal of Social and Clinical Psychology*, **6**, 278–296.

Kaplan, R.M., Bush, J.W. and Berry, C.C. (1976). Health Status: types of validity and the Index of Well-Being. *Health Services Research*, **11**, 478–507.

Karnofsky, D.A., Abelmann, W.H., Craver, L.F. *et al.* (1948). The use of nitrogen mustards in the palliative treatment of carcinoma. *Cancer*, **1**, 634–656.

Katz, S., Ford, A.B. and Moskowitz, R.W. (1963). Studies of illness in the aged: The index of ADL — a standardised measure of biological and psychosocial function. *Journal of the American Medical Association*, **185**, 914–919.

Kong, B.W., Clive, J. and Kong, S.H. (1990). Quality of Life as a vital clinical sign. *Journal of Human Hypertension*, **4**, 121–123.

Rosser, R.M. and Kind, P. (1978). A scale of valuations of states of illness: is there a social consensus? *International Journal of Epidemiology*, **4**, 347–358.

Slevin, M.L., Plant, H., Lynch, D. *et al.* (1988). Who should measure quality of life, the doctor or the patient? *British Journal of Cancer*, **57**, 109–112.

Smith, G.T. (1990). The economics of hypertension and stroke. *American Heart Journal*, **119**, 725–727.

Spielberger, C.D., Gorsuch, R.L. and Luchene, R.E. (1970). *Manual for the State–Trait Anxiety Inventory*. Consulting Psychologists Press, Palo Alto.

Stones, M.L. and Kozma, A. (1980). Issues relating to the usage of conceptualisations of mental constructs employed by gerontologists. *Journal of Ageing and Human Development*, **11**, 269–281.

Torrance, G.W. (1986). Measurement of health state utilities for economic appraisal. *Journal of Health Economics*, **5**, 1–30.

Tyrer, P. (1990). Personality disorder and social functioning. In: Peck, D.F. and Shapiro, C.M. (Eds), *Measuring Human Problems: A Practical Guide*. Wiley, Chichester, pp. 119–142.

Wilkin, D. and Jolley, D.J. (1979). *Behavioural Problems Among Old People in Geriatric Wards, Psychogeriatric Wards and Residential Homes, 1976–1978*. Research Report, Psychiatric Unit, University Hospital of South Manchester.

Zigmond, A.S. and Snaith, R.P. (1983). The Hospitals Anxiety and Depression Scale. *Acta Psychiatrica Scandinavica*, **67**, 361–370.

10

Looking Ahead

PETER TYRER and PATRICIA CASEY

It will only be too apparent to the readers of this book that the subject of social function is in a developmental phase. In fact, it is reasonable to conclude that it is at a very early phase of development, summed up in the words of Groucho Marx, 'risen from nothing to a state of absolute poverty'. Forty years ago the subject was only mentioned in parentheses in expanding the descriptions of mental state phenomena. In the new psychiatry phenomenology and psychopathology conquered all and social features were by-products to be left to the attention of other disciplines, notably social workers. Conditions such as 'endogenous depression' could be dealt with in isolation from their social context. The clinical features which together made up an endogenous 'factor' were all-explanatory. Nothing more needed to be said; a description of the clinical syndrome should be sufficient to infer cause, treatment and outcome, and therefore demonstrated the same economy as a medical diagnosis such as lobar pneumonia.

Much has happened to change this view of the psychiatric world. Social function, from its uncertain beginnings as 'social attainment' (Feffer and Phillips, 1953) has steadily grown in stature so that it is now the subject of complete investigations independent of the other two main axes of psychiatry, mental state and personality disorder. In clinical practice it is becoming increasingly recognised that it is social dysfunction that usually trumps clinical symptoms in deciding important issues such as admission of patients to hospital or placement in residential or independent accommodation.

At present, however, this impression is largely a qualitative one and the subject is not established firmly as independent. There has also been a great deal of confusion over which aspect of social function is being measured or, indeed, which is the most important. This ranges from broader issues such as social class through to measurement of quality of life, a seductive concept that John Green and Fiona Henderson address in the previous chapter. It seems likely that the independent measurement and definition of social

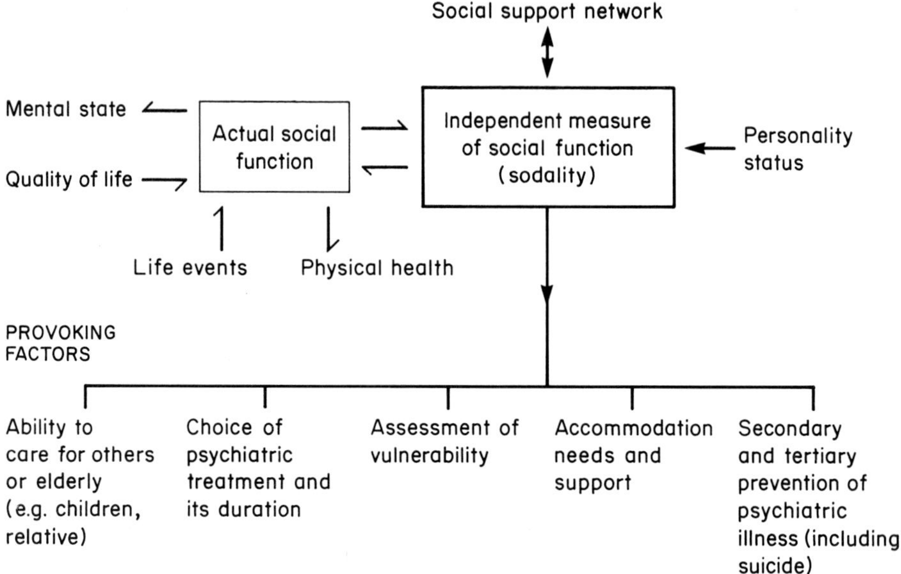

Figure 10.1.   The value of an independent measure of independent social function in psychiatry.

function in its various forms will be expanded and improved over the next few years and we can speculate with some confidence that at least some of the suggestions below are likely to be implemented.

CLASSIFICATION

As the title of this book indicates, although social function is a formal axis of classification in both DSM-IIIR (and its successor DSM-IV) and ICD-10, it remains largely ignored and is seldom measured in the course of clinical practice. However, for research purposes, and probably for clinical ones also, ICD-10 is a much better classification than its predecessors (Mezzich, 1988), and with the introduction of multiaxial classification in both schemes social function will at least get an adequate airing.

Although social function is not formulated in the published ICD-10 classification (World Health Organisation, 1992) it is currently being evaluated in field trials. The draft version of the WHO Disability Diagnostic Scale is illustrated in Table 10.1. The scale, which has some similarities to the Global Assessment of Function Scale (Endicott *et al.*, 1976) (Table 3.4), covers all aspects of social function in a single scale. This has the merit of simplicity

Table 10.1. WHO Disability Diagnostic Scale — (WHO–DDS).

Rate global and specific areas of functioning (A–D) using any of the values from 00–99, including intermediate values. The following anchor values and definitions are provided to facilitate rating:

00	No dysfunction	The patient's functioning conforms to the norms of his/her reference group of sociocultural context.
20	Minimum dysfunction	Deviation from the norm in one or more activities/role is present. The disturbances are minor but persist over the greater part of the time period. More conspicuous dysfunctions may appear for very short periods, e.g. one or two days.
40	Obvious dysfunction	The deviation from the norm is conspicuous and dysfunctions interfere with social adjustment. Dysfunction in at least one activity/role persists nearly all the time. More severe dysfunction may appear only for a few days.
60	Serious dysfunction	Deviations from the norm are marked in most activities/roles and persist more than half of the time.
80	Very serious dysfunction	Deviations in all areas are very severe and persist nearly all the time. Action by others to remedy or control the dysfunction might be required (according to the rater's judgement), but it does not need to have taken place in order to make this rating.
99	Maximum dysfunction	Deviation from the norm has reached a crisis point. A clear element of danger to the patient's own existence or social life and/or to the lives of others may be present. Some form of action or social intervention is necessary.

XX   Not applicable (please state reason on coding sheet).

An overall rating is made and also one each for each of the following areas:

A   Personal care and survival.

B   Occupational functioning: performance of expected role as remunerated worker, student or homemaker.

C   Functioning with family: interaction with spouse, parents, children and other relatives.

D   Broader social behaviour (functioning in other roles and activities): interaction with other individuals and the community-at-large, leisure activities.

---

but may suffer problems of reliability through combining several aspects of social function. In particular, there may be difficulty in estimating 'the maximum level of expected social function in the socio-cultural context of the patient'. It is expecting a lot of a rater to know the maximum level of functioning of any individual, and if the person concerned comes from an unusual cultural background this estimation can be little more than an inspired guess. However, it is understandable that this issue has to be taken into account in estimating social function and emphasises how far we have moved from the concepts of normative social function introduced by the earlier authors in the United States (Feffer and Phillips, 1953; Phillips and Zigler, 1961; Barrabee et al., 1955).

At present social function is an axis which receives one overall rating in the WHO scale. It seems likely that other elements will be rated and classified before long and this is likely to go far beyond the four elements comprising the WHO Disability Diagnostic Scale (WHO–DDS).

THE INTER-RELATIONSHIP BETWEEN SOCIAL FUNCTIONING AND PSYCHIATRIC DISORDERS

The psychiatric disorders which have been most comprehensively investigated are depressive illness and schizophrenia. Unfortunately the amount of research into aspects of social function is considerably less than comparative research into symptomatic change, and is also less than is warranted by the importance of social incapacity. The lack of data on social functioning both during an episode of disorder as well as following intervention is particularly striking in relation to phobias and eating disorders. The commonly held perception that non-psychotic and eating disorders are less serious than schizophrenia and affective psychoses deserves exploration since preliminary findings described in Chapter 5 vitiate this view. Many a patient with one of these non-psychotic disorders is upset to learn that they are regarded as 'minor' ones, even though they can be handicapping to the point of death. Qualification of the extent and nature of social dysfunction associated with these categories may serve to alter the perception of these being less worthy of psychiatrist's time than psychotic illnesses.

The burgeoning interest in personality disorder as a subject for research is to be welcomed, and this needs to be pursued in conjunction with social function research. An area of concern however is the *ad hoc* growth in the number of categories classified with each new edition of the DSM and ICD systems, and there is a danger that a similar proliferation could be generated by introducing operational criteria for social function also. Investigation of social dysfunction is but one step towards validation of these numerous categories. Again some work already completed and described in Chapter 6 suggests that these categories cannot be separated from each other, at least in relation to social function.

PHARMACEUTICAL INDUSTRY

Traditionally the pharmaceutical industry has been interested only in the response of symptoms to biological interventions. The recognition that functioning is an all important aspect of the patient's life has recently prompted some companies to include measures of functioning and, more broadly, of quality of life in their drug trials. To be successful these instruments need to be wide-ranging and a recent development of medications to treat the negative symptoms of schizophrenia must surely augur this step. It is to be hoped that this will become common practice in the future.

PHYSICAL ILLNESS

Quality of life measures are especially pertinent in assessing the outcome of such varied procedures as hip replacement, heart transplant, mastectomy, coronary by-pass and a host of other surgical interventions. Given the array of conditions and treatments it is hardly surprising that so many quality of life schedules exist. No doubt this practice of assessing quality of life will continue not least because of the recent attempts to make comparisons between dissimilar disorders with a view to prioritising financial input (see Chapter 9). The ethical issues which this approach (QUALYs) raises are a cause of deep concern to many and particularly to psychiatrists. It is pertinent to ask if QUALYs are refined enough to be used in making treatment decisions of such magnitude. Moreover there are philosophical problems in comparing dissimilar conditions and reducing each to a single score which is then utilised as if each is similar to the other. Can the impact of treating a patient with chronic schizophrenia be compared with the social effect of a liver transplant or can the treatment of a severely depressed patient with ECT be usefully compared with the emergency treatment of a patient with ketoacidosis? Whilst the effect of interventions on quality of life in each individual disorder is worthy of study in itself and indeed is to be encouraged the technical difficulties and moral dilemmas must be addressed.

There are many disadvantages in multi-axial classifications, not least of which is that they can encourage unnecessary splitting of diagnostic groups. If a single mental state disorder is sub-classified into four others through classification of social function, and each of these is further classified into three others on the basis of social factors such as life events (the Z-codes in ICD-10) then one condition immediately becomes 12! However, this need not necessarily lead to splitting, as an independent taxonomy of social function would cross diagnostic boundaries and could be a valuable predictor of service needs, clinical outcome, duration of different forms of psychiatric treatment and specific issues such as suicide risk. In short, it would have clinical validity (Kendell, 1989).

In order to achieve this degree of usefulness we need to have measures of social function that are not dependent on adverse life events, mental state changes or other, often short-term perturbations in normal levels of function. To some extent the measures of social function described in Chapter 3 of this book are such independent measures, particularly when they take a long time interval of assessment and are used in epidemiological studies. All however, are affected greatly when there is serious mental state disturbance.

In Figure 10.1 the value of such an independent measure of social function is indicated. In instances where physical and mental health and other provoking factors are impaired in the long term (e.g. multi-infarct dementia) the actual social function becomes the same as the independent measure of social function, named sodality (from the Latin *sodalitas*, meaning fellowship) for short. In other instances, however, the actual social function is much worse than sodality for a short period only and it is reasonable to predict that function will improve once the immediate provoking factors have disappeared.

Some separation of social function from the other aspects of health that have constantly recurred throughout this book — demographic features, life events, mental state, personality status, quality of life — is necessary before the subject can achieve its deserved place as a separate topic of inquiry. This book illustrates that we are not quite at the point where every student in the mental health profession should have the training to be able to define, describe and classify social function, but not too far off. We need a new Linnaeus to show the way forward for multi-axial classification in psychiatry, and once we have a sound system in place social function will at last come out of the shade.

REFERENCES

Barrabee, R., Barrabee, E.L. and Finesinger, J.E.F. (1955). A normative social adjustment scale, *American Journal of Psychiatry*, **112**, 252–259.

Endicott, J., Spitzer, R.L., Fleiss, J.L. and Cohen, J. (1976). The global assessment scale: a procedure for measuring the overall severity of psychiatric disturbance. *Archives of General Psychiatry*, **33**, 766–771.

Feffer, M. and Phillips, L. (1953). Social attainment and performance under stress. *Journal of Personality*, **22**, 284–297.

Kendell, R.E. (1989). Clinical validity. *Psychological Medicine*, **19**, 45–55.

Phillips, L. and Zigler, E. (1961). Social competence: The action–thought parameter and vicariousness in normal and pathological behaviours. *J. Abnormal and Social Psychology*, **63**, 137–146.

Mezzich, J.E. (1988). On developing a multiaxial schema for ICD-10. *British Journal of Psychiatry*, **125** (Suppl. 1), 38–43.

World Health Organisation (1992). *International Classification of Diseases, 10th Revision*. WHO, Geneva.

Index